Sports Journalism

A Multimedia Primer

Rob Steen

LONDON AND NEW YORK

First published 2008
by Routledge
2 Park Square, Milton Park, Abingdon, Oxon OX14 4RN

Simultaneously published in the USA and Canada
by Routledge
270 Madison Ave, New York, NY 10016

Routledge is an imprint of the Taylor & Francis Group, an informa business

Typeset in Perpetua and Bell Gothic by
Florence Production Ltd, Stoodleigh, Devon
Printed and bound in Great Britain by
MPG Books Ltd, Bodmin

British Library Cataloguing in Publication Data
A catalogue record for this book is available from the British Library

Library of Congress Cataloging in Publication Data
Steen, Rob.
Sports journalism: a multimedia primer/Rob Steen.
p. cm.
1. Sports journalism. I. Title.
PN4784.S6S87 2007
070.4′49796–dc22 2007001878

ISBN13: 978–0–415–39423–9 (hbk)
ISBN13: 978–0–415–39424–6 (pbk)
ISBN13: 978–0–203–94574–2 (ebk)

ISBN10: 0–415–39423–6 (hbk)
ISBN10: 0–415–39424–4 (pbk)
ISBN10: 0–203–94574–3 (ebk)

To Laura, Josef and Evie –
all a father could ever pray for

Contents

Preface

'To be a journalist, you have to either be cynical or a communist.' Or so a member of the sports desk at the *Daily News* in Mumbai recently insisted. I prefer the word 'socialist', but so long as he means 'communist' in the non-Stalinist, all-for-one, equality-for-all, be-nice-to-your-fellow-homo-sapiens sense, I am with him most of the way. After all, believing that the planet's multitudes can coexist peacefully and creatively on a flat wage with the bare minimum of material comforts is nothing if not an ideal worth pursuing. And I'm far too accomplished a hopeful romantic to be an outright cynic.

With regard to the content of the coming pages, wherein I will attempt to guide you through the most pleasurable area of this particular minefield, namely sports journalism, I find myself recalling a comment made by the celebrated football writer Brian Glanville while we were on the same stage at London's Institute for the Creative Arts in 1993, at an event entitled, with suitable grubbiness, 'Sweaty Letters'. To be a sports journalist, he reasoned, did not oblige you to know anything about sport. What he meant, I suspect, was that a journalist need not know much about sport in order to report it, since a journalist would ensure he or she did sufficient research to bring off a competent bluff. While I am not sure I entirely agree – the sporting audience seems to me far better-informed than it was a generation ago, if only because television now allows billions more to witness events and matches – I firmly endorse the implicit logic: that covering sport is less about memorising results than analysing people.

In keeping with a subject so inextricably linked to its own past, I have attempted to contextualise both the evolution of sport and of sports journalism, in all its forms, the better to appreciate how the profession arrived at its current state, where it should go from here and how you can help ensure it gets there. There are, furthermore, a number of exercises I believe will be beneficial. I feel compelled, however, to offer a few health warnings, riders and apologies:

1. Although my own experience is by no means confined to the erstwhile Street of Shame, newspapers remain the primary home of sports journalism – as opposed, that is, to the mere reporting of scores. So while magazines, the web, non-fiction books and broadcasting are all analysed, most of the advice herein focuses on the production of daily and weekly sports pages, albeit with a constantly peeled eye or two on the wider context.

2 To learn how to be a sportswriter it is first necessary to appreciate the standard required. Whenever somebody asks me how to write, rather than prattle on about technical matters such as the use of understatement and double negatives, of short sentences and long, of dictionaries and Thesauri – all of which are heartily endorsed – I would rather point them in the direction of a good writer. So, even though good writing is even harder to define than bad, and equally subjective, I have included a liberal sprinkling of lines from the genre's finest storytellers (a journalist is nothing if not a storyteller, albeit one rather more constrained by space than the brothers Grimm or sisters Brontë). The fact that they are all composed in English – whether American, Australian, Indian or even English English – is less evidence of myopia or snobbishness, I like to think, than an incurable ineptness with foreign languages.

3 Please forgive any and all lapses into wholly inadvertent sexism, not least in my selection of extracts and writers to emulate. It would be disingenuous, not to say pointless, to pretend that sports journalism has moved far beyond the boys' own pool of yore (though much the same can be said of those other macho citadels, film, theatre and music criticism). A recent Danish survey of magazine and newspaper articles about sport across the world concluded that women were the subjects of 14 per cent and the authors of 5 per cent. 'This is not a profession that lends itself to family relationships very easily,' emphasises Vicki Michaelis, President of the Association of Women in Sports Media. Another study, published in the winter 2005 edition of *Journalism & Mass Communication*, found that most women working in sports media have suffered sexual discrimination and verbal abuse.

On the other hand, it would be wrong not to express optimism. The roll of honourable exceptions is lengthening: to the trailblazing likes of Margaret Hughes (who in 1954 became the first woman to cover an Ashes cricket series for a newspaper), Adrienne Blue, Cynthia Bateman, Sue Mott, Michelle Savidge and Louise Taylor we can now add the likes of Chloe Saltau (*Melbourne Age*, who in 2005 became the first woman to cover an Ashes cricket series since Ms Hughes), Tanya Aldred (*Guardian*), Sharda Ugra (*India Today* sports editor), Lewine Mair (*Daily Telegraph* golf correspondent), Alison Kervin (*The Times*), Eleanor Oldroyd and Alison Mitchell (BBC Radio Five Live), Donna Symmonds (*Test Match Special*), Janine Self and Vicki Orvice (*Sun*), Amy Lawrence (*Observer*), Emma John (*Sunday Times* and *The Wisden Cricketer*), Vaneisa Baksh (Caribbean-based cricket writer), Jenny Thompson (Cricinfo.com) and Kate Laven (*Daily* and *Sunday Telegraph*). As I write, moreover, Jacquelin Magnay (*Sydney Morning Herald*) and Natasha Woods (*Glasgow Sunday Herald*) occupy the throne of chief sportswriter. In other words, should you not possess a fully functioning Adam's apple, please, *please*, don't imagine the obstacles are insuperable.

4 Reading this book and completing the exercises will not guarantee you a full-time job. Indeed, while the breadth of opportunity has expanded, courtesy of the growth in broadcasting and new media and the seemingly insatiable public appetite for sport, full-time positions in sports journalism, especially on local and regional newspapers, are nowhere near as widespread as they were when I began. How big is the difference between demand and supply? Think of the chasm separating Tiger Woods and other

contemporary golfers: now double it. Declining sales and diversification have spawned a generation of multi-tasking freelancers: a few regular newspaper and magazine gigs, some subbing shifts, a spot of broadcasting, perhaps the occasional book or TV documentary. Transferable skills and versatility are never vices.

5 For all its laudable principles, journalism is rife with contradictions, prejudices and self-loathing. 'If there is such a thing as a journalistic "family", it is a highly dysfunctional one,' Kim Fletcher, former editor of the *Independent on Sunday*, recently acknowledged. 'Reporters on popular papers are not keen on reporters from so-called quality ones, regional newspaper journalists don't trust national newspapers, television journalists only like themselves.' Revealing what the powerful and privileged would prefer Joe and Joanne Public not to know, furthermore, is hardly a passport to popularity and trust. Only those with the self-motivation of a ravenous lion, the hide of an insensitive rhino and the reticence of an angry bull need apply.

Acknowledgements

Researching and writing a book while relocating from Cornwall to Sussex, holding down a job as a university lecturer and writing about a cricket season does not, I am fairly confident, sound like the sort of recipe likely to win the approval of Delia or Nigella. Whether the result is as digestible, juicy and nourishing as those good ladies would require is for you to decide, but without the help of a good many kind and generous people it would not have progressed beyond the first sentence.

I would like, therefore, to first thank Samantha Grant at Routledge for rejecting my original idea and persuading me to do hers, as well as her endlessly patient and supportive colleagues Ygraine Cadlock, Hannah Tylee and Kate Manson. After a dozen or so non-fiction books, writing one for an academic publisher was always going to be a steep learning curve.

No less helpful and understanding have been my colleagues at the University of Brighton, notably Alan Allchorn, Dan Burdsey, Jo Doust, John Doyle, Jackie Errigo, Mandi Green, Chrissy Hutchings, Marc Keech, Gill Lines, Sheridan McCoid, Ian McDonald, Graham McFee, Paula O'Shea, Steve Redhead, Dianne Reeves, Patrick Smith, John Sugden, Mary Thair, Alan Tomlinson and others at Chelsea School too numerous to list here. Our external examiner, that erudite Celtic fan Raymond Boyle of the University of Stirling, was another indispensable source of support and encouragement. For the 100-odd students on the BA Sport Journalism course who unwittingly volunteered to be guinea pigs for my early musings and rough drafts, no amount of thanks could suffice.

Thank you, too, to those fellow journalists who were so philanthropic with their time, memories and wisdom: Andy Afford, Simon Barnes, Scyld Berry, Andy Colquhoun, Ted Corbett, Ed Craig, Peter Deeley, Ralph Dellor, Steven Downes, Tim de Lisle, Matthew Engel, Stephen Fay, Gideon Haigh, Murray Hedgcock, David Hopps, Andrew Jennings, Ahmer Khokhar, Rob Kitson, Duncan Mackay, Mike Marqusee, Christopher Martin-Jenkins, Kevin Mitchell, Paul Newman, Jeremy Novick, Brian Oliver, Steve Pinder, Nick Pitt, Mark Ray, Huw Richards, Neil Robinson, Brian Scovell, Sharda Ugra, Mike Walters and Richard Weekes. My gratitude, naturally, also extends to those who granted permission for me to reproduce their prose as an inspiration to those who will one day have the pleasure of doing for a living what we were fully prepared to do for fun.

I am also grateful to the following for granting permission to republish material: Simon Barnes, Bob Cooke, Jason Cowley at *Observer Sports Monthly*, Peter Deeley, Leon Hickman, Mukul Kesavan, Mike Marqusee and Matthew Syed. Almost every effort has been made to seek permission for other material quoted; I only trust the authors have no objection to being complimented on their skill, perspicacity and literary verve.

A writer needs uncommon tolerance and encouragement from family and friends, so mercis unconfined to Shirley and Ralph Dymond, Anne Taylor, Jill Taylor, Jeremy Novick, Gilly Smith, Mary Hetherington, Mick Burton, Tamara Jones, Steve O'Rourke (thanks for the peaches!) and above all, for their love, patience and forbearance, my children, Laura, Josef and Evie, without whom even a triple-century before lunch by Andrew Flintoff against Australia would pale into pathetic insignificance.

Glossary

Add	Addition to a story already sent.
Agencies	Agence France Presse, Associated Press (US), Reuters, The Press Association and other suppliers of news and features to newspapers; formerly called wire services and hence still referred to as 'the wires'.
Angle	Different ways to present the same story; theme of the story.
Back bench	Production hub of a newspaper, where decisions are taken and implemented, usually comprising production editor, chief sub-editor and news editor.
Beat	Reporter's geographical territory or area of expertise.
Beat-up	A flimsy story exaggerated by dramatic/inflammatory language.
Bed	Sending the finished edition/page to the printers, as in putting it 'to bed'.
Breaking story	Unfolding event.
Brief	Short item.
Broadsheet	Traditionally, larger and allegedly serious newspapers (aka 'Qualities').
Byline	Reporter's name on top/below a story.
Catchline	Word (such as 'Arsenal' or 'Drugs') atop each page of a printed-out story to identify author and theme/subject, followed by page number, as in 'Steen/Arsenal/4'.
Check-call	Phone call (not email) to office to check safe arrival of copy and whether sub-editor has any queries.
Colour piece	Article supplementary to main match report, picking out a particular player or theme; like, microcosmic rather than macrocosmic, man.
Crosshead	Short phrase to break up long passage of copy for reader's benefit, previewing an aspect of the copy beneath.
Cross-reference	Line at the bottom of story denoting that the topic also features elsewhere in the publication, or that there is a related story in the news section: 'MP's tennis shame, page 7'.

Cut	Copy that needs to be deleted in order to make story fit its designated slot on the page: 'This needs a 15-line cut . . .'.
Deadline	Religiously-fixed time by which copy must arrive at the desk to enable sub-editor to check it in good time. Also refers to time a page is scheduled to be sent for printing. To be stretched at one's peril; to be defied on pain of immediate and uncomfortable death.
Diary	Constantly updated record of upcoming fixtures and events maintained primarily by news editor, noting which reporter/agency is assigned to which task.
Door-stepping	Camping out at the home/office of somebody who has scant wish to see you.
Dummy	How a page/publication looks at the planning stage.
Exclusive	Banner above a story allegedly to be found in only one publication; frequently seen, seldom to be trusted.
Furniture	Collective term for crossheads (see opposite), headline, picture captions, pullout quotes, sub-head, standfirst (see page xvii).
Hack	Unpretentious reporter.
Head	Headline.
Holding story	Story written strictly for early editions when a fixture kicks off too late for a report to be carried, later replaced, at the same length, by the match report.
Intro	Opening paragraph (see Lead, Nose, Top).
Kill	As in 'Kill that story on the Queen: she wasn't Osama bin Laden's secret lover after all'.
Lead	Main story on page/intro.
Legs (1)	Number of columns a story spans.
Legs (2)	The potential of a story to run for a few days or weeks, as in 'Has it got legs?'.
Line	The most newsworthy/interesting angle to a story, as in 'What's the line?'.
Literal	Misspelling or capitalisation/punctuation error; often emanating from harassed copytakers. One soccer reporter returned from a World Cup to find a typed copy of a report pinned to the office noticeboard: 'John Barnes' had metamorphosed into 'gendarmes'.
Masthead	Name of newspaper/magazine on the front or editorial page.
Mock-up	Page at design stage.
Nannygoats	Direct quotes.
No. 1	Chief correspondent for a particular sport/editor.
No. 2	News-oriented second-in-command/deputy editor.

Nose	Opening sentence or paragraph.
Obit	Obituary.
Opposition	Any other newspaper in your segment of the market.
Outro	Final paragraph.
Page proof	Printed copy of a page to be read for errors before publication.
Par	Paragraph.
Point	Full stop, term used when dictating copy by phone.
Pops	Shorthand for 'popular', i.e. tabloid papers, whose mastheads were originally red (see Red-tops).
Puff	Free plug for company mentioned in story.
Puff-piece	Story that serves as a blatant advert for subject and hence has no journalistic credibility whatsoever.
Rags	Less complimentary slant on Pops.
Red-tops	See Pops and Rags.
Rent-a-quote	Sizeably-egoed person in the public eye who likes to see their name in print and can hence be relied upon for a quote, no matter how bland, predictable or insightless.
Results sub	Sub-editor entrusted with overseeing accurate publication of results; since these are printed in six-point text, good eyesight is as important as a keen grasp of mathematical principles.
Revise sub	The sub-editor's sub-editor: entrusted with giving subbed copy the once-over before approving it for publication, checking in particular that house style has been properly adhered to.
Rewrite	Story rewritten for later editions to account for post-deadline developments.
Runner	Stage-by-stage match report, delivered in prescribed chunks at prearranged times during the course of a game, thus easing the pressure on the sub-editor.
Scoop	Antiquated term for 'exclusive', albeit fractionally more trustworthy.
Screamer	Exclamation mark: avoid as you would a particularly vicious epidemic.
Sidebar	Supplementary/complementary story to match report/news story.
Sign-off	Byline placed at the bottom of a story, for visual variation.
Six-point	Type size used for team lineups and results.
Slip	Page inserted in the main print run of a newspaper targeted at a particular area or focusing on a particular event.
Snappers	Photographers.
Spike	Thin, pointed metal object on wooden base used to store unwanted stories; now strictly figurative.

Splash	Front-page lead story.
Staffer	Member of full-time staff.
Standfirst	Sentence or two below main headline of a feature and sometimes a news story, outlining the theme; never used in conjunction with a sub-head (see below).
Stringer	Freelancer.
Sub	Standing not, as some aggrieved reporters have been known to suggest, for subnormal, but sub-editor.
Sub-head	Smaller, wordier and more explanatory headline beneath main head, usually used in features; never in conjunction with a standfirst.
Tail	Last paragraph or two in a runner; see outro.
Take	First or subsequent page of a running story.
Top	Opening paragraph(s).
Top-and-tail	Final take of a runner.
Update	Rewriting story using fresh facts.
Widow	Single word at the top of a column; more or less illegal.
World's Biggest Tabloid, The	Popular alternative title for the *Sunday Times*.
Wri-tor	Serious-minded/pretentious reporter.

Chapter 1

The hardest job ever craved

An almost shameless confession

People view sports like they do organised religion. Some see nothing but a history of oppression, hypocrisy and mind control of the wilfully stupid in the service of a corrupt and dangerous institution. Some see nothing but glory, beauty and the opportunity to worship something greater than themselves. Some merely go on watching sports because their forebears did, as did their forebears before them. I recognise there's a lot about sports that's distasteful. But sports itself is not the problem. Sports doesn't create assholes, assholes do.

I love sports. I love the action. I love the drama. I love the artistry displayed in even the most barbaric of physical activities (I'm thinking boxing, not cockfighting). I love the emotion invested by players and fans – the true fans, not the college dopes who light cars on fire when the bars close on championship game night. I love the sense of community sports can build.

To preserve my love for sports, I gave up sportswriting for a living. Being a professional sportswriter can suck the joy out of sports. The grind of beat reporting, of hearing the same clichés spouted day after day (of course you take it one game at a time!), of having to put yourself on red alert the moment your Spidey Sense picks up the sound of a tailback's hamstring twinging, of having parents calling you around the clock to demand why you're not covering their 'All-State candidate' – at the start of your career, you're told no cheering in the press box. It doesn't take long, unless you're a college football reporter at a mid-sized daily in the South, to not have to be reminded. Sportswriting is a lot like doing a movie nude scene. There's something that sounds appealing about it, and it looks like fun, but you're so worried about your lines and all the stuff around you that it can become just as passionate a task as cleaning grout.

Thus, a couple of years ago, did Bob Cooke introduce his first column on the American website flakmag.com. I begin with it partly because, despite the occasional unBritishism (and I trust I've saved my University of Brighton students the bother of writing witheringly sarcastic letters by changing all the -izes and -izeds and -ors in this book to -ises and -iseds and -ours), it underlines the universality of sport, and sporting language; partly because it is written with such infectious verve and conviction; but mostly because it echoes so many of my own thoughts and thus enables me to wriggle free of most if not all allegations of overt bias. And if there's one trick you soon learn as a sports journalist, it is to use the views of others as a vehicle for your own.

After the best part of a quarter of a century earning varying amounts of my corn as a sports journalist, I still regard it as a privilege. With its daily dose of breathtaking winners and gallant losers, trailblazers and exemplars, cheats and leeches, what more could a writer possibly wish for in a subject? A few years ago, Martyn Lewis, the BBC newsreader, insisted that bulletins should place greater stress on 'good news'. He was pooh-poohed at the time, and rightly so, but is it really any coincidence that sport now commands increasing amounts of coverage on *The Ten O'Clock News*?

This is a world that never stops still for two consecutive seconds, where what was hip one week can be 'so last year' the next. Creative activities such as art, music and dance have evolved in ways unimaginable to their exponents 50 years ago. With its familiar landscapes, ancient customs, slowly evolving rules and nigh-on total imperviousness to fashion, sport, by comparison, has been an oasis of stability, a Tower of London with a fraction of the brutality. With its readily accessible fund of shared memories – thanks to record books and TV channels such as ESPN Classic – even those too young to have experienced games and feats first-hand can join in. Nothing unites generations quite so effortlessly.

In theory, merely telling heroic stories, or those that expose wrongdoing, or light the way ahead, can never be as satisfying or enjoyable as actually being the hero, capturing the corporate criminal or inspiring the masses by your own deeds. However, as Alan Felix's departed wife informs him in Woody Allen's *Play It Again, Sam*, this planet of ours is divided into watchers and doers, and neither mud nor blood are on my list of favourite things. Witnessing, forecasting and striving to comprehend greatness, on the other hand, ranks right up there with lockshen pudding, Peking duck, London parks, Paris cafés, Barcelona cinemas, New York record shops, African smiles, Australian sunsets, Caribbean dancehalls, fresh bedsheets and newly mown grass. Or, as Simon Barnes, chief sportswriter of *The Times*, put it:

> *As I seek constantly a good tale to tell, so I seek – almost for private reasons, for personal rather than public gratification – greatness. I seek a definition of greatness, I seek an understanding of greatness. I seek, perhaps, the highest thing of all, to write greatness: and write it true. But, above all, I seek to be where greatness is. That is the greatest thing in the life of a sportswriter.'*[1]

Mr Cooke and I differ on two counts, one minor, one major. Once, in my formative years as an aspiring wimp, I persuaded myself that boxing constituted safe, acceptable and palatable violence leavened with a dash of art and a bucketful of drama. The professional project with which I have been least dissatisfied, furthermore, was a biography of the fearsome hombre Muhammad Ali stunned to win the world heavyweight boxing title, Sonny Liston. Nevertheless, I have long recoiled from the ignoble art much as I do from video nasties, happy slappings and *Big Brother*: none present humanity in an especially complimentary light. As a boy, I fell head over heels, not just for the artistry, arrogance, rebelliousness and political drive of Ali, but also for his 1920s predecessor Gene Tunney, the ex-Marine smitten by a high society gal who swore to make the million dollars he felt he needed to make her his, did so in the ring, then quit.

The knowledge I began acquiring around that time, and the vague interest I reluctantly kept up, meant that I covered the odd world title fight – Terry Marsh in a tent in Basildon, Prince Naseem Hamed at the Royal Albert Hall – and even the trial for tax evasion of Don King (I was in New York researching the Liston book, a good example of that essential journalistic skill: being in the right place at the right time). Published in the *Sunday Times*, it was probably the most sheerly vindictive article I have ever written – bar one for the *Guardian* during the hate phase of my love–hate relationship with Brian Lara. Riddled as I am with Jewish guilt complexes, this was one instance where being sarcastic and disrespectful and downright rude carried no downside whatsoever. Best-known, deceptively, for that electrified shock of mad professorial hair, King, the manager, promoter, wheeler-dealer and murderer once accused by another ex-champ and client, Tim Witherspoon, of specialising in 'black-on-black crime', was one of the prime causes of my disillusionment with boxing. Ditto all those WBCs and WBAs and WBOs and IBFs, denying us as they do the answer to the question sports aficionados ask before all others: who's the best? Not to mention the one all human beings feel they have a right to know: who can we trust? At bottom, though, what ruined it was the blood and gore, the intended, unapologetic, *unnecessary* violence of it all. Sport should compensate us for civilisation's failings, not endorse them.

Mr Cooke and I also differ in that I did not have to give up sportswriting to preserve my love of sport. I did, however, give up writing about football – twice, in fact. Over-exposure and close proximity to its inner workings had hardened a journalist's innate scepticism into grumpy old man cynicism. I quit to preserve what little affection I still felt and to rid myself of the rising guilt of an ex-disciple; when it comes to sanctimonious claptrap, not even a reformed smoker can match someone who has renounced all faith in something that once gave them a reason to wake up. On the first occasion I was persuaded to recant by the *Sunday Times* and actually began to enjoy myself again. This was because I was assigned to cover a lowly club every week, and encouraged to turn what was ostensibly a lengthy match report into something more akin to a profile of a community. Then my wife and I decided we needed an adventure, left London and downshifted to deepest Cornwall; at the height of an advertising recession that 9/11 would only accentuate, and with freelance budgets shrinking, my patch dwindled to Plymouth. Besides, as a father of three young children to whom weekends had long been a Daddy-free zone, I wanted to realign my work–family balance. Indeed, the reason I am writing this book is that that balance has changed in a way I would never have suspected: I now spend more time attempting to teach others how to be sports journalists than I do plying my trade, as Hugh McIlvanney once modestly inscribed in my copy of *McIlvanney on Football*, as 'a fellow toiler in a scruffy vineyard'. Writing about what you love, for a living, can be a curse full of blessings. More often than not, it can be a blessing full of curses.

I was drawn irresistibly to sport. With hindsight, the psychological catalyst, I suppose, was that it offered a way of ordering a terrifying world that otherwise defied comprehension: a tributary of certainty winding gently off a river of doubt. Whether one team thrashed another or a sprinter edged home by the thickness of a vest, you couldn't argue with the result, or at least not with any expectation of changing it. Slowly, the associated virtues dawned:

the physical artistry; the knowledge that I couldn't hit or pass or bowl a zillionth as well even if my life depended on it; the miraculous variety of games devised around the possibilities generated by balls of differing sizes; the indescribable buzz of a close contest or a victory against the odds; the dignity sport alone lent to patriotism; the operatic nature of its plotlines; what it taught me about politics and geography and history; how it brought together mutually mistrustful races and buried, however fleetingly, their social and economic differences. Oh yes, and the possibly self-deluding belief that knowing vast amounts about who won what and when afforded me precious insights into Life Itself.

In the interests of full, frank and fearless contextualisation, I should relate that I lost my sporting virginity at the age of eight and two-thirds, in 1966, which for a romantically inclined Londoner was incredibly fortunate. England won the World Cup; Everton became the first – and still only – side to win the FA Cup final after going 2–0 down; between May and November, Muhammad Ali, Garry Sobers and Pelé, the most important black sporting figures of the age, all graced the capital with their otherworldly presence: Ali cracked Henry Cooper's eggshell eyebrows at Highbury, furnishing the Sunday papers with their goriest front-page snaps in years; Sobers beat England's cricketers singlehanded – nobody else has ever scored 600 runs and taken 15 wickets in the same Test series, much less the 700 runs and 20 wickets he actually managed; only Pelé, injured knee targeted mercilessly by Bulgarian, Hungarian and Portuguese studs, disappointed. For the first time since the 1880s, England felt like the centre of the sporting universe, a backdrop that enhanced my fanciful teenage dreams – becoming the next E.W. Swanton or Brian Glanville. Unlike so many fellow cricket writers, above all my unfortunate friend John Ward in Zimbabwe, I am fortunate enough to live in a country whose wealth makes the fulfilment of such dreams feasible. Nor did it hurt that it accommodates more influential newspapers per square mile than anywhere else.

Back then I loved to distraction virtually any contest between individuals or teams where the key element was a spherical object; even snooker. I even quite liked most of the various racing genres – motor, horse and foot if not sailing – but it was the skill involved in hitting, kicking and handling balls that really tickled my fancy. Mostly because I knew from bitter and shameful first-hand experience how tricky those skills were to acquire and hone. What roused me more than anything, however, was:

1. the possibility that small could embarrass big, and right beat might (that Glasgow Rangers were tossed out of the Scottish FA Cup by Berwick Rangers in my first season as a football fanatic scarcely hurt);
2. the sheer *justice* – in most cases – of the scoreline, which explains, in good part, my quiet lust for cricket: by dint of the longevity of its contests, albeit not exclusively so, it all but precludes flukish or freakish reversals of form or ability;
3. nobody wins all the time. Not Tiger Woods. Not Roger Federer. Not even the treasurers.

And now? As I write these words amid a steady trickle of leaves in the winter of 2006, having covered most of the entries in *The Oxford Companion to Sports and Games* for most of the titles that once resided in Fleet Street, in addition to sundry magazines and publications in Australia, South Africa and India, I am still smitten, irreversibly I suspect. While I can trace my youth and teenagehood via the pop charts, my life is mapped out by Test matches and

World Cups. I began my preparations for the 2006–07 Ashes series by watching the DVD of England's triumph in the 2005 encounter for the umpteenth-and-first time. Small wonder my wife tired of me.

So, unlike Mr Cooke, being a sports journalist has not eroded my passion for sport, at least not fatally. If it had, I would not have had the gall to write this book: the very last thing you should be reading is a how-to guide by a practitioner who has forgotten the why.

THE LURE OF SPORTS JOURNALISM

The way the profession is perceived has evolved radically during my time as a member of the National Union of Journalists, the Sports Journalists' Association and the proudly unreconstructed Cricket Writers' Club; chapters 2 and 3 examine this in detail. Suffice to say that sports desks, once derided, slimly-populated and barely tolerated, are now dignified – all right, grudgingly valued. This may seem extraordinarily naive, not least given that journalists, by and large, command a level of public esteem matched only by dentists, insurance salesmen, estate agents and car-towers. I would argue otherwise – but then I would, wouldn't I?

My tastes and loyalties, meanwhile, have shifted and realigned. I like to feel that that enduring childlike interest has been aided by neutrality. Unless, of course, one of the protagonists is poorer, unluckier, more deserving, more inclined to cheat or play with neither wit nor imagination – or the England cricket team. Intriguingly, to me and my therapist if nobody else, my passion for cricket, the sport I have covered with comfortably the greatest regularity, has actually grown. It is a moot point, mind, whether this says more about cricket than it does about my refusal to age gracefully, if at all.

I also adore baseball (my favourite sporting event is the World Series, a best-of-seven affair and hence the fairest and most democratic test of athleticism and nerve there is), occasionally thrill to a goal or try or smash or putt and take a passing interest in about half the remnants. The exceptions, besides boxing, are motor racing, horse racing and sailing (too reliant on non-humans and hence immeasurably less interesting), athletics and cycling (neither of which appears to be possible to perform in a spectacular or even captivating way without the whiff of drugs), and darts, which shares much the same affinity for athleticism and variety as a kebab shop. To be ashamed of such prejudices is to be ashamed of the contents of your iPod.

But why – beyond their common worship of such boyish delights as hits, throws, runs, outs, catches and averages – cricket and baseball? I love the sense both give, in this noisy, nosy, non-stop age, of defying the tyranny of time (baseball, indeed, has no clock, literally or even figuratively). I love that each game combines the best of all cultural worlds: like novels and biographies, they are long enough and languid enough to suck you in; like movies, plays and television dramas, they twist and turn, and with even greater disregard for probability. I love the utterly fortuitous fact that my introduction to baseball – Game 6 of the 1986 World Series between New York's Mets and Boston's Red Sox, courtesy of Channel 4 – happened to conclude with the most dramatic climax to a sporting event it has ever been my fingernails' displeasure to witness, a climax that could never have been scripted for a cinema or plasma TV because it was too far-fetched. I love the way that, after 23 years – admittedly, I have just completed my first summer in that span without reporting a game of cricket – I still feel a sense of deflation, and renewed longing, whenever a Test match in

England ends, no matter what the result. Above all, I love that you can read about cricket and baseball with as much delight as you can watch them, often more so.

I have unquestionably been fortunate. Even though my knowledge of the subject had been gleaned solely from the safe side of the white line – terraces, grandstands, libraries, bookshops, newsagents, radio and television – various editors have been kind/potty enough to employ me to report, and comment upon, something about which I have no right ever to call myself an expert. It probably says quite a lot about me, none of it terribly flattering, that of the three sometime saintly Michaels I have interviewed – Jordan, Stipe and Atherton – I only felt intimidated by the third. I've talked the hind legs off such gifted gabblers and personal deities as Martha Reeves (minus Vandellas, sadly), Rickie Lee Jones, Todd Rundgren, Carlos Santana, Harold Pinter, Ron Shelton and Rory Bremner, even all five members of Squeeze in a dressing room in the bowels of the Albert Hall, but I've only once been more nervous than the day the *Independent* asked me to corner Ian Botham in a tent in Ilford, and that was when George Best agreed to meet me at his Mayfair club. Or, for rather different reasons, the week I spent, while researching the Liston book, being absolutely paranoid that I was being followed by men in pulled-down trilbys (well, the tragically luckless Sonny was managed and sponsored by the Mafia, the same kindly family types I remain convinced commanded his early death).

Better yet, a cricket press box, the nearest I have ever had to a regular office, is a unique beast. Because games last for days, and tours for months, reporters, almost exclusively beta males, spend an enormously unhealthy amount of time together. For that not to result in a daily diet of laddish mayhem, vendettas and sulks suggests cricket tends to attract patient and tolerant human beings. It does. I am exceedingly thankful it has made me friends all over the world, the vast majority of them journalists, none of whom I would have encountered without that shared enthusiasm – and an enthusiasm shared, after all, is an enthusiasm squared. That mutual affection is often a direct consequence, for better or worse, of the people we are. Or the children we still are. Best of all, because of their relative accessibility (especially at non-international matches, far from those prying cameras), which is in turn due in no small part to the time they have on their hands between innings, it is not that difficult to get to know the players to some extent. Wherein lies the greatest pleasure of all. I doubt many, beyond their immediate family and friends, cared more about the careers of Graham Thorpe, Mark Ramprakash and Nasser Hussain, felt their failures more keenly or took such pride in their successes. True, this did have something to do with the fact that I met them when they were teenagers, and perhaps even more to do with the fact that I spent so many days extolling their virtues and didn't want to look a fool.

A LESSON IN LIFE

Sport, in most cases, is full-contact ballet. In all instances it is the art of competition. At bottom, in its demands on body and soul, on head, heart and spirit, it is a celebration of human possibility. As a cultural phenomenon, as an agent of change, it is without equal. Would the horrors of apartheid have ended with such relative suddenness but for the international sporting boycott that savaged white South Africa's sense of worth? Nelson Mandela and I are as one on this. Would African-Americans be called African-Americans were it not for the courage and persistence shown during the Civil Rights struggle by Ali, Jackie Robinson, Tommie Smith and Althea Gibson (go on, look them up)? Maybe, maybe not, but anecdotal evidence suggests that Stevie Wonder, Marvin Gaye, Bob Marley, Richard Pryor, Bill Cosby and Spike Lee all derived a much bigger thrill from pressing the flesh with Ali or Jordan or Viv Richards than vice versa. All too readily could they testify to the difficulties of expressing oneself without the aid of editors, scriptwriters, producers, engineers, synthesisers, background singers and cue cards. Every time they compete, professional sportsfolk tread a vertiginously high wire without a net, a stuntman or even a bottom double. They are always aware that one fall, one slightly over-stretched lunge, one inadvertent collision or even an altercation with a disobedient kitchen implement could lead directly to the dole queue. Worse, there's always someone trying to stop them doing their job. If the skill required to run, jump or manipulate balls for a living is primarily geared towards entertaining others, the additional difficulty in being a professional is that it is not enough merely to entertain; defeat can turn even the most spellbound spectator into a whinging critic and, potentially, an ex-spectator.

This is why one of the three Cs every sports journalist ought to possess, or acquire, is compassion, the others being courage – both to ask the difficult questions and withstand the sense of rejection every time your work is rewritten or your ideas rejected – and curiosity. Compassion for stressed-out press box colleagues who think nothing of flinging a typewriter out of the window or foul-mouthing all and sundry? Yes. For fellow workers stuck behind the same computer terminal in the same stuffy office every day while you jaunt the world, city or county? Absolutely. But mostly for the fragility of our subjects.

As someone captivated by the idea of being a professional storyteller, the crux of sport's appeal, or at least the basis of my desire to write about it, lies less in the results and performances and theatre, the graceful athleticism or even the social and political ramifications, than in its practitioners' humanity: there is no limit to the stories you can tell. About their emotional and intellectual responses to glory and disaster, yes, but mostly their inescapable vulnerability; a vulnerability magnified, at the highest level but also on the lower rungs, by the omnipresent camera. Not, mind, that they always help themselves. After Pakistan's batsmen Mohammad Yousuf and Younis Khan had added 363 in the Headingley Test of August 2006, the fifth highest partnership ever conceded by England, both made a point of stressing that the secret of their collective success – despite a torrent of boundaries excessive even by modern standards – was the sort of mutual understanding that facilitates quick singles. Two days later, in the second innings, came a mix-up that risked a run to the home team's best fielder, Paul Collingwood. Yousuf was run out and the match turned, irretrievably, towards England.

We are now all but conditioned, because of the stakes involved in professional sport, to regard defeat as failure, as a sin, even a crime. Yet as the television cameras seldom fail to remind us in their incessant quest for emotion, losers are as fascinating as winners, frequently more so. Only relatively recently has mankind come to dissect the downside of success, to sympathise with the winners, but failure is more valuable. It is the lessons learned in defeat, the way we learn to cope with it and change our approach accordingly, that strengthen. Once learned, they may not pave the way for major triumphs, but life is about small victories and hard-earned draws.

People spend their lives making ends meet, coping, treating rough and smooth with sturdy equanimity. In other words, settling, however reluctantly, for the draw. Professional sportspeople (all right, golfers excepted) are next to useless if they do not win pots or shields or winner's medals, at least once every blue moon. In a team sport, moreover, no matter how well you might play, no matter how efficiently, even spectacularly, you might do your job, and even cover for others, one daft or luckless colleague can commit the sort of error that changes everything in a trice. Unfortunately, you are obliged to rely on contraptions such as bones, tissue and flesh, and when they go awry there is no tomorrow. Which is why I can be relied upon for an impressive impression of a deranged Staffordshire Bull Terrier whenever I spot an article from yet another deeply envious ex-player wheeled out to whinge on about footballers' wages. As I write, the big studios in Hollywood are busy making it abundantly clear that the days of Tom Cruise making $20m per picture are over. Salary caps are all the rage. Yet of all the causes for journalists to espouse, that of deflating salaries for work that until comparatively recently was grossly under-rewarded (set against the money raked in by club owners and governing bodies *and* by comparison with their own monthly cheques) seems much the least worthy and easily the most pointless.

The difficulty with sportsfolk in the twenty-first century is that the sheer scale of their earnings is regarded by far too many as insulation against misfortune and even fallibility. In late September 2006, word broke that Terrell Owens of the Dallas Cowboys, one of the leading American footballers of his generation, had attempted suicide. His PR assistant Kim Etheredge had called 911, informed police the wide receiver was 'depressed' and tried to prise some pills from his mouth. The very next day, however, she was claiming that a leaked police report was a fabrication and that Terrell had '25 million reasons to be alive'. 'I'm still stunned by the ugliness of that statement,' wrote Dave Zirin. 'Twenty-five million is how many dollars Owens will be paid over the life of his three-year contract with the Cowboys. For Etheredge, Owens' life must be worth no more than his pay scale. Presumably, if cut from the team, his "reasons to be alive" would dwindle to nothing.'[2]

'Athletes have been taught to appear invulnerable, to repress emotion, to never, ever let 'em see you sweat, much less show panic or pain,' observed the veteran American boxing writer and novelist Robert Lipsyte, once a confidante of Muhammad Ali and now, in his own words, a 'recovering sportswriter'. 'This is why for so many pro athletes, with their shallow marriages, false friendships and dysfunctional family relationships, the only places where true emotion can freely emerge are the locker room and the playing field. There, they can finally hug and cry. For many, these are the only times they feel truly alive, and one can understand how they might be tempted to do anything to stay in the arena, including drugs.'[3]

However unwittingly, Bruce Springsteen, who has been entertaining the public for the best part of four decades, recently alighted on one of the chief differences between athletes and other cultural icons. Asked why he wanted to carry on making what were once called 'records', he replied: 'You know how to make records. Your writing craft is more honed, and you have more confidence, which comes from being around for so damned long. You're not worried if you make a mistake . . .'[4] Sportspeople have a much shorter shelf-life, and those that matter most to the widest audiences – i.e. those involved in team sports, whether it be rugby league or Formula One – always fear mistakes, no matter how many mountains they've climbed.

After a 26-year gap, Green Gartside, frontman of cult 1980s popsters Scritti Politti, recently resumed playing concerts, stage fright conquered, apparently. Fortunately, just as actors do voiceovers and radio plays, he, too, could do his job in another office, namely a recording studio. Imagine the outcry were Wayne Rooney to withdraw for such a reason, claiming that fans were abusing him and distracting him into errors and temper tantrums. The pitch, his stage, remains his one and only office. To aggravate matters, the world can see inside. While technology has transformed almost every other walk of the working week, sport, notwithstanding the prevalence of helmets, advanced surgery, psychologists, action replays and video analysis, remains as naked as entertainment gets.

Make no mistake. For all those regular intrusions by harsh, unforgiving reality, sports journalism is still for the juvenile at heart, the fun-lovers and the thrill-seekers, the romantics and the idealists. For one thing, fretting about what minute a goal was scored or whether the attendance was 2,347 or 2,348 is not for those of a serially serious or mature disposition. For another, as aficionados with laptops, however jaded, we care – possibly too much. The older we get, the more proprietorial we get, not to say more maternal/paternal. The closer you get to the players (a task, take it from me, that grows increasingly difficult as soon as you notice you are ancient enough to be one of their parents), the more you empathise with their hopes and feel their disappointment. These sentiments become increasingly plain as soon as you actually become a parent yourself. On the other hand, as that wonderful cricket writer David Foot, the sports journalist I hold in the highest esteem, admitted when I asked how on earth, at 70, he maintained his enthusiasm: when you're old enough to be an up-and-coming batsman's *grand*parent, empathy is harder to find. Which leaves you reliant on the pleasure principle, the joy sport brings. And if that joy is no longer attainable – even those fleeting spasms of delight that remind you of why, a lifetime since childhood, you are still turned on by the sight of men in shorts – this is no longer the job for you.

Fortunately, for me, the appeal endures. Now in his fifth decade at *Sports Illustrated*, Frank Deford deems Tiger Woods the most interesting contemporary sportsman, purely by dint of the chasm between himself and his rivals. My boxes are ticked most ably by Muttiah Muralitharan, the Sri Lankan cricketer, for dozens of reasons, most prominently: a) he is a spinner and a profoundly unorthodox one at that, and hence, for me, the ultimate sporting sorcerer; b) he has made me appreciative of a part of the world I barely knew existed and which would otherwise have held precious little interest; c) he has risen to the top of his profession, as a member of a team, despite endless if unjust allegations that he is knowingly cheating; d) he is a proud but peace-hungry Tamil, renowned for his charity and relief work, and e) his teammates, representatives of the people he is supposed to regard as his oppressors, the Sinhalese, depend on him like a camel depends on humps.

For all the impartiality it requires, this is no more a job you can do dispassionately than you can do blindfold. I say this fully aware that I am being as politically incorrect as it is possible to be, and that if you cannot see what is happening on the field that doesn't mean you cannot observe, but those observations will always be secondhand and hence less valid. A sizeable portion of the pleasure, moreover, will be missing. This is an ongoing debate on the BA Sport Journalism course I teach at the University of Brighton, and applies equally to being a television, movie or theatre critic. It promises to rage on, but it is best to be realistic, however ruthless this may seem. Besides, there is no newspaper or magazine editor I know who would hire anyone for such a position who did not have the wherewithal to be one-eyed.

INSPIRED WRITING

By dint of their male-designed origins, sport, and by logical extension sports journalism, both have their politically and morally incorrect overtones. Both are still shamelessly sexist and still, in places, institutionally racist. By comparison with sport, however, sports journalism is relatively non-ageist, albeit in good part because typing is as strenuous as tying shoelaces (unless, that is, you are sitting on an ergonomically incorrect chair). In contrast to so many other walks of professional life, experience is everything. Many lament that times are changing, but I have met many more septuagenarian sports journalists than those of any other persuasion, much less estate agents or computer programmers or accountants – and most of those are still at the top of the tree. The fact that Foot is still reporting as I write these words, a few summers after his sobering admission of mortality, shows what is possible; likewise the continued presence in press boxes and newspaper columns of other pre-TV babes such as Brian Glanville, Hugh McIlvanney, John Woodcock and Frank Keating.

The last of these still stands, for me, as the most complete spinner of sporting morality tales, the Pixar of the press box, fusing as he does the awe of a permanent child and the perspective of an adjusted adult. Nobody did more to fuel my dreams of becoming a sportswriter. Nor Simon Barnes's. 'In the main,' he says, 'I was inspired by the great literary writers, such as James Joyce, but Frank was the exception. I first read him when I was living in Asia. I wasn't a *Guardian* reader but I got a subscription when I was out there and read him all the time. He had this fantastic sense of humour and insight into the humanity of sport. He didn't pretend to be an expert: he wrote like a novelist rather than an expert.'[5]

My conviction that the best writing should be pleasing to the ear took root when the *Guardian* launched a series of TV adverts during the 1980s featuring the luxuriantly tonsiled actor Peter Ustinov reading one of Keating's articles. A sports producer with ITV in the 1960s, Frank is conversant with more games than Sony. Steeped in the now as well as the then, he is brimful of warmth and compassion, passion and purpose; a lover of language yet unafraid to expand the dictionary; a devout disbeliever in the laughable notion that politics and sport should never mix; a persistent thorn in the side of authority – few attacked apartheid with such well-channelled rage – yet at heart a celebrant. He also let his boyhood affinities hang out: hailing from the West of England, local rugby and cricket heroes from Somerset and Gloucestershire were a frequent focus for his most lyrical waxings, just as they were for his friend, colleague and regional comrade David Foot. By the same token, he seldom if ever gave the impression of believing that yesterday was superior to today, merely that sport was once markedly less complex. A post-modern romantic, if you really want to pigeonhole.

The following extract, while culled from a published diary, distils all that made him so unputdownable. It also demonstrates how the columnist's nose for a story is informed by a reporter-fan's awareness of topicality. The subject, the Gloucestershire cricketer Jack Crapp, best-known for being a walking headline and for muffing a crucial catch in an Ashes Test, was as inextricably linked to Keating's childhood as ration books and Mrs Hitler's son.

The pretext, though, was sombre in its simplicity: after a lifetime's service to the game, Crapp had just retired.

> *Two summers before I was born, Jack Crapp kissed his beloved mother goodbye, put his cardboardy attaché case under one arm, his bat under another, and strode down the hill to Bristol Temple Meads to start a long life's journey in professional cricket. The final week of April 1979 was the first since 1936 that he was not setting off again. For twenty-one years he played cricket at the highest level, and then umpired at the highest level for twenty-two more. He knew it was going to be hard to stomach this first free, summer's Monday morning. He knew it would be when the dreaded 'Dear Jack' letter arrived from Lord's in February. He had heard on the grapevine that two younger men had applied in the autumn. Anyroad, he knew he was lucky to have been given the summer of 1978. His obvious pleasure when I knocked on the door of the tidy-trim council house where he lodges warmed my cockles more than I can describe. He had not been forgotten after all, on this bleakest Monday morning of all his sixty-seven summers.*[6]

I like to think that sports journalism appeals, above all, to unscarred souls, those who are not only keen on justice but firmly believe it is far more likely be dispensed within those white lines than inside any courtroom – especially one in a land whose current rulers appear to believe that juries are dispensable.

The point, both for the purposes of this book and – much more importantly – your ambitions, is this: whether in the guise of an underdog battling incalculable odds, a team shattering a century-old record or merely one scraping the point required to avoid relegation, sport captures contemporary imaginations like nothing else. It can enchant the senses and embolden the soul, feed the need for identification and, at the other, less admirable extreme, for *schadenfreude* – that little voice inside us all, however shy and shameful, that rejoices in the misfortune of those we fear or resent. In mediating between game and audience, sports journalists meet a widespread need.

GLORY DAYS

'Sportswriting was a dubious profession when I was in college,' recalled Frank Deford, who joined *Sports Illustrated* straight from Princeton and grew up to be one of North America's most respected sportswriters and broadcasters. 'It was not something a serious person went into. Though there were a few good writers, it was a pretty low-class profession. I thought it was something I was only going to do for a little while, but I woke up one morning and realised that this was what I was – I was a lifer . . . after I'd been doing it for a while, I realised, "It's okay Frank, you're not just one step up from being a hooker."'[7] Like so many others, he came to feel a sense of duty. As the history of sport lengthens, as the context of players, games and records becomes ever richer, so that obligation intensifies. To protect and serve, yes, but also to help reform and improve, by question, challenge and prod.

Before going back to college to study how to be a journalist, I cut my teeth on pop papers, reviewing gigs and albums (now there's two words that date me horribly). I enjoyed the freebies and the opportunity to brush shoulder pads with style leaders. I also dabbled in cinema, but soon realised that, much as both music and movies would both continue to provide untold pleasures and insights into the human condition, neither repaid repeated, daily, ritualistic observation. Musicians took years to make new records; film directors were barely more prolific. Those were my pre-neutral days, before uneasiness, over football hooliganism, patriotism and overt partiality, took their toll. I was a longtime fan of Chelsea FC, Celtic FC, Middlesex CCC, New South Wales CC, Harlequins RFC, St Helens RFLC and just about every St George or rose-wearing team in existence. I was also a zealous hoarder of sporting factoids, trivial and nearly important. Covering muddied oafery and flannelled tomfoolery seemed the natural step.

What ultimately motivated me, though, was the absolute conviction that, as a cricket and rugby writer, I might help, in however miniscule, anonymous or invisible a way, to bring down apartheid and end all racism. I like to think – or perhaps kid myself – that I did my bit by joining the chorus railing against the iniquities of 'rebel' tours of South Africa and the way cricket was run by white nations. Fortunately, I also harboured a more realistic ambition: to highlight cricket's flaws and thus help modernise, and hence preserve, my favourite game. Sports journalists should never resist idealism.

I started the sensible way: sub-editor at *Marketing Week*. Weekends were spent reporting football for Hayters, the country's leading sports agency, though a potential libel (the offending item, fortunately, was excised in time) cost me three months in the cold: I rang the office dutifully every Thursday morning to see if I had been forgiven. Three months after joining *Marketing Week*, I received a phone call from Reg Hayter, the agency's avuncular proprietor, father of a teenage cricket teammate and, more usefully, a highly respected cricket reporter in his heyday and, better yet, the 'Hughie Green' of sportswriting (Hughie Green hosted the then-popular TV show *Opportunity Knocks*, a precursor to *Stars In Their Eyes* and *Pop Idol*). 'Do you want to be a sportswriter or not?' he demanded mock-gruffly. Of course I did, and spent the best part of the next two years in his turret of a sweatshop in Gough Square, just off Fleet Street. He was Ian Botham's agent, Henry Cooper's too. His phone burned hot all day with calls from the *Sun* or the *Express*, *Shoot* or *Titbits*, the South African *Argus* or the BBC. Between calls he would hammer out interminable notes to himself on an antediluvian typewriter, an ageing drummer still chasing that perfect beat.

I ascended those three narrow flights of stairs every morning to the polyrhythmic sound of chattering typewriters. While it may have been the mid-1980s, it could just as easily have been the 1930s. Staff were arrayed over two floors divided by a half-landing and a toilet. Reporters were squashed in next to the distinctly non-palatial offices occupied by Reg, columnist Jason Tomas, chief sub Ron Surplice (who taught me all I could ever wish to know about definite articles) and editor Frank Nicklin, the modest, warm and witty tabloid legend, of which more anon. Making tea, updating statistics and cuttings, juniors scurried about below, watched by the kindly office manager, Paul Maher, and Lawrie Dalby, an ageing wisecracking accountant. Upstairs, the Class of '86 included Peter Hayter (aforementioned teenage cricket chum and long-serving cricket correspondent of the *Mail on Sunday*), John Etheridge (highly respected in the same role at the *Sun*), Martin Samuel (chief sports columnist at *The Times* and 2006 sportswriter of the year), Mike Walters (*Mirror* cricket correspondent), Glenn Moore (former *Independent* football correspondent, now football editor), Rob Kitson

(*Guardian* rugby union correspondent) and Rob Shepherd, a former West Ham youth player who rose to chief football correspondent at *Today*, the *Daily Express* and the *Mail*, and enjoyed his 15 minutes of off-page fame by embarrassing Graham Taylor in the documentary that scuppered the then-England manager's reputation. Rob would later be jailed for a more literal assault, but having never climbed higher than deputy sports editor at the *Sunday Times* (for the princely sum of seven weeks), I still consider myself the underachiever and black sheep of that particular pen. That said, being a freelance, and hence theoretically my own boss, I have been free to pursue full-time fatherhood, book-writing, editing, lecturing and other activities. If I could do it all over again, I am not sure I would change anything.

Besides, being born where I was when I was – London, 1957 – my less than inexorable path towards becoming a sports journalist (via trainee accountant, trainee surveyor, advertising, record and department store salesman, estate agent, computer programmer, theatrical promoter, barman and dole-queuer) was enhanced by the climate in which I took those initial faltering steps. By the time I landed my first newspaper job, on Robert Maxwell's shortlived and barely remembered *London Daily News* in December 1986, my first three years as a fledgling hack had encompassed the very best sport had to offer.

That said, by comparison with today, the competitive arts in Britain that Christmas were, on many levels, barely recognisable. And not merely because Oxford United were in the same division as Liverpool and Manchester United, because the following spring's FA Cup final would feature just one imported player, Tottenham's Osvaldo Ardiles, or even because Scarborough's achievement in becoming the first club to gain promotion from the Conference was still a few months away, likewise the inaugural League playoffs. The International Association of Athletics Federations was still the International Amateur Athletics Federation: 'compensation' – nothing as vulgar as 'payment' was mentioned – had not been officially tolerated until 1982. The 1986 FIFA World Cup had attracted 110 entrants, barely half the number 20 years later. Tennis players still wielded wooden rackets. Soccer referees were aided by linesmen rather than assistants. There were no neutral or third umpires or replay assistants, no Premiership or Champions League, no Test Championship or central contracts in cricket. Sunderland's home ground was Roker Park, Middlesbrough's Ayresome Park, both primarily standing-room only. There was no Reebok Stadium, no Pacific Bell Stadium. The Wightman Cup, in which America's women tennis players habitually beat up their British counterparts for fun, was still a going concern. County cricket and rugby union had yet to embrace promotion and relegation. The latter game, in fact, was almost unrecognisable. For one thing, it was an inferior spectacle to rugby league (rather than the virtually indistinguishable copy it would become). For another, the first Rugby World Cup was still a year away, a European Cup more than a decade distant. There were no directors of rugby. Nor, indeed, professional rugby union players – or at least none who dared admit as much.

Although a troubled boxer by the name of Mike Tyson was about to simplify the task (the New Yorker became the youngest-ever world heavyweight champion in 1986), finding and berating villains was a sight harder than discovering and cherishing heroes. At the end of the decade, the Canadian singer-songwriter Leonard Cohen, better known as an accomplished miseryguts, captured the zeitgeist more perceptively than most: 'In the 60s music was the mode, the most important means of communication; that's where the highest values of the race were being articulated. I don't think that's the case today. I think today it's sports –

that's where our most intense imagination is invited to manifest itself. The sports figures in America are much more attractive, much more interesting and their lives are much more dangerous than the rock figures. They are in the traditional heroic mode.'[8]

Television had shrunk the world: the more we saw, the more we slavered. In 1986, albeit with a little celestial help from his friend the 'Hand of God', Diego Maradona became the first man to win a football World Cup singlefootedly; Viv Richards, Carl Lewis, Michael Jordan, Joe Montana, Martina Navratilova and that trio of Buzzing Bs – Ian Botham, Serge Blanco and Seve Ballesteros – were all in their prime. The leading teams in European football and world cricket could be found, respectively, on Merseyside and in the Caribbean, neither exactly abundant in economic wealth. In 1985, six years after Britain and Ireland had finally bitten the bullet and fielded reinforcements against the seemingly invincible Americans, victory in the Ryder Cup had become sport's first pan-European show of unity. In 1984, conducted by a sublime Aboriginal fly-half, Mark Ella, and featuring an inspirational soloist in winger David Campese, the Australian tourists had completed a Grand Slam of wins against British opposition with handling, running rugby of the most expressive and creative kind. In 1986, baseball's Championship Series and World Series had produced a three-act play of Shakespearian proportions, culminating in the game between the Mets and the Red Sox that transformed my sporting preferences. Even I could concede that motor racing was a gas: a brash, daredevilish young Brazilian, Ayrton Senna, had made his Formula One debut in 1984 on a circuit already boasting, in Niki Lauda and Alain Prost, two of the finest, bravest drivers in four-wheel annals. If it wasn't the most fertile and exciting time to be residing on Planet Sport, it certainly felt like it.

Small wonder ESPN (Entertainment and Sports Programming Network), a small North American cable TV offshoot owned by the network giant ABC, made its move in 1987, draining the budget to land a contract to screen live NFL games on Sunday evenings: the first audacious step on the road to a marketing empire and a broadcasting revolution. Rupert Murdoch and his cronies were not slow to take note: come the start of the next decade, Sky Sports would be open for business. Newspapers caught the mood, too: England's first regular broadsheet sports section, in the *Daily Telegraph*, also debuted in 1990.

Then there was John McEnroe, who in 1984 came closer to winning tennis's Grand Slam than any male player since Rod Laver in 1969 and who wins my vote for the most fascinating sporting champion of that or any era. A rare blend of touch, power, speed and innovative technique, many sound judges regard him as the finest all-round player of the professional era, as audacious on the baseline as he was dextrous at the net. It is almost impossible to imagine anyone resisting popularity quite so resolutely as baseball's Ty Cobb, a wizard at hitting, catching, throwing and running, a competitor without peer, but also a paranoid psychopath reviled with equal vehemence by teammates and opponents. McEnroe gave him a run for his money, alienating those who would otherwise have been only too willing to kiss his feet. Yes, Tyson would be fitter fodder for the tabloids, but that, with the exception of the night he bit Evander Holyfield's ear, was attributable to his antics outside the ring. Maradona, Best and Paul Gascoigne also saved most of their excesses for extra-curricular activities. What set the skinny New Yorker apart was the way he shattered his sport's jealously guarded self-image.

While tennis may be the nearest sport gets to non-contact hand-to-hand combat, decorum is demanded. The umpire is not only never wrong, he sits down in a high chair throughout, presiding over all he surveys like some celestial authority. In many eyes, it seemed that McEnroe and his inner demons – Richard Evans, his biographer, characterised him as a boy who wanted to outdo a father who appeared impossible to satisfy – regarded authority as a glass house that deserved a good stoning. He raged at umpires, line judges, photographers, even the crowd, incurring points penalties, lost games and countless fines for verbal and racket abuse. The introduction of electronic devices for line decisions (in tennis and other sports) can be traced in good part to the days when his fury was justified. Yet those outbursts did not make him the world's first protest sportsman. They were a means of redirecting the anger that churned inside and drove him on, a self-directed anger that overflowed not as part of some Machievellian plot to disrupt the concentration of his opponent – many assumed just that – but because, on court, he simply couldn't contain it. His nickname, 'Superbrat', barely skimmed the surface.

The contradictions were plain. 'Who else could have behaved with such grotesque insensitivity on court,' wondered Evans, 'while proving himself to be such a doting father and caring supporter of children in need?'[9] Evans also captured the journalist's dilemma when assessing troubled genius (is there any other sort?): 'What we have here is a hard man: born to achieve, destined to be misunderstood; unable to compromise; driven by an inner rage for perfection the ordinary man cannot comprehend. It is no use, therefore, asking of him the ordinary and the commonplace.'[10]

In early 1986, by when his star was clearly on the wane, McEnroe seemed to have matters in perspective. He was fast approaching 27, the age at which so many high fliers begin to reflect and sometimes go off the rails; at 27, Barry John, that prince of fly-halves, and George Best, for the first time, both retired; in one way or another, the rock musicians Jimi Hendrix, Kurt Cobain, Janis Joplin, Jim Morrison and Brian Jones all killed themselves. 'Hey, but I did it for eight years, didn't I?' McEnroe exclaimed to Evans. 'I stayed in the top two in the world for eight years without training, that wasn't bad, was it?'[11] The poacher, though, would be reborn as gamekeeper. These days, McEnroe is a newspaper columnist.

JOURNALISTIC SKILLS

'Sports journalism offers a fascinating case study in how global and local media interact in contemporary societies,' avers Professor Raymond Boyle of Glasgow University.[12] It can also be more stimulating, more rewarding and – yes – more fun than any other semi-respectable trade in town. If nothing else, you know you are providing a service that is appreciated, however silently. Handsomely paid full-time writing posts with expense allowances the size of a Third World nation's GNP are not quite as commonplace as they were, and the vast majority of match reports are submitted by freelancers, yet there are still more opportunities today than there have ever been, thanks to the growth of broadcasting and the Internet. Because it is my primary area of alleged expertise, this book will be most valuable to those reporting and writing for English-speaking audiences – the British, American, Indian and Australian branches of the business are all represented and discussed – but those seeking to enter other media channels will, I trust, find plenty to chew on. The point being that covering sport on an hourly, daily, weekly, monthly or annual basis, whether for readers, listeners or viewers, involves certain standard disciplines that underpin journalism of all colours and shades. Switch specialism and, with a blend of research, technical skills and anti-slothfulness, you should be able to cover bookkeeping or beekeeping with equal alacrity, if not necessarily the same proportion of joy.

Ask a leading sports journalist to sum up their virtues and they would be indistinguishable from those of any other journalist: a deep, abiding love or fascination for their subject, a faith in their capacity to discern right from wrong, a hunter-gatherer's reluctance to throw away newspapers, magazines, books and match programmes, and an amply stocked, regularly replenished contacts book. When I was interviewed for my job at the University of Brighton, I was asked to give a brief talk explaining how, if at all, sports journalism differed from other forms. The short answer is: not very much, other than that it is more fun and matters to more people. The long answer ran along the following lines.

One major distinction between sportswriters and other journalists is that the former can evade the pigeonholers. We're all-rounders. I write news stories, match reports, previews, features, colour pieces, statistical analyses, columns, TV, DVD and book reviews. Even when I report a match I am doubling as critic: what was the game like? Did the crowd get their money's worth? Did Boris Beckham play well enough to warrant selection in the next England squad? Which leads us to the key distinction, freedom. The sportswriter's freedom is facilitated and enhanced by the audience's familiarity with the subject. Because of its constant presence, the extent to which it is chronicled and the ease with which it can, seemingly, be interpreted, sport attracts the anoraks and obsessives in a way that music, cinema and even television cannot.

Far more people, I would suggest, could cite the name of Sunderland's home ground than Madonna's home town. An American businessman's takeover of Manchester United recently led the front page of *The Times*. I talk up to my readers, if only because I suspect, as passionate fans rather than allegedly dispassionate professionals, they could probably do my job standing on their head. This freedom was captured vividly in *A Sportswriter's Year*, written in 1988 by Simon Barnes, an informative entertainer whose reporter's nose, historian's eye and columnist's ear make him, in my view, the best contemporary British sports journalist. 'In most areas of journalism,' he reasoned, 'you are dealing with the material of the historian. You are painting a picture that will never be completed. There are always too many qualifications. Nothing in real life is ever clear-cut. But sport is not real life. We can break free from the tyranny of "news" and write about our characters with something that approaches the novelist's freedom. If sportswriting is always trivial, then so is humanity, for that is our subject.'

I take strenuous issue with Barnes only in so much as, for me, sport is 'real' life writ large, and hence not always trivial. As sportswriters, it is certainly real to our subjects, and those devoted to their fortunes. Boxers die in the ring; fans kill themselves over a disappointing result, or assault officials; corners are cut and rules flagrantly bent. Where, pray, does 'real' life differ?

In other ways, sport is an improvement. The heroes we, as sports journalists, hail are losers as often as winners, extraordinary mostly in their ordinariness, their accessibility. The villains are easily identified yet capable of swift redemption. Because, by dint of statistics and trophies, it lends order to a confusing world – and because its adversarial nature enables it to tap far more strongly into local, national, regional and racial awareness – sport is, above all, a common language, a bridge-builder. Best of all – because its physicality can narrow the gap between rich and poor, and because its mental demands narrow the gap between strong and weak – David regularly beats Goliath. No other journalistic discipline, I would contend, is so concerned with celebrating life's possibilities.

Do not, however, underestimate how hard it is to be a sports journalist, or *should* be. Merely keeping up to date with each and every hourly development is more than most proper jobs demand, although the Internet (once you know who to trust) has eased that task immeasurably. Because of this, and unlike other journalists, it is far from unusual to cover numerous stories every day. The onus is that much greater: you are trying to satisfy an audience that not only has access to most of the same information but cares far more about sport than about politics.

The late Jimmy Cannon, a distinctive, fervent, at times feverish voice on New York's daily tabloids for nigh-on half a century, explained his preference for sportswriting over political journalism thus: 'When I was a young guy they sent me to Washington to cover the White House. I did it for a while, but the town bored me and I left. I can't stand politicians. They lie more than football coaches.' The sports pages, he averred, were home to 'some of the best and some of the worst writing in newspapers . . . when sportswriting is bad, it's the worst in the paper. When it's good, it's the best.'[13]

Cannon also scorned the notion that the press box is devoid of cheering:

> *It's one of the great boasts of all journalists, and especially baseball writers, that they are not influenced by their relationships with people off the field. This is an absolute myth . . . But I never cheered out loud. I've heard guys cheering. Most of the guys travelling with ball clubs are more publicists than reporters, [referring] to the ball club as 'we'. I've seen sportswriters with World Series rings, and they wear them as though they had something to do with the winning of the World Series.*

Wherein lies a lesson for all local journalists who cover a single team. Balancing objective reporting with local loyalty, the expectations of your readers and editor, and the need to maintain a working relationship with clubs and officials with whom you may have daily contact, is as difficult as journalism gets. The rump of sportswriters are employed by local and regional titles, moreover, and hence face just such a tightrope every day. All the more reason to use temperate language and resist rushing to judgement.

That sportswriting has survived, Cannon argued, is attributable to 'the guys who don't cheer . . . the truth-tellers. Lies die. Go into any town where they have placid baseball writing, where they're all for the home team, and you'll find out that in that town baseball is not considered an exciting game. Telling the truth – and writing it with vigour and clarity – that's what makes it exciting.' The last thing a sportswriter should be, he contended, is a fan. 'I want them to be the guys who neither love nor hate the sport and whose life is not wrapped up in the sport and who remember they are working newspapermen and not baseball people. No more than a police reporter is a cop.'[14]

Which is why, for all my enduring gratitude, I no longer feel guilty over my good fortune. So much so, I am now going to scale the very heights of self-indulgence and list Ten Moments When I Wouldn't Have Traded My Press Box Pulpit For All The Chocolate In Belgium:

- the 1999 World Cup cricket semi-final in Birmingham, when the player of the tournament, the fearless Lance Klusener, lost his nerve and South Africa snatched a tie from the jaws of victory, putting Australia in the final (always the first to spring to mind: my father, by way of levelling the pain–pleasure score, died eight hours later);
- Game Three of the 2001 World Series in the Bronx, seven weeks after 9/11, when the local Yankees grabbed victory from the teeth of defeat and the crowd sang Frank Sinatra's 'New York, New York' all the way to the exit;
- Game Four the very next night – same life-affirming, hopelessly romantic, gloriously Hollywooden finish that New York does twice as well as Hollywood;
- that misty moisty afternoon of athletic poetry and ceaseless carnage in Huddersfield when the All Blacks ran in 101 points against Italy at the 1999 Rugby World Cup. It was like watching Michael Johnson run or Jimi Hendrix play a guitar, Gene Kelly dance or Marilyn Monroe sashay down that train platform in *Some Like It Hot*: impossible to imagine anybody doing their job any better;
- Karen Smithies and chums taking time away from their day jobs to beat favourites Australia at Lord's to win the 1993 World Cup for England while the menfolk were being crushed in the Ashes: impossible to imagine anybody doing their part-time job any better;
- being among the 66,000 at the MCG the night in the first week of 1989, when Steve Waugh, the most singleminded competitor and gifted self-publicist I have ever met, confounded the omnipotent West Indies by winning a one-day floodlit international with a running catch that locked his canary-yellow kit in a glorious technicolour struggle with the white ball, the green turf, the maroon-clad batsmen, the royal blue Melbourne sky and the pitch-black sightscreen: irrefutable proof, for this particular Pom, that cricket had come to terms, finally, with the twentieth century;
- the 1991 World Series in chilly Minnesota and steamy Atlanta, which brought together two clubs that had finished bottom of their respective division the previous year yet produced the most gripping week of sport I have ever attended;
- that sunkissed morning at Edgbaston in 1997 when Andrew Caddick, Darren Gough and Devon Malcolm scattered Australia to the Birmingham breezes, setting up England's first 'live' Ashes victory for more than a decade;
- that hazy summer's day at Trent Bridge in 2005 when Andrew Flintoff and Geraint Jones staged the partnership that underpinned the victory that put England ahead for good in the Ashes series and en route, after the thick end of two decades, to finally bettering those blasted . . . whoops, nice Australians;
- that spring afternoon in Hereford in 1997 when the trapdoor to non-league non-distinction beckoned for one or other of the financially unsound teams. Despite the spell the hosts strove to cast by wheeling on the town's ugliest bull before kick-off, Brighton drew and survived, on goal-difference. I'd felt fear before but never smelled it, much less tasted it.

The only alibi I offer for the such apparent boastfulness is to make a wider point: for a journalist, however tempting and increasingly practicable it may be to stay at home or log on to the Nokia or Blackberry while shopping, super slo-mos and constantly refreshing virtual pages can never begin to compensate if you can't smell the crowd or taste the mud.

The intention is to equip you for the climb, to convey the reality. The oxygen is your department.

Note: Please note staunch resistance to phrases such as 'in my view' or 'in my humble opinion': partly because every piece of writing, every piece of journalism, is slanted or shaded in some way and hence opinionated; partly because my opinion, I'm afraid, isn't terribly humble. If it was, I would never have had the temerity to express it in print, much less expect payment for it, still less accept the invitation to write this book.

Chapter 2

Batting and balling

A short history of sportswriting

CELEBRATING SPORT

Let's kick off with one terrible cliché and a few random observations:

> *There are few words in the English language which have such a multiplicity of divergent meaning as . . . sport.*
>
> (*H. Graves,* Sport and the Body: A Physical Symposium, *1974*)

> *People come back from a game saying, 'We won, we won'. No, they won, you watched.*
>
> (*Monologue from* Seinfeld, *1994*)

> *Malcolm Muggeridge is supposed to have said that a man ultimately has to decide whether to be a saint or a sod. Ian Botham has not quite made up his mind yet. He is, however, not mucking about with the messy grey areas in between.*
>
> (*Matthew Engel,* Guardian, *1988*)

> *With rare exceptions . . . sportswriters are a kind of rude and brainless subculture of fascist drunks whose only real function is to publicise and sell whatever the sports editor sends them out to cover.*
>
> (*Hunter S. Thompson, 'Fear and Loathing at the Super Bowl',* Rolling Stone, *1973*)

> *I owe sport a great deal. Not only has it enabled me to earn a comfortable living; it helped me to grow up.*
>
> (*Grantland Rice, Prologue to* The Tumult and the Shouting, *Cassell & Co., 1956*)

Ever since Athenians and Spartans sought to prove their manhood by running and jumping their way to applause and sexual favours at the Ancient Olympic Games (with a little help from some early performance-enhancers), civilisation's fascination for sporting prowess, in the east as well as the west, has grown inexorably. Never, moreover, have what I like to call the competitive arts been written about so widely, or relentlessly, as they have been during the first decade of the twenty-first century.

Once upon a time, not so terribly long ago, newspaper editors referred to their sports desks as 'the Toy Department'. In recognition of the seemingly unslakeable public thirst for information, and the profits engendered by satisfying that demand, the sneering has all but abated. Indeed, erstwhile sports editors such as Simon Kelner and Charles Burgess have attained more 'serious' and senior editorial positions on national titles. Lent lustre and status by novelists ranging from Bernard Malamud to Nick Hornby, sport occupies a parallel universe while constantly being cited as a metaphor for life. Hence the assimilation of sporting phrases into everyday speech, not least by politicians seeking connections with the great unwashed. Check out how many sporting colloquialisms or metaphors George W. Bush packs into an average speech, or Tony Blair, or how many times you hear any official of any description spouting phrases such as 'It's just not cricket' or 'They haven't even got to first base' or 'You're well offside, Minister'. Sport, in short, is an Esperanto that works. More often than not.

Not that we lack dissenters. Jean-Marie Brohm, a Parisian PE teacher, deemed the professionalisation of physical games to be one of the least edifying products of capitalism; nor did he have much time for the Olympic ideals propounded by his compatriot Baron de Coubertin – as may readily be ascertained from a quick glance at the titles of his collected essays from the 1970s: 'Enough of the myth of educative sport', 'Sport, culture and repression', 'Sport, an ideological state apparatus', 'Draft appeal for the setting up of an anti-Olympic committee'.[1] Yet for all the drug-taking, match-fixing, financial corruption and incompetence, racism, sexism, gratuitous violence and ugly nationalism, sport today is generally regarded much as it has been since its late nineteenth-century explosion: considerably more worthy of celebration than damnation. Few areas of human expertise have been judged so derisively by sceptics; even fewer have been served so admirably by its witnesses. The aim of this chapter is to chronicle and contextualise the evolution and development of sportswriting, albeit exclusively in the English language. 'We have lost religion and found sport,' warranted Mihir Bose in the *Daily Telegraph*. While not strictly accurate, he has a point.

Reviewing Simon Barnes's book *The Meaning of Sport*,[2] Peter Wilby, formerly editor of the *Independent on Sunday* and *New Statesman*, wondered, rhetorically, whether the accompanying surge in sports journalism had brought a commensurate improvement in quality. His answer was not flattering.

> *The politics pages have long given up verbatim reports of parliamentary debates, but the sports pages record every banal syllable of football managers' comments. Player interviews dominate the weekend features; strictly supervised by PRs and agents, they are wholly unilluminating and, significantly, sport has no equivalent of Lynn Barber, renowned for her probing questions. Equally uninteresting are most columns by players and ex-players, usually hastily cobbled together in the office after a disjointed phone conversation with the alleged 'writer'.*
>
> *Match reports can be sloppy. A few weekends ago, I found significant errors in reports of the same rugby union match in three of the four Sunday heavies. This is not uncommon. Sports news meets lower standards than most other news. 'Stories' about impending player*

transfers are planted by clubs and agents hoping to ramp up a player's value. Meanwhile, real stories – about football 'bungs', for example – are left to the BBC's Panorama team, which then gets a good kicking from sports journalists because it couldn't film anybody actually handing over a wad of used fivers.

Then there is the star sports journalist – often called 'chief sportswriter' – who commands a six-figure salary and five-star hotels. When a story breaks, he has to be present, in spirit if not in person, regardless of his knowledge and understanding of the sport involved. So, when ball-tampering allegations forced the abandonment of a Test at The Oval – a subject that required, if ever a sports story did, probing inquiry, technical knowledge and historical perspective – the chief sportswriters rambled on about honour and morality.[3]

Tempting as it is to erect a 10-man defensive wall and repel each and every sling and arrow, it would be churlish not to acknowledge and accept much of Wilby's critique (though the ensuing pages will strive manfully to balance the books). As with any branch of the entertainment/infotainment industry, or any other profession you could mention for that matter, sports journalism is amply stocked with mediocrity. A salary, moreover, is never a reliable indicator of worth. The reason sports journalism lacks a Lynn Barber is plain. While Barber herself is a terrific journalist and writer, she seems to like nothing better than the cheap thrill of cutting the famous down to size, believing, no doubt, that she is merely fulfilling her readers' baser wishes. And while the admirably persistent and trenchant Andrew Jennings – to take the worthiest example – specialises in interrogating and undermining the powerful and corrupt (primarily FIFA and the International Olympic Committee), there is no sportswriter of my acquaintance who embarks on interviews with so pointlessly venomous an agenda as Barber's. This is not to say that some of us do not envy our subjects – their wealth, their lifestyle, their adulation, their skincare products – and write accordingly; merely that, as a general rule, we appreciate both the unique emotional investment our audience places in the highs and lows of its heroes and how fiendishly difficult it is for those heroes to stay heroes.

Tracing his abiding love for Liverpool FC in *Far Foreign Land*,[4] Tony Evans attests to the incongruousness of the sporting fanatic's condition while investing it with the nobility that absolves sports journalists of most if not all our crimes and justifies our continued existence:

There are people who contend that the state of obsession that many of us exist with is an affectation, a lifestyle choice. It's not. Right from the beginning, from the first moment that my consciousness registered as a memory, I've known that it is part of my being. And it can skew the way you look at life.

The intrinsic physicality of sport, furthermore, makes Zinedine Zidane or Andrew Flintoff infinitely more vulnerable than Jack Nicholson or Mick Jagger, both of whom, as I write, are in deep into their seventh decade and still strutting their inimitable stuff. It is our awareness of these differences, and the fragility of our subjects, that imbues us with the requisite compassion to carry out our jobs fairly and justly. If only because we, the chroniclers of the hero business, are sorely aware of our own fragility. If there is one thing you can depend on in the wacky world of employment, it is that enjoying one's work is apt to fuel the insecurities.

THE 'TOY DEPARTMENT'

In the summer of 1956, just as my eventual parents were being introduced by a well-intentioned if misguided friend, Jim Laker produced arguably the greatest one-off in the entire history of the competitive arts. In taking 19 of Australia's 20 wickets at Old Trafford, Manchester, he secured the Ashes for England, a feat that would duly see him voted the BBC's Sports Personality of the Year. On the drive back to London – he was playing against the tourists again the following day, this time for Surrey, which may lessen your sympathy for today's cricketers when they complain about 'burnout' – he stopped off at a pub for a sandwich, and found the regulars watching televised highlights of his accomplishment. He wanted peace and quiet, of course, but may well have been a trifle miffed to have been left unmolested: not a soul recognised him.

Barely a decade later, after England's footballers had won the World Cup in front of a live armchair audience of more than 20 million Britons, such cosy anonymity would have been unthinkable for the likes of Bobby Moore or Geoff Hurst. Rupert Murdoch would be the first to admit that, by now, but for the planet's seemingly unquenchable thirst for men in shorts, his empire might have gone the way of its Egyptian, Greek and Roman predecessors. By paying over the odds for football broadcast rights, and stocking his schedules with cricket, golf and rugby to a degree that the BBC would never have conceived (or even deemed desirable), he took the sort of risk proscribed to all but those with a surfeit of wealth and ambition. More significantly, he and his advisers unwittingly echoed Leonard Cohen's theory: the gamble was based on that growing sense that sport, not dance music, nor the cinema, was now the common currency, allowing generations and nations and cultures to trade and connect. In terms of newsprint, airtime and net-space, sport is now the dominant language of twenty-first-century culture, West and East.

The Victorian era

In *The Victorians and Sport*,[5] Mike Huggins, a lecturer at St Martin's College, Lancaster, devoted more space to the media than to the era's leading sportsmen. As far back as 1895, he records, *The Times* was claiming – apparently without much fear of contradiction – that 'all the schoolboys in England read the cricket news', and that sport, moreover, had become 'a positive passion, thanks to the publicity given by the sporting press'. These days, it is impossible to imagine anybody making the first assertion, and inconceivable that any institution bar *The Times* could make the second.

It was in the Victorian era that newspapers became the main means of conveying information. The *Glasgow Herald* and *The Observer* had been launched nearly half a century previously, in 1783 and 1791 respectively, but it was the abolition of stamp duty in 1855 that opened the floodgates: that year, the *Daily Telegraph* became the first 'penny national' daily paper, while the *Manchester Guardian, The Scotsman* and the *Liverpool Post* all started printing every day of the week. In 1868 came the Press Association, an agency providing copy for newspapers. Distribution enhanced by advances in transport, the *Telegraph* daily sale in 1861 was 130,000, double that of *The Times*; by 1877, it was up to more than 240,000 – a new planetary record. Helpfully, the status of sport as the people's opiate began to take shape in Britain after 1855, as the following list of 'firsts' indicates:

1857: First golf championship (Scotland)
1859: First overseas tour (English cricket team to North America)
1860: First major international tournament (golf's British Open)
1864: First County Championship (cricket)
1868: First Australian cricket tour of England (by Aboriginals)
1870: First America's Cup (sailing)
1871: First rugby union international (England v Scotland)
1872: First football international (England v Scotland)
1872: First FA Cup final
1877: First cricket Test match and Wimbledon Championships (tennis)
1883: First Home International Championship (football) and International Championship (rugby union)
1888: First Football League season
1889: First Football Associations formed outside Britain (Denmark and The Netherlands)

It was in August 1882 that a newspaper first left an indelible imprint on sporting history. In response to England's shock loss to Australia in the final Test at The Oval in south London, Reginald Shirley Brooks, editor of *The Sporting Times*, published a mock obituary:

In Affectionate Remembrance
OF
ENGLISH CRICKET,
WHICH DIED AT THE OVAL
ON
29th AUGUST, 1882,
Deeply lamented by a large circle of sorrowing Friends and acquaintances.
R.I.P
N.B. – The body will be cremated and the ashes taken to Australia

A few months later, at a Christmas party during England's tour of Australia, a damsel from the backwoods named Florence Morphy presented the touring captain, the Honourable Ivo Bligh, with a modestly proportioned terracotta urn, a token of her considerable esteem. Inside this romantic gift, for the man she would soon marry, are held by scholars to be the ashes of, variously, a bail, a ball or a veil. Whatever its contents, the urn would endure as the trophy for which the two nations would henceforth compete.[6]

With horse racing patronised and encouraged by royalty since the fourteenth century, turf 'Classics' (the St Leger was the first to be run, in 1778) and steeplechases (the Grand National followed in 1839) were already staple dishes on the annual social menu, tapping into Britain's fondness for a flutter and affinity with non-carnivorous animals. Yet this, in keeping with contemporary notions of sport as 'masculine Christianity'[7], was the era in which the ball game came of age – sports that placed a premium on individual skill and, in the case of football, rugby and cricket, collective responsibility. By the end of the century, the religion was gaining fresh apostles. The French staged their first (strictly domestic) tennis championships in 1891; pre-empting the Football League by forming baseball's National League in 1876, the United States launched its own tennis (1881) and golf (1895) Opens, and in 1892 hosted the first heavyweight boxing title fight of the gloved era. This fledgling internationalism culminated, initially, in the inaugural modern Olympic Games of 1896, in Athens, prehistoric home of the prototype.

The man generally agreed to be the father of sports journalism was Pierce Egan, a writer who offended many Regency sensibilities in London and beyond. Born in 1772 to an Irish roadmender, relates Steven Carver of Fukui University in a profile for the *Literary Encyclopaedia*,[8] Egan achieved a modicum of notoriety with a satire about the Prince Regent and his lover, Mrs Fitzherbert; indeed, when Victorian reviewers sought to castigate a book, they would often invoke Egan's name as representing the bottom of the barrel. It was in the burgeoning sporting arena, nevertheless, that he made his name. He published his first collection of pugilistic-themed musings, *Boxiana*, in 1812, reported on bare-knuckle fighting and horse racing for the *Weekly Despatch* from 1816 and, eight years later, suitably emboldened, launched a Sunday newspaper, *Pierce Egan's Life in London, And Sporting Guide*. Another leading pioneer was William Denison, Surrey County Cricket Club's first honorary secretary: he first reported cricket matches for *The Times* in the 1840s, a decade that also saw him produce a magazine, *Cricketer's Companion*.

'The media's importance in constructing the Victorian sporting world cannot be overestimated,' attests Huggins[9]. Though the odd publication was already in circulation by the time Victoria ascended the throne in 1837 – *Bell's Life in London*, for instance, was first published in 1822, the same year the *Sunday Times* became the first national or regional newspaper to cover sport in any depth or to any length – the fad became ever more fashionable as the century progressed: the more capable bandwagon-jumpers included *The Illustrated Sporting News*, *Athletic News*, *The Racing Times*, *The Sporting Chronicle*, *The Fishing Gazette*, the extant *Horse and Hound* (recently immortalised on film by Hugh Grant in *Notting Hill*) and even the *Illustrated Sporting and Dramatic News*. By 1851, the *Sunday Times* was a 'literary, dramatic and sporting paper',[10] albeit favouring horse racing by some considerable margin.

In terms of influence, Keith Booth makes a plausible case for citing the major player as Charles Allcock, the versatile enthusiast widely credited as the progenitor of professional and international sport. Allcock achieved most dreams on the field – playing for MCC at Lord's, scoring a goal for England, skippering a side to victory in an FA Cup final and even refereeing one – but is best remembered for his role off it. A skilful and innovative administrator, in which capacity he served as secretary of the Football Association from 1870 to 1895 and of Surrey County Cricket Club between 1872 and 1907, Allcock was also a sports journalist of significance, as sub-editor, reporter and editor. When football first showed signs of challenging cricket, he went into newspapers and became, in turn, football sub-editor at *The Sportsman* and *The Field*, then reported cricket for the former. It was he who hit upon the idea, as football began to eat into cricket's editorial inches, of charging minor clubs two shillings to ensure the results and details of their matches were properly reported and widely publicised in *The Sportsman*. Scoresheets to facilitate this, he added, could be obtained for ninepence a dozen, or 10d post-free. A couple of centuries later, racing would seek to charge newspapers for the privilege of printing lists of runners and riders; one day without such free publicity was sufficient to persuade the authorities that Allcock's approach was much the more acceptable. He also edited all 28 editions of *James Lillywhite's Cricketers' Annual* (1872–1899), launched *Cricket – A Weekly Record of the Game* (1882) and edited it until his death in 1907. It was Allcock, too, who in 1868 launched the FA-authorised *Football Annual*, the first attempt by the winter game to follow the trail blazed by *Wisden Cricketers' Almanack* five years previously. Even back then, as Booth relates, criticism of the referee was de rigeur, even from so measured and seemingly compromised a correspondent as Allock: 'Had the referee had only an ordinary knowledge of the provisions of the offside rule, two, if not three of the goals given them by his casting vote would never have been allowed.'[11]

Amid an age longer on sporting corruption than many would wish to acknowledge, these initial steps were accompanied, not unnaturally, by a tangible determination to be accepted by serious students of these growing games. 'Our creed,' claimed *The Sportsman*, founded in 1864, 'is catholic; our position independent; and our resources as large as enterprise or research can make them.'[12] It even dropped a noble literary name, namely the Roman poet Horace, an early indication of the veneer of respectability and credibility sportswriters have always sought to introduce to their work by way of justifying spending their precious time and words on such an alleged frivolity.

> *Horace has said that the fountain of all good writing is to know something about the subject, but this, so far as we can see, has not always been a principle adopted by all who have come forth to instruct the public in sporting matters. No one is or will be admitted into our establishment from the writer to the typesetter who is not capable of avoiding the gross errors, which so frequently disfigure accounts of sporting transactions.*

Note the word 'instruct'.

By the 1880s, *The Sporting Life*, a racing paper, had a circulation of 300,000, while *Athletic News*, a journal trading in football match reports produced in Manchester since 1875, was claiming weekly sales of 100,000. With interest in soccer progressing apace, the number of Saturday 'classified' sports papers following the fortunes of local and regional teams – commonly known as 'Pink 'Un' and 'Green 'Un' because many were printed on pink or green paper, an early example of branding – rose from four to 18 between the 1880s and the 1890s; by 1900, stated the historian Richard Holt, these were 'ubiquitous'.[13]

The twenty-first century

By the end of Queen Victoria's reign in 1901, the newspaper industry was expanding at a rapid lick: 13 new dailies entered the London market between 1890 and the outbreak of World War I, including the *Daily Graphic*, the first illustrated daily, and the *Daily Mail*, *Express* (the first to put news on the front page) and *Mirror*, whose owners, unlike their posher counterparts at *The Times* and the *Telegraph*, were less interested in political influence than advertising revenues and bottom lines.

Football and cricket results and reports, together with racing cards, were the principal attraction, with cricket's pre-eminence over football more than plain. Tellingly, *The Times* regarded the 1914 FA Cup final as being 'of comparatively little interest except to the Lancashire working classes'. As the Labour movement gained momentum, and the working classes earned a modicum of money and status, so the pendulum swung. The demise of *Athletic News* in 1931, according to Holt, spurred Fleet Street to fill the gap. 'Taking their lead from the "gee-whizzers" of American journalism, a more colourful, gossipy style of writing took over from the rather self-consciously poetic late Victorian style with its "hapless custodians" and "leather spheroids".'[14] Thus did 'popular' Sunday circulations surge in the inter-war period. As printing processes quickened and transport – and hence distribution – improved, so newspapers were able to produce multiple daily and evening editions. This facilitated regular rewrites and updates, especially handy during a Test match or golf tournament.

The endlessly controversial 1932–33 'Bodyline' Ashes series in Australia, cause of sport's first significant international row, had a sizeable impact. Indeed, the word 'bodyline' was a reporter's invention. In filing his report of the Test match in Sydney, Hugh Buggy of the *Melbourne Herald*, having already used the phrase 'bowling on the line of the body', tried to cut the costs of the telegram by abbreviating this to 'bodyline bowling'. Little can he have suspected that his invention would come to symbolise the precariously thin line between fair and unfair play, between sportsmanship and gamesmanship.

For Australians, like Americans, the principal function of sport from the late nineteenth century onwards was to define, and enhance, national identity. (Strange, then, that publications in both countries decided to refer to sporting teams as 'it' rather than the more human 'they' preferred in Britain, a curious distinction that persists to this day.[15]) As a direct consequence, Australian journalists – in particular those covering cricket and rugby, the predominant team games in international terms and hence that much more symbolic than individual causes such as tennis or golf – have gained a reputation for over-parochial cheerleading, albeit increasingly less so as Australia continues to punch well above its weight in just about every sport you might care to mention. During the 1986–87 Ashes series, which England won at a canter, cricket coverage regularly took second place to effusive celebrations of Alan Bond's America's Cup yachting triumph. Australia is far less inclined than England to celebrate losers.

All the same, as Depression-hit Australians endured that 'Bodyline' series – their finest batsmen were battered unmercifully by England's fast bowlers and diplomatic relations threatened – not every member of the home press corps attacked England captain Douglas Jardine's reprehensible tactics without a second's thought. One exception was Arthur Mailey, a Test player-turned-reporter and thus more sympathetic to the quandaries faced by the combatants. What he objected to far more vehemently was the ripple effect of the encounter in journalistic terms.

> *On the next England tour [1936] came an army of 'incident-spotters', just in case there were repercussions which were too newsy to be adequately handled by the ordinary cricket writer. This was a bright idea on the part of London editors. Men who were excellent journalists but who had never covered a cricket match before were thrown into the fray; and what made it worse was that the regular cricket scribes tried to compete with their slick fellow-workers and in most cases made an awful mess of the attempt. It was then we saw a blast of criticism*

> *about umpires' decisions, about playing conditions, about the advisability of players having two or three eggs for breakfast and of fried liver being on the menu. We were supposed to get seriously concerned about whether the senior amateur was becoming engaged to a girl from Wagga Wagga or was it Woop Woop? These news morsels were more or less amusing but when one . . . wrote that an umpire's lbw decision was putrid because, with his own eyes, he had seen the mark of the ball on the bat, some of us viewed the future of cricket journalism with a certain apprehension.*

As to the ensuing editor-led emphasis on accentuating, even exaggerating, the drama, Mailey concluded: 'I treat it as I would an American film version of a famous battle, merely as a piece of unconscious burlesque.'[16]

'Perhaps the ultimate *Mirror* story of the late forties,' proposed Matthew Engel,[17] concerned the flamboyant American tennis player, Gussie Moran, just prior to the 1949 Wimbledon Championships. Dubbed 'Gorgeous Gussie', Moran took the court in lacy knickers visible to all and sundry. 'GAME, SET AND UNDIES!' was the headline, under which ran the following intro: 'To the solid twang of racquet and ball will be added a new sound . . . the rustle of ruffles and the frou-frou of frills. Oomph is coming to the Centre Court – in satin-trimmed frocks and lacy undies – undies you are meant to see too.'

One 'popular' title quick to latch on to and exploit sport's commercial possibilities was *The People*, which boasted of a giddy 'four pages of sport', and advanced its circulation from 600,000 in 1924 to 4.6 million immediately after World War II. By the outset of the 1950s a third of the paper's pages revolved around sport, soccer first, last and almost everything. In the 1960s, moreover, it was *The People* that financed the year-long investigation into English football that ultimately led to the biggest sporting scoop of the era: the revelation that a group of Football League players had pulled off a betting sting in order to take advantage of the Treble Chance, where winnings could be gleaned by forecasting the number of draws. This marketing ploy had recently been instituted by the pools companies, led by Littlewoods, whose owners, the Moores family, controlled Everton FC and would make a similar investment in arch-rivals Liverpool. The ringleaders were banned for life and imprisoned; so were Tony Kay, Peter Swan and David 'Bronco' Layne, who had bet on their own team, Sheffield Wednesday, losing to Ipswich, though Kay still claims this had nothing whatsoever to do with the conspiracy – 'It was just a bet' – and is quick to tell interviewers that *The People* named him man of the match: 'I gave my all.'[18] In a just twist, Kay, apparently as gifted a player as Bobby Moore and a good deal more so than Nobby Stiles, his chief rivals, thus lost his chance of immortality at the 1966 World Cup.

Wherein lay the heart of sport's appeal, for readers, writers, editors and publishers. As a purveyor of life lessons and dispenser of justice, on or off the field, it was deemed superior to, and more trustworthy than, Parliament and the courts (although this gap would close as sport became ever more inclined to believe its best interests lay in kow-towing to corporations and buttering up broadcasters). Because of the sheer volume of people to whom sport represents material and social advancement, and the myriad locations represented – local newspapers have always traded heavily on the premise that success for team or individual is a victory for 'us', for the community – there is always somebody whose day is made by victory on the field of play. Because of this, and also because of the relative (if decreasing) accessibility of both players and game – the former England midfielder Alan Hudson once described football as 'the working man's ballet' – the stories were a good deal more likely to inspire than depress.

For a nation as vast, as diverse and – crucially – as young as the United States, sport acquired an even more onerous responsibility: creating history. Sportswriting there, about boxing and baseball especially, acquired a caché and credibility unmatched elsewhere. There are two obvious differences between the way sport is covered there and in Britain. 1) As a direct consequence of the enormity of the country, there is a virtual absence of national newspapers – not until the populist *USA Today* in the last quarter of the twentieth century did one actually emerge. This means that city, state and regional stories and issues are deemed of greater import than those of national or international interest. 2) Freedom of expression has traditionally been afforded greater encouragement. That said, the immensity of the various newspaper empires did lead to the birth of the syndicated columnist. Even in his dotage, Grantland 'Granny' Rice, one of the early giants of the keyboard, was turning out six columns a week for 'some 80 newspapers'.[19] E.W. Swanton's biographer, David Rayvern-Allen, related with no little awe that his subject had written some 8 million words about cricket over the last 70 years of the twentieth century; from 1901 to 1954, by his own modest estimation, Rice wrote 'over 67,000,000 words, including more than 22,000 columns . . . over 1,000 magazine articles – plus radio outbursts for 32 seasons'. And he still had time to pour out '7,000 sets of verse'.[20]

In many respects, American sportswriting was about self-mythologising, and nowhere was this tendency more apparent than in baseball, which, barely a decade after its alleged birth in 1842, was already inspiring the writer Walt Whitman to call it 'our game . . . America's game', with its 'snap, go, fling of the American atmosphere'. Just as cricket has always attracted its fair share of literati – *The Faber Book of Cricket* (1987) numbers P.G. Wodehouse, Arthur Conan-Doyle, Dylan Thomas, Siegfried Sassoon, Lewis Carroll, George Orwell and a couple of Mitfords – so baseball has trumped it. *Baseball – A Literary Anthology* (2002) features Bernard Malamud, John Updike and Philip Roth, Damon Runyon and Ring Lardner, Whitman and Dom DeLillo: how cricket must envy a constituency of celebrated aficionados that includes the living.

The world's best-known sports publication is *Sports Illustrated*, a weekly feature-led North American magazine born of the postwar sports boom. Despite taking ten years to turn a profit, it has evolved into a brand (South Africa now has its own edition), thanks primarily, admittedly, to its annual 'Swimsuit Issue', which has nothing to do with men in trunks, everything to do with barely-clad women and generates the profits that pay the magazine's way for the other 51 weeks of the year. The success of specialist sports papers in France and Italy reflect a similar cause-and-effect. In England, where weekday sales of national papers even amid the steep declines endured this century averaged in excess of 12 million in 2006, no attempt to replicate the widescreen multi-subject focus of *Sports Illustrated* has survived for long. While American affection for sport is no more passionate than it is in Britain, insularity is more evident. The first international sporting encounter of any hue pitted the USA against Canada at cricket, in 1844, yet of the continent's four major sports – baseball, basketball, American football and ice hockey, team sports all – only the last (oddly enough, the most Canadian of the quartet) ran an official world championship prior to the current century. In the United States, unlike Europe, Africa, Asia and even South America, international sport runs a distant third to regional and racial loyalties.

That insularity, though, is changing, due in part to what may be construed as cultural empire-building – witness the launch in 2006 of a baseball World Cup (its formal title is the Baseball World Classic) – in part to a tacit if belated acknowledgement that international sport might conceivably be of a higher standard. 'In the past, all that mattered in golf was how you played for yourself and by yourself,' noted Thomas Boswell, the man who did most to turn me on to the wonders of baseball and my favourite contemporary American sportswriter.[21] 'Now it also matters how you play for your country and with a partner. Sports and tastes evolve. Is it fair that a Ryder Cup standard that never applied to Bobby Jones, Ben Hogan or Nicklaus will be part of what measures [Tiger] Woods's career? Maybe not. But it surely will. Champions must adjust to their times, even Tiger Woods.' It is doubtful whether he would have written those words but for the fact that the United States' traditional dominance of the Ryder Cup changed radically after Great Britain joined forces with Europe in 1979. Similarly, the failure of the Americans to field a fully representative team at that inaugural baseball World Classic (many players and managers considered the risk of injury before the impending Major League season too great, while one or two leading Hispanic-American performers such as Alex Rodriguez dropped out because they feared that plumping for one country rather than another might impact on their status and endorsements), and the subsequent failure to reach the final, is expected to concentrate minds next time round.

RED SMITH – A STUDY IN ECONOMY

At the end of the last millennium, the magazine *Editor and Publisher*, respected as the so-called 'bible' of North American print journalism, commissioned an illustrious panel to nominate the 25 most influential newspaper folk of the twentieth century. Remarkably, on the final list, shoulder-to-shoulder with publishers such as Joseph Pulitzer and Katherine Graham, and columnists such as H.L. Mencken, lurked a sportswriter: Red Smith.[22] The same ginger-mopped, peppery-witted Smith, droll yet incisive doyen of the *New York Herald Tribune* for five decades spanning World War II and the Falklands War, who was once instructed by his sports editor, Stanley Woodward, to 'stop Godding up those ball players'. Of all the crimes a self-respecting journalist could be accused of, that of bowing and scraping to scantily educated, over-muscled oafs is arguably the most grievous. For the most part, Smith subscribed to the Rhett Butler theory: he gave not a damn.

Reflecting on his career in Jerome Holtzman's oral history of American sportswriters *No Cheering in the Press* Box,[23] Smith expressed a modicum of embarrassment – 'I am sure I have contributed to false values' – but tempered this with a broader view:

> *I won't deny that the heavy majority of sportswriters, myself included, have been and still are guilty of puffing up the people they write about . . . If we've made heroes out of them, and we have, then we must also lay a whole set of false values at the doorsteps of historians and biographers. Not only has the athlete been blown up larger than life, but*

so have the politicians and celebrities in all fields, including rock singers and movie stars.[24]

Syndicated in some 250 newspapers, Smith had to find 800–1,000 words worth saying every day of the week. Surprisingly, his ego was modestly proportioned. Dave Bergin, who went on to edit a number of major North American newspapers, recalled a nervy early encounter with Smith when the latter popped into the *Tribune* office and asked which sub-editor had worked on a column of his a fortnight earlier. It had been the young Bergin, who had transposed two of the paragraphs. The sports editor was furious when he learned this – editors have neither the time nor the inclination to read everything every day – and told the tyro he was 'on probation' for meddling with the untouchable. Smith, though, was not aggrieved. Indeed, he congratulated the sports editor: the column, he felt, had been improved.[25]

Smith's aims were modest:

I like to report on the scene around me, on the little piece of the world as I see it, as it is in my time. And I like to do it in a way that gives the reader a little pleasure, a little entertainment. I've always had the notion that people go to spectator sports to have fun and they grab the paper to read about it and have fun again.[26]

Not that he was all sweetness and light. Doing something daily for more than half a century is unlikely to tint the vision. Indeed, as Holtzman discovered when he interviewed the then 69-year-old, Smith's grasp of proportion was firm:

When you go through Westminster Abbey, you find that excepting for that little Poets' Corner, almost all the statues are of killers. Of generals and admirals whose [speciality] was human slaughter. I don't think they're such glorious heroes. I've tried not to exaggerate the glory of athletes.

On the other hand, he felt sport fulfilled a function, even during wartime.

During [World War II, Stanley Woodward] felt games were non-essential and that we should all be fighting . . . that there shouldn't be a sports page, no baseball or horse racing, not even football – and he loved football. Well, of course, there shouldn't be necktie salesmen or florists or any of the non-essential industries, if you're fighting an all-out, one hundred percent war. I disagreed with him. I felt there was some morale value to games.[27]

Smith was a master of the drop-intro, the delayed punchline. Witness this report of a World Series game in 1947:

In 1942 the president of the Dodgers, whose name is lost in antiquity, hired Louis Norman Newsom as pennant security. Mr Newsom, one of the most distinguished of latter-day poets, responded with a telegram:

'Have no fear
Bobo is here.'

Brooklyn didn't win in 1942, but Bobo Newsom is a man of honour, to whom a promise is a gilt-edged bond. Yesterday he put the Dodgers into a World Series. He did it belatedly and not altogether voluntarily, but when he had pitched an inning and two-thirds for the Yankees in their third and most sordid encounter with Brooklyn, the Dodgers were on their way to victory, 9 to 8.[28]

Even if you cannot tell a pitch-out from a pinch hit, it is difficult not to find something to delight in somewhere in those two paragraphs: the profoundly irreverent opening that glosses purposefully over the name of a bumptious administrator; the easy flow of elegant, hype-free but bouncy sentences that give you the warm sensation of being in the hands of somebody who knows what they are doing and what they are talking about and thus should be wholeheartedly trusted; the light but precise touch; the spry, spare, bone-dry wit ('not altogether voluntarily'); the thoughtful deployment of the Queen's (as opposed to President's) English; the not untasty fact that Newsom – so far as his teammates, employers and most of the Bronx were concerned – turns out to be the villain.

Smith recognised that every story he wrote had a hero and a villain, even if only a temporary hero and a pantomime villain. He also knew that, since his reports and theories were always a hostage to fortune, and that he could just as easily be made to look idiotic come the next day or match, it was better to be temperate, and wary of generalisations. Today more than ever, in a world that only has time for black or white, it is the shades between that capture and define the human predicament. For those dealing with sport, having licence to paint pictures does not – or should not – mean confining yourself to black and white.

Perhaps Red Smith's greatest gift was his ability to plunge a dagger between a perceived wrongdoer's shoulderblades while they were too busy tittering to notice he was not wearing a red nose and a daft wig. As on the first day of the 1970s, when he related the latest development in the ugly battle between the baseball club owners and Curt Flood, the St Louis Cardinals outfielder who had shocked the nation by taking, as Smith put it, 'a stand for human freedom'. Flood had defied his profession's most basic and primeval law, refusing to do his bosses' bidding when the Cardinals decided to trade him to Philadelphia, whose reputation as the so-called 'City of Brotherly Love' had not been earned on the basis of its affection for Flood's fellow African-Americans. Flood resolved to challenge the 'reserve clause', the prehistoric concession baseball had been granted by Congress that enabled the owners to reserve the right to do as they wish with a player at the end of his contract. (In 1972, he lost, narrowly, in the Supreme Court, betrayed, he believed, by the refusal of fellow players to speak on his – and hence their own – behalf, but the battle he led was won three years later.) Smith scanned the scene with that mischievous-sounding-but-deadly-serious glint: '"You mean," baseball asks incredulously, "that at these prices they want human rights too?"'[29]

THE BRITISH TABLOIDS

As the twentieth century wore on, the *News of the World*'s circulation soared to 8 million. Like its direct daily and Sunday rivals, it valued quotes above detail. 'The quotes system, an idle form of journalism, has two fathers,' believes Ted Corbett, who spent the best part of the second half of the century covering football and cricket for the populars.

> *The Manchester United air crash of 1958 killed seven football reporters. They were replaced in time for the following Saturday's matches by lads from the news desk. When they did not understand something they behaved as they would in their other life, by asking an expert, usually the club manager, and quoting him. Quotes were a rarity until that time. It was quite common when I reached the* Daily Herald *in 1964 to start a story 'John Smith scored four goals for Derby County on Saturday and said: Blah, blah . . . ' until the end of the piece. Then came TV with its interviews at the end of matches. Sports editors loved* Match of the Day *and insisted on quotes although I remember that every season at the* Daily Mirror *we would have a get-together in which the sports editor would say 'No more bloody quotes pieces' but by the beginning of October every Monday morning story would be full of quotes.*[30]

The *News of the World* would claim to be the world's best-selling newspaper. But, for all that it published allegations (unproven, if unconvincingly so) that the Leeds United manager Don Revie had tried to bribe his way to the League title in the early 1970s, the zeal for campaigning seldom resurfaced once the populars had been reborn – and redefined – as the 'tabloids', a process that picked up speed when Murdoch's ailing young *Sun* downsized in 1969. As the austere, self-conscious 1950s gave way to the revolutionary, promiscuous 1960s, so journalism and journalists cut their cloth accordingly. No longer was it only the Sunday papers that rattled cages and offended sensibilities. As the *Daily Mirror* sought to lure back the readers it was losing to the *Sun*'s diet of Page 3 dollybirds, racy storytelling, TV gossip and sport, and the *Daily Mail* and the *Daily Express* jettisoned broadsheet for tabloid, the style of the 'popular' papers reflected a readership less inclined to defer to authority or censorship. Once, while editing the *Sun* in the 1980s, Kelvin McKenzie, a man inhibited by neither taste, tact nor propriety, ran a competition to win razors belonging to the javelin thrower Fatima Whitbread, whose sexual orientation the paper, and many reporters, often questioned, though mostly in private. If George Best cannot truthfully be classed as the first sporting celebrity created by the British tabloids to lead the front page and boost sales – unruly Beatle-like hair, a model's figure, a penchant for boutique fashions and outrageous talent made him sport's first pop star as early as 1965 – his rows with management and dalliances with blondes and bottle made him the premier inspiration.

The order of the day became celebrity, gossip, humour and irreverence. Having seemingly run out of verbal abuse during the build-up to the 1990 World Cup – 'World Cup Wallies', 'Pathetic Boring Rubbish' and 'We're a carbuncle on the face of Soccer' were among the choicer pieces of anti-patriotism[31] – the *Sun* was obliged to change tack abruptly when Bobby Robson's side came within a penalty shoot-out of the final. Four years later, the paper infamously committed vegetable abuse, depicting Robson's successor, Graham Taylor, as a turnip. The struggle for market share with the *Mirror* begat renewed sensationalism and rushed, rash judgments. The perils of the latter became ever more apparent once news reporters began to be unleashed on sport, unsympathetic eyes and not-so-well-hidden agendas in hand. As uninvolved, temporary observers, they had nothing to lose by offending their subjects. This can be, should be, every journalist's outlook. Trouble is, it can also lead to scruple-free reporting.

On 19 April, 1989, three days after the Hillsborough stadium tragedy in Sheffield that cost 93 Liverpool FC supporters their lives shortly before an FA Cup semi-final was due to kick off, the front-page headline in the *Sun* roared 'THE TRUTH'. Beneath ran allegations that 'drunken Liverpool fans viciously attacked rescue workers' and 'rifled the pockets of injured fans as they were stretchered out unconscious'. One group, apparently, had 'noticed the blouse of a girl trampled to death in the crowd had risen above her breasts. As a policeman struggled in vain to revive her, they jeered: "Throw her up here and we will **** her."'[32] The allegations were never substantiated, Liverpudlians started boycotting the paper and sales in the region withered. News Limited executives are still trying to heal the scars.

The brains and spirit behind the renewed emphasis on a more blatantly populist, personality-based brand of sports coverage was Frank Nicklin, sports editor of the *Sun* when it went tabloid. While he would have held no truck with the excesses quoted above, he encouraged his reporters to be snappy and exclamatory in their language, personal and provocative in their angles and analysis; nor should they take anything or anyone too seriously. And if the story was too tame, too literary or failed to inspire a suitably audacious and/or funny headline, the sub-editors would add the appropriate twists and hyperbole. (Not for nothing are tabloids, and some mid-market titles, known as 'subs' papers'.) Indeed, Nicklin blazed a hugely influential trail with his brash and adventurous approach to headlines, not to mention page design, headlines, boxes, career-at-a-glances and photographs, but necessity, as ever, served as the ignition. When the *Sun* was relaunched in 1969, the paper was only printed in London, necessitating early deadlines so that it would reach northern climes in good time, which in turn reduced live match coverage, so Nicklin began assigning reporters to compose ghosted columns under the name of sporting celebrities. 'They were so popular,' notes Engel, 'that when deadlines did improve and there was more live match reporting in the paper, people screamed to have the old stuff back.'[33]

Circulation battles, moreover, meant that, where honour, discretion and self-protection had once governed the coverage of incidents in dressing rooms or on tour, the rise in the number of sports pages and the concomitant hunger for the inside scoop changed all that. Pleas that a remark was being made 'off the record' often went unheeded. If trust between players and reporters did not entirely evaporate, it certainly curdled. The descent into distrust began in late 1977 with a spat in a taxi on the way back from the Islamabad High Commission between Ian Botham, England's first superstar of the tabloid age, and the then cricket correspondent of the *Sun*, Steve Whiting, ushering in an era of off-field reporting. Eleven years later, Mike Gatting, a married man, was sacked as England captain, ostensibly for inviting a female member of the hotel bar staff to his bedroom on the eve of a Test match. The selectors, admittedly, had been looking for a reason to dispense with him after failing to do so following a rancorous and unseemly altercation with a Pakistani umpire a few months previously that had caused the suspension of an entire day's play in a Test match. The fact remains that the press had hitherto drawn a polite veil over Gatting's extracurricular activities, just as they had done for his likeminded predecessors, if mostly because they themselves were far from innocent in this regard. Now anything, anybody, was fair game.

Not that the players always helped themselves. Dragged from his bath to be interviewed by the BBC's Peter West after bowling England to an astonishing victory over Australia at Headingley in 1981, Bob Willis did not seem quite himself. Some would allege, with little foundation, that the wild-eyed look in his eyes was induced by drugs. The pace, bounce and spite he served up that afternoon had been terrifying, winning the match while saving his

THE TRAVELLING BROTHERHOOD

In 1926, when Shirley Povich became sports editor of the *Washington Post* at the improbably tender age of 21, he had a staff of six. Bylines were rare, and only awarded for conspicuously well-written or important stories. In 2005, the paper's sports desk had expanded to 65 personnel. It took Povich a year before he persuaded his bosses to allow him to cover an event outside the national capital. Commercial flights at affordable prices were still to come. For an American journalist, because of that aforementioned insularity, overseas assignments were largely confined to the Olympics and the occasional boxing title fight. Having an Empire/Commonwealth to play games with, as well as a more competitive newspaper market, gave his British counterpart more reason to travel.

Indeed, as pleasure once more became permissible after the end of World War II, foreign reporting broke fresh ground. Since England did not enter a World Cup until 1950 – the four British FAs had fallen out with FIFA in 1928 over payments to amateur players – and with the 1948 Olympic Games having taken place in London, it was left to cricket and rugby to lead the way. For the first postwar British Lions tour to New Zealand, believes Huw Richards, author of the first comprehensive history of rugby union, *A Game for Hooligans*,[34] the travelling corps could be counted on the fingers of one hand and still leave enough to make a rude gesture: 'I think Dai Gent of the *Sunday Times*, who was about 80, went for part of the tour, but that was about it. From 1955 in South Africa you get a few more – the beginning of the deluge of JBG Thomas tour books dates from here – but still only in single figures.'[35] Cricket, though, was a different matter. According to research by the late Dick Streeton for the Cricket Writers' Club, there were no fewer than 14 members of the press corps that clambered aboard the Stirling Castle in early September 1946 bound for the six-month MCC tour of Australia and New Zealand (England teams played abroad under the Marylebone banner until 1977). To put this in perspective, mind, in September 2006, two months before another Ashes series, Lachy Patterson, who handles media accreditation for Cricket Australia, reported having received around 1,200 applications, which would in due course be whittled down to around 100 per match.[36] (It would be remiss not to mention here that the genial pipe-smoking Streeton – or 'Streeton of the London *Times*' as he preferred to announce himself on foreign missions – taught me a number of idiosyncratic if easily resisted tricks when we toured Zimbabwe together in 1990. Not only did he conserve his boxes of Swan Vestas as if wood was on the verge of extinction – 'This is the third world, you know' – he would methodically, even ruthlessly, rip out each page of every paperback he brought with him as soon as he had read it: the better, he reasoned, to avoid paying excess baggage.)

Unsurprisingly, given the time spent in each other's company, it was shortly after first postwar Ashes tour, in June 1947, that the Cricket Writers' Club was founded. Though pre-empted by the Baseball Writers' Association of America (BBWA) (1908), the International Sports Press Association (1924) and the Boxing Writers' Association of New York (1926), it kick-started a trend in Britain; the Football Writers' Association (September) and the Sports Writers' Association (November) were both established before 1947 was out. As befits its longevity, the BBWA has long exerted the greatest influence, not only improving the profile and working conditions of its members as all such bodies seek to do, but also through its inception of sport's arguably best-known and most celebrated answers to the Oscars: selection for the Baseball Hall of Fame at Cooperstown (since 1936) as well as for each season's major awards in the National and American Leagues. Others followed suit, but the BBWA was solely responsible for the adoption of MVP (Most Valuable Player) as a popular acronym in other fields.

The point about such associations is that, whatever your chosen speciality, it is advisable to seek membership as soon as possible. The best way to achieve this is to make yourself known to established professionals whenever you are in a press box or at a news conference: nurture your contacts. I am delighted to report that there are no written exams, nor, in contrast to many monosexual clubs one could mention, any mysterious initiation ceremonies involving Greek symbols, chaps in hoods, rabid squirrels and other curious forms of male bonding. The more members, in short, the more the relevant authorities are compelled to listen to complaints about dodgy mobile phone signals, clapped-out air conditioning and one-legged chairs. The annual dinner, moreover, can be relied upon as a source of fun as well as an opportunity to make or renew useful acquaintances, whether with players or editors, but be wary and discreet. The talk is usually of the shop variety but nobody likes to be buttonholed while they are busy trying to drink the house dry. Under these circumstances, men are rarely as good as their word.

international career. Yet instead of revelling in what is still the greatest fightback by an England XI, Willis castigated the media for writing the team off, and for obsessing over the former captain, Botham. Fair enough: even the philosophical Mike Brearley, recalled to lead the side, shared his distaste for the depths to which the press had apparently plunged. That same day, however, Willis, judgement doubtless impaired by relief and emotion, accepted an offer of £1,000 to contribute a ghosted column to the *Sun*. He subsequently apologised for this gross if unconscious hypocrisy in his column for *Wisden Cricket Monthly*, but the battle lines had been drawn.

By the second half of the decade it had all gone mildly beserk: Botham was being handsomely paid by the *Sun* for a column while his employers let rip with front-page headlines about his latest off-field escapade. Only when the paper rang up requesting another column in 1988, shortly after he had spent a night in an Australian jail after allegedly assaulting a fellow airline passenger, did he and his advisers decide that enough was enough. That said, the *Mirror* was not slow to offer a contract, nor Botham tardy in accepting.

Instructively, Botham's glorious if infamous heyday – Sir Len Hutton, the former England captain and then an *Observer* columnist, declared him the first 'rock 'n' roll cricketer' – coincided with both a downturn in the fortunes of all three of England's major national sports teams, and, even more tellingly, the bitterest phase yet in the circulation war, ignited by the 1979 sale of *The Times* to a sharp-minded bounder from the colonies. As 'Dirty Digger' Murdoch (*Sun*, *News of the World*) and Robert 'Bouncing Czech' Maxwell (*Daily Mirror*, *Sunday Mirror*, *People*) slugged it out for the title of Britain's Most Reviled Émigré, so Botham himself, caught in an unprecedented tug-of-lust between the two dailies, was frequently brandished as a weapon by both sides. The final score was joyful neither for *Mirror* employees, whose pension fund was raided by Maxwell (who had died in mysterious fashion by the time the case came to court), nor for British journalism, which lost even more in credibility.

CAUGHT IN THE WEB

That the tabloid diet of rumour and confrontation now set the sporting agenda was plain by the 1990s, by when Murdoch was slashing the cover price of *The Times* in a briefly successful attempt to haul back the *Daily Telegraph*'s vast advantage as the market leader. As football became the new rock 'n' roll, so celebrity columnists and gossipy diaries inveigled their way into the broadsheet lexicon. The advent of the Premiership, the flotation of clubs on the Stock Exchange, squabbles over broadcasting rights, the ramifications of the Bosman ruling on freedom of contract and movement, not to mention salaries and the transfer market – all combined to add high finance to the mix. Hitherto underemployed as a topic of debate within the parallel, hermetically sealed world of sport – boxing and horse racing aside – money now emerged as the handiest stick with which to beat the underachievers and the disloyal. The gradual disappearance of the one-club man incited heated debate, and no little hypocrisy.

Then, in the mid-1990s, came the Internet, with its instant service and improbably long tentacles, allowing baseball games and Test matches to be followed, play by play, over by over, from tens of thousands of miles away. Cricinfo, indeed, was set up by English expats living in the US who were eager to satisfy their thirst for up-to-date scores. The Web created more employment for sporty wordsmiths in exchange, again, for what was widely perceived, if not always fairly, as a shallower approach. This time, the Luddites were less stubborn. It did not take long for newspapers to decide that joining the new boys was more pragmatic than striving to beat them. The *Guardian*, through *Guardian Unlimited*, were first to produce a Web version, accompanied by articles that could not be accommodated in print: one of the wonders of the Internet is the freedom it afforded to break the tyrannical hold so long imposed by page sizes and the column format. Soon it was deemed commercial suicide *not* to follow suit, even though nobody had quite, as yet, worked out precisely how to make such sites pay.

The impact, for journalists, was immense. The relentless speed at which information was now gathered, processed and delivered shrunk the planet, let alone mere nations. Where once news desks were littered with posted copies of the *New York Times*, *Le Monde, Suddeutsche Zeitung*, the *South China Morning Post* and the *Sydney Morning Herald*, an increasingly paper-less society can transmit news all but instantaneously. What with bloggers, 'citizen journalists' and impromptu mobile-phone snappers further aiding the process, a crowd riot in Peru or a record-breaking long-jump in Chicago will not only be reported far earlier than has hitherto been possible, but in infinitely more detail.

The *Argus Lite*, the compact product of a long-established Brighton newspaper, exemplifies this shrinkage. A condensed, allegedly easier-to-follow edition of the main paper, *The Argus*, it is aimed squarely at commuters. Launched in 2006, it was inspired by *Standard Lite*, the London *Evening Standard* offshoot that had in turn drawn inspiration from the cheaply produced *Metro* freesheets whose owners – Associated Newspapers, proprietors of the *Standard* – had in turn followed the business plan increasingly beloved of cash-strapped local and regional papers: deploying the Internet, wire services and sub-editors in place of reporters. On the two pages dedicated to sport, neither of the two main stories was Brighton- or even Sussex-centric: the 'bungs' inquiry launched in the wake of a *Panorama* TV investigation into the questionable antics of English football managers and a report of the previous night's televised match between Watford and Fulham. Of the remaining 13 stories, just one (complete with 'Sussex Sport' tagline) concerned sport in either county or city. Although it was about Brighton and Hove Albion FC, much the most popular sporting team in the area, it still propped up the page alongside a quiz. Even the 'TV sport highlights' column was granted greater prominence.[37] Where TV leads, newspapers follow.

Saturday 5 August, 2006 proffered another sign of the times, aptly enough in *The Times*. The previous year the paper had been reduced, amid much heated debate, to a so-called 'compact' size: bar the tabloid-sized pages it was barely discernible from the broadsheet, but the reduction, notwithstanding an increase in pagination, meant word-lengths had to be trimmed and many stories excluded. The *Independent* was also in the vanguard of this radical change, one justified in part by the purportedly tiresome business of having to fold a broadsheet in order to read it on a crowded Tube train. The *Guardian* found a happy medium with its 'Berliner' format (halfway between tabloid and broadsheet) and, having dabbled with it previously with pullouts on Saturdays and Mondays, launched a daily sports section; the *Daily Telegraph* responded with a daily tabloid sports supplement, all of which left the term 'broadsheet' bereft of meaning. 'Quality' became a popular if inaccurate alternative, 'serious' a grave, snooty one, 'heavy' a more literal and accurate one, however ponderous.

This left the Sunday papers, traditionally the thickest of the week and seen as an opportunity for longer articles and broader perspectives, in something of a quandary. Following the Australian lead, the parallel expansion of Saturday papers – which by the end of the century were matching the following day's papers for paperboy-snapping bulk – had also impacted on Sunday sports desks. When he was appointed cricket correspondent at the fledgling *Independent on Sunday* in 1990, recalls Tim de Lisle, 'the Sunday papers were a lot more reflective and analytical than the dailies, which went well with cricket. The dailies have become more Sundayish since, which has made the Sundays' job harder.'[38]

Unlike their 'popular' rivals, these products did not quite cram virtually every nook and cranny with football, but the accent on the game was still hefty, leaving other reporters more cramped for room than at any time since the dawn of the 1990s. Unsurprisingly, they greeted this with about as much enthusiasm as a bull ordered to wreck a shop brimming with unbreakable china.

On the day in question, there were 16 sports pages in *The Times*, including three devoted to racing: coverage of world news was far skinnier. The trouble, on the face of it, was that, being a Saturday, there were few major fixtures of interest to a British audience to report bar the continuing sagas – the third Test between England and Pakistan and the Women's British Open. Murdoch's ownership of both *The Times* and Sky Sports, needless to add, meant oodles of plugs – by way of features and columns – for what the latter was covering. Far more alarming, for lovers of paper and ink, were the county cricket reports. Even though the top four teams were playing each other, and Surrey's Mark Ramprakash had made the first 300 of his illustrious career to take his season's average to a colossal 113, the fixtures were all relegated to a round-up. If nothing else, this made no economic sense. Even though they could quite easily cobble together something from the Press Association feed and the Internet, *The Times*, along with the *Daily Telegraph*, send reporters to every Championship fixture, of which there may be up to nine in a week, each lasting up to four days. If we include subsistence, travel expenses and fee of £100–£130, the cost per reporter per day, bearing in mind the vast majority were freelancers, would have been £200–£250. The get-out clause came in the shape of a few lines advising deprived readers that full reports could be found at *The Times Online*. Which was all fine and dandy if you weren't suffering from the delusion that an Internet café was a place trawlermen frequented between voyages.

In many ways, newspaper websites are shop windows for the product still sold in newsagents. Or so the executives theorised. As the millennium drew to a close, many predicted that the end of newspapers was nigh. As I write, for all that sales are in decline and certain titles appear to be living on borrowed time – notably the *Daily Express* and *Independent* – such fears have been confounded. According to a 2006 report by Ofcom, the British broadcasting watchdog, a quarter of respondents aged between 16 and 25 said they read newspapers less frequently as a consequence of spending more time online,[39] yet vast swathes of the Great British public were still prepared to buy what they could get for free.

Why? Three theories. First, habit. Second, paying for something somehow invests it with greater credibility, a sense of ownership: the Internet may not be free, but it does not cost 70p a day. Third, niche marketing may be all the rage but the British, in particular, remain avid newspaper readers, from which one can reasonably infer that reading about a variety of subjects in one tidy(ish) package, and the mere act of turning pages, retain an appeal. For those born and bred in a world of typewriters, telexes, teleprinters and stubbornly immobile telephones, constantly flicking between menu items on a virtual page, not to mention straining one's eyes to follow the words on a screen, is often a cultural leap too far.

Over the past decade the nature of sports journalism has altered radically, irrevocably – and, many argue, not necessarily for the better. Not for nothing did the Sports Writers' Association vote in 2003, after 55 years, to change its name to the Sports Journalists' Association, an accurate reflection of the number of commentators, presenters, producers and photographers now swelling its ranks. Rival media, more immediate, more accessible, less costly media, have circumscribed the sportswriter. No longer is he necessarily the first source of information, and rarely so when it comes to match reporting or interviews. Always a step behind the beat, gossip, analysis and nostalgia are now the most valuable of his wares. Throw in all those over-protective coaches, hypocritical chairmen, image-obsessed shareholders, mustard-keen PR departments and ambitious agents, and the number of obstacles strewn in their path leaves the press obliged to run the equivalent of the Grand National in search of that elusive 'exclusive'. Of the genuine variety, that is, not the Dave Blogginsworth contract dispute 'exclusive' that first appears in the *Northern Echo* then miraculously crops up in the *Sun*, then disappears for the second edition when an observant Scottish sub-editor on the late shift respectfully informs his news editor that the *Daily Record* had run a similar piece three days previously.

Given the choice, leading sportspeople would always prefer to be interviewed on the air. That way, what they say cannot so easily be filtered or edited, or left to stew for a few days, or longer, to be reheated for another time, another context. By and large, furthermore, TV and radio reporters, more constrained by time than the press tend to be by space, chase the short and the sharp: the immediate reaction, the predictable and the reassuring. Because rights fees and primetime exposure are of such mutual benefit, sports and broadcasters, generally speaking, are content to scratch each other's backs. To spend a day eavesdropping in the media centre at Lord's is to be acutely aware that the erstwhile 'gentlemen of the press' feel as if they have been herded into a box marked 'Barely Necessary Evil'.

Yet as non-terrestrial and Internet-based organisations proliferated in the early years of the twenty-first century, so the growth of niche TV and radio stations has proved a boon for frustrated print journalists. Whether their beef is with the budgetary constraints imposed by a declining newspaper market, or with the intellectual handcuffs slapped on as a consequence of the perceived dumbing-down of the mass media, consolation has come in the shape of the documentary. Step forward Ken Burns's *Baseball*, a superlative chronicle of the USA's so-called national pastime; BBC4's examination of the so-called 'D'Oliveira Affair' that brought the iniquities of sport under apartheid to a head; *The Fight* and *World Cup Stories*, two more BBC series, the first an illuminating six-part dissection of the keystones – primarily racism and corruption – of boxing history, the latter a similarly broad-spectrumed venture focusing on FIFA World Cup winning-nations. Books, too, help fill the yawning void: witness Simon Wilde's thorough and measured account of cricket's match-fixing crisis of the late 1990s, *Caught* (Aurum 2001); Howard Bryant's *Juicing the Game* (Viking 2005), an insightful account of baseball's 'see no evil, hear no evil' approach to drugs since 1994 based on the author's columns in the *Boston Globe*; David Conn's hard-headed yet heartfelt tomes on the social and economic realities of soccer, *The Football Business* (Mainstream 1998) and *The Beautiful Game?* (Yellow Jersey 2005). Andrew Jennings, best of all, has hounded sport's wealthiest and most powerful governing bodies, FIFA and the International Olympic Committee (IOC), whether via *Panorama* documentaries or in books such as *The Lords of the Rings: Power, Money and Drugs in the Modern Olympics* (Simon & Shuster 1992) and *Foul! The Secret World of FIFA: Bribes, Vote Rigging and Ticket Scandals* (HarperSport 2006). Work of this order, contemporary histories all, written and researched by journalists – albeit not necessarily sports journalists – reinforce the growing conviction that the most important and far-reaching reporting these days is more likely to be found on television screens and between hard covers.

Indeed, argues one leading newspaperman, reporting standards in Britain are not what they were. In terms of ethos and practice, there is a considerable difference in the way British and North American newspapers operate, or so contends Leonard Downie Jr, one-time London correspondent and now editor of the *Washington Post*.

> *Obviously the fact that British papers tend to have an ideological position is very different from papers in this country. And there is a tendency in the British media [for writers] to be essayists rather than reporters. There's a lot of detail that doesn't appear in most British reporting – it's more impressionistic, more analytical, and it's less deep and less facts-seeking . . . The depths of investigative reporting and accountability reporting*

> *in the US, and the premium on accuracy, is paramount. In Britain, the* Daily *and* Sunday Telegraph, *for example, are both very aggressive newspapers right now, but every time they report something that interests us, the first thing we have to do is check it out. Just because they have reported it doesn't mean it's true. I would hate for people to see the* Washington Post *that way.*[40]

Another view would be that whereas the United States' insistence on fastidious fact-checking is completely justified and laudable – 'fact checkers' are integral to any high-profile newspaper or magazine in the US but not, regrettably, in Britain – the timidity of so many of that nation's reporters – however fearful they may be, understandably, of litigation – leads to a more compliant, less purposeful media.

For aspirants of every hue, there are realities that must be faced. Being a fan with a laptop, an anorak's stash of sporting trivia, a vast hoard of books, magazines, programmes and scrapbooks and a neat turn of phrase is no longer enough, if it ever was. In broadcasting, especially television – which, being a visual medium, is more susceptible to the lure of a familiar face and/or voice – the accent on celebrity is unmistakeable. Of the 15 analysts hired by CBS Sports to cover the 1998 Nagano Winter Olympics, for instance, just one was neither an ex-athlete nor a former Olympian.[41] Most of these illustrious ex-players, though, are not practising journalism in the strictest sense. They offer expert comment and insight; few, if any, ever break a news story or deliver a string of running 30-second match bulletins.

The print media is still dominated by trained journalists but many of the most coveted jobs, notably in cricket and rugby union, have been cornered by former players. While the path from pitch to press box is well-trodden – C.B. Fry, in the 1920s, was probably the first notable to cross it – the balance, in England at least, has altered dramatically in recent years. At the outset of the 2006–07 Ashes series, the chief cricket correspondents on three of the four main English daily heavies, the *Guardian* (Mike Selvey), *Independent* (Angus Fraser) and *Daily Telegraph* (Derek Pringle), as well as the *Observer* (Vic Marks), were all ex-professionals, with Selvey and Marks in situ for two decades. Ditto un-ghosted columnists and reporters such as Atherton (*Sunday Telegraph*), Mike Brearley (*Observer*), Peter Roebuck (*Independent*), Simon Hughes (*Daily Telegraph*) and Steve James (*Guardian* and *Sunday Telegraph*). The same, in rugby union, is true of Eddie Butler (*Observer*) and Paul Ackford (*Sunday Telegraph*), while Stuart Barnes (*Sunday Times*) is also an eminent voice. When England toured the West Indies in early 1986, the only English daily or Sunday broadsheet to be represented by an ex-international in an unghosted capacity was the *Sunday Telegraph*. Then there are those whose fleeting encounters with the sporting heights afford them closer glimpses into the athletic mind. Matthew Syed, once a Commonwealth table tennis champion, has become a perceptive all-round sports feature writer for *The Times*; Paul Kimmage, a former professional cyclist whose remarkably frank account of his experiences, *Rough Ride*, won him the William Hill Sports Book of the Year award, is now the *Sunday Times* sports section's chief interviewer, effortlessly turning double-page spreads into an intimate exploration of the competitive soul.

Almost without exception, these ex-players bring their expertise to bear in a manner that most of us who have never tasted the thick of sporting battle at exalted levels, however superior we might believe our intrinsic journalistic skills to be, could not hope to better. The good news for unathletic types is that the public schools and Oxbridge are no longer such fertile breeding grounds for cricketers. Yet rather than bemoan our purported misfortune at seeing the plum jobs vanish from view, we must focus on those key journalistic skills: digging, questioning and, yes, painting. Or, as Raymond Boyle put it so pithily, 'get out of the office'.[42] The Internet age has been virtuous in many respects, especially for journalists, but it has also encouraged them to embrace laziness with greater gusto than ever before. The next chapter elaborates on how you can reverse this depressing tide.

EXERCISE

To climb even the first rung of this rickety ladder, certain minimum requirements must be met, starting with literacy and the correct use of words. Use the following to write a piece of continuous prose, ensuring the meanings and distinctions in each case can be fully and properly understood. Some, it bears stressing, are abused virtually every day of the week in publications from Tripoli to Tipperary.

Disinterested
Uninterested
Currently
Presently
Affect
Effect
Principal
Principle
However (with and without commas)
Who's
Whose
It's
Its

Chapter 3

Whose agenda is it anyway?

Sports journalism in the digital age

> *Sport invites a rejection of prejudice. You can have as cock-eyed a view of life as Adolf Hitler but you can't stop Jesse Owens from winning four gold medals . . . Sport is not a moral force in itself, as the Victorians believed. Rather, sport is morally neutral, but as such, it is a vector for truth. With South Africa, sport showed that an entire system of government was immoral, and that sport then set about destroying it.*
>
> *Black people are as good as white people. Muslim people are as decent as anyone else on the planet. Women are strong. Sport not only tells us many truths, sport also forces us to listen to them. That is a fact about the history of South Africa, a fact about this history of this country, a fact about the history of every other country on earth. Anyone who rejects the truths told by sport is living in cloud-cuckoo land.*
>
> *Simon Barnes,* The Times, *28 July, 2006*

Those words formed part of an article written to commemorate one of the more significant breakthroughs in sporting history: the first day as captain of South Africa's cricket team of Ashwell Prince, a Cape Coloured. The headline was: 'Coronation of Prince is an inevitable end to story of changed world'. The line chosen even more adroitly by the sub-editor to highlight, via a pullout quote, was: 'The death of apartheid is all about the power of sport'. To anyone with aspirations to write about sport for a newspaper, it is important to recognise this micro-context in order to understand and appreciate that journalism is not a solo endeavour.

THE RELATIONSHIP BETWEEN SPORTS JOURNALISTS AND CLUBS

As outlined in the previous chapter, the profession has undergone seismic changes since Barnes wrote his seminal book *A Sportswriter's Year*. Technology and computer programmers have seen to that. The *Sports Illustrated* baseball columnist Tom Verducci related a revealing conversation he had in September 2006 with the general manager of the New York Yankees,

Brian Cashman, about the waning form of Alex Rodriguez, whose $250 million, 10-year contract is still, as I write, the juiciest in that or any other game. 'Imagine,' wrote Verducci, 'how bad it would have been had he gone through this 10 years or so ago, when Steinbrenner was still Steinbrenner.' George Steinbrenner is the Yankees' owner, and a shipping magnate, until fairly recently the planet's most meddlesome and egotistical sporting executive. Not all that long ago he characterised his Japanese pitcher Hideki Irabu as 'a fat pussy toad'. He lost some of that hard-won repugnance, mind, when he became a cosily familiar sitcom figure: Larry David, the co-creator of *Seinfeld*, impersonated him (he was always filmed from the rear), milking the rapid-fire speech and daft utterances for all they were worth. While defensive, not unnaturally, of his boss, Cashman saw another reason to dispute this view: 'Today George doesn't have to say anything. That's because we live in a 24-hour-news-cycle world where the critics are everywhere: newspapers, talk radio, TV, the Internet. There are a thousand different Georges.'[1]

This in turn begs a question: have the rules, unwritten as they are, changed for those actually paid to be Georges, the journalists? Up to a point, yes. The practicalities and logistics have certainly undergone transformation. The timeless verities, though, remain intact.

Being a sports journalist, especially in the twenty-first century, is about a good deal more than 'Godding up' these post-modern gladiators, let alone describing and explaining their daring deeds. Consider the sheer tonnage of sports coverage in the media and the pleasure, even stability, the heartbeat of its seasons brings, itself a reflection of changing social values, values that have seen ballgames and races flare into quiet obsessions and mass communion, affecting lives on a private, regional, national, racial and even sexual level. I especially love the fact that the sports that command the most fanatical followings happen, by no coincidence whatsoever, to be team games, which demand a degree of selflessness, collective consciousness and unity of expression so conspicuously absent in most other walks of post-Thatcherite life. To me, this signifies that it really is community we crave, not individualism; that society is not, contrary to what Margaret Thatcher herself asserted, deader than a dodo. What does it say about a mongrel nation's gradual acceptance of multiracialism than that, in the summer of 2006, dominated as it was by a FIFA World Cup millions of Englishmen had apparently been deluded into imagining Sven-Goran Eriksson's team could win, the homegrown sportsperson to inspire the most affection, and be made an early favourite for the BBC Sports Personality of the Year, was a Luton-born Sikh named Monty? But then the rapid rise of Mudhasen Panesar, England's first world-class spinner since my teens, was but Exhibit A of a changing thoughtscape. Paul McKenzie, editor of *Touch*, Britain's only magazine devoted solely to black music, told the *Guardian* about his 'moment of epiphany' during a Manchester United v Tottenham game at Old Trafford: 'I noticed how many black kids were wearing David Beckham shirts. Before, black kids would only wear black players' shirts. But all these black backs suddenly sported a white player's name.'[2] In my language, that represents progress. This does not mean, though, that more, a great deal more, is not required.

If more is now written and said about events outside those white lines than within them (inevitably and not unreasonably), only a minority can be classified as celebratory. The ratio of whinges to appreciation has soared. But there are good reasons for this, of which the most obvious are: a) ever-lengthening fixture lists and increasing chunks of editorial space have combined to denude appetites and engender staleness; b) for all the administrators' claims of transparent governance and the ubiquitousness of the press release, information is still tightly controlled and expertly suppressed, needling and prodding the written press into an increasingly adversarial role; c) the gap in earnings between player and journalist, let alone player and reader, has never gaped wider.

In the perennially complex relationship between sport and the media, the dynamic has changed dramatically. Long grateful for the column inches and airtime, the producers – the chairmen, boards, marketing directors and chief executives – have cottoned on to the fact that their wares have a market value. They have also realised that their assets – the players – have a scarcity value.

Access to footballers in particular is monitored and restricted by clubs and agents, the better to increase that scarcity value and glean the right sort of exposure. The flattering sort. Of late, you might have seen a tell-tale sentence, usually in italics, at the end of apparently exclusive interviews, informing you that Maud Linn buys her contact lenses at Magnet-Eyes. Not all that long ago, when reporters dutifully wrote 'here at the Foster's Oval' or 'England finished the second day of the second Cornhill Test in command' – well, they did lay on lunch, tea and drinks, stationery, stats and the odd free gift, not to mention a helpful coterie of pretty non-males – the 'Foster's' or the 'Cornhill' would in many instances be briskly deleted by a sub-editor: partly to save space, mostly to make a withering point about the sordid, over-commericalised state to which sport had sunk; a point far easier to make in a London office than a press box in Leeds. In retrospect, my own reluctance to mention ground or competition sponsors seems extremely petty (though I still steadfastly refuse to call The Oval by its latest incarnation, the Brit Oval): without the money paid to clubs and governing bodies to secure such an honour, there might no longer be a ground to report from or an event to describe.

'THE WORLD'S BEST ADVERTISING AGENCY'

Such was the headline in a recent newsletter from the Sports Journalists' Association,[3] alluding to the editor, Steven Downes's belief, widely unappreciated, that the sporting press is just such a helpful beast. The ensuing article spotlighted findings from a recent worldwide survey by 'a Danish think tank' into the ways publications in different nations cover sport (though India, Pakistan and Malaysia were all mysteriously overlooked). The commonalities, setting aside sports of specific national interest such as baseball, were considerable. In Britain, 53.8 per cent of the articles monitored were about football, slightly higher than the ratio in continental Europe (50.9 per cent); in both cases, the next most popular sport (golf and cycling respectively) accounted for less than 10 per cent, emphasising both soccer's dominance and the competition among the also-rans.

Other conclusions were even more instructive. More than half the articles monitored (58 per cent) dealt with current events, by way of match reports, previews and results. Surprisingly – to those of us convinced that horizons have expanded – roughly one in 20 articles covered the economics of sport, and just one in 30 the political aspects. In fact, the proportion of stories about drugs and doping (1.5 per cent on average) had *declined* since the previous such survey. More predictably, men were the focus in 86 per cent of the articles, 95 per cent of which also happened to be written by the hairier of the species.

That headline, though, was what lingered longest in my mind. Sport has always differed from journalistic coverage of other commercial pursuits. How many adverts do you see in newspapers or magazines that have been taken out by Manchester United publicising a match? Now consider the acreage of advertising space hungrily devoured at colossal prices by film and record companies, TV channels and book publishers. Instead, fixture lists, results, reports, previews and interviews serve as free advertising. Unfortunately, governing bodies and clubs, and the local bigwigs and/or media conglomerates behind them, seldom see it in those terms. Which puts sports journalists at a severe disadvantage. If you are a music writer who wants to talk to, say, Puff Daddy (all right, Mr Diddy), you will probably be accommodated. His record company will probably fly you halfway round the world, give you all the time you desire in whatever ornate Babylonian palace he might live in and even pick up the expenses tab. If you are the chief sports feature writer of the *Sun* and want a one-on-one with David Beckham, you had better make your own way to Madrid, finish inside the prescribed twelve-and-a-half minutes and promise to give a prominent mention, not to the subject's next match, but his latest hairspray. And all for some hoary platitudes and rusty clichés that will be dutifully repeated for the grateful pleasure of every other interviewer.

This unhappy state of affairs is borne out by Neil Robinson, whose extensive experience at the business end on both broadsheet and tabloid newspaper desks – formerly deputy sports editor at the *Evening Standard* and the *Guardian*, as well as a reporter and feature writer, he now works at the *Daily Mail* – incorporates many years at the front end of a newspaper.

> *I'm not sure there is much journalism in sports journalism these days. Perhaps that is a little unfair but so much information is now filtered through official channels that the public is being constantly fed a very sanitised version of events. One of the great ironies of the past few years is that the more coverage has increased, the less we have come to know. When players do speak, they seem instinctively suspicious and adopt a uniform blandness. This even extends to the spate of ludicrous football autobiographies which have become a completely discredited medium.*
>
> *Newspapers are struggling with all this. Faced with acres of pages to fill, they are forced to rely on recycling quotes from club websites, where the official line is routinely trotted out. Opinion regularly appears as fact and the bloated sports sections of the broadsheets seem to lack the vitality of old. But I suppose the same could be said about me. It is not a healthy state of affairs. Newspapers used to lead the way in knowing which player would sign for which club and which manager would be sacked. But this information is much more tightly controlled and tends to come out via the official websites. I think this has led to a collective lack of edge among the tabloids.*[4]

THE IMPACT OF TELEVISION

That evergreen football correspondent Harry Harris, best known for his work on the *Daily Mail* and the *Daily Express*, does not like what he sees either, blaming the seemingly unstemmable flow of TV money for what he regards as a deterioration in the relationship between media and clubs.

The problem is that access is at an all-time low, and I think the relationships between football clubs and the media is also at an all-time low. The industry no longer needs the written press and whereas the mistrust existed before now, the football industry no longer needs to put up with it, so there is a huge chasm between the two industries.

The modern footballer now has image rights and they become big celebrities. David Beckham can't possibly be classed as big a player as Bobby Moore, but his image is much greater as a footballer than players of the past, and that's what television has done. Newspapers still play a big role, but you see comments from players such as Rio Ferdinand saying: 'I don't trust newspaper journalists, I'm not bothered about being in the newspapers'. Modern-day footballers say 'I don't need to be on the back page any more because I'm on television', but at the same time, if a newspaper pays one a quarter of a million pounds to have a column, they don't say no, [although] that same newspaper could be turning them over on the front page.[5]

On the other hand, Robinson does espy reasons to be cheerful as well as fearful, notably in what he regards as

the greater attempt to explain the technical aspects of sport in a way which readers and viewers understand. You could call it a democratisation. Some of the inventiveness shown in this respect is breathtaking and a real leap forward. Of course television leads the way in almost every aspect of the genre, a trend which will never be reversed. Some of what appears on our screens is as close to art as sport can get. It is astonishingly creative.

Harris, however, believes the gulf between reporters and players is harming print coverage.

Now you get an awful lot of articles written by really good journalists in an authoritative way, but they really do not know the subjects they're writing about. They don't know them intimately on any personal level whatsoever. There is still the ability to get to know people on a private basis, but it is very limited and very difficult to achieve. At first, clubs needed the newspapers to have shirt sponsors visually advertising themselves, but when there was wall-to-wall coverage in places like Sky there was a better outlet for sponsors to be on TV screens rather than newspapers.

Is this a jaundiced view? I do not believe so, but then I am probably irretrievably biased as well. Two questions arise. Are sports broadcasters journalists? And if television is the only medium sportspeople can trust, where does that leave the legions that still pay mortgages through the written word? From where I sit the answers are 'Yes' and 'In a bit of a pickle'.

THE IMPACT OF CHANGES IN THE NEWSPAPER INDUSTRY

Yet television was not the sole catalyst. The technological advances and union-bashing of the mid-1980s led to faster printing and, inexorably, to more, cheaper and thicker publications.

This changed the newspaper industry irrevocably, sports coverage above all. To fill those pages, it has risen at an unparalleled rate: there is so much more to do. But while there may be more games and sets than ever before, match coverage – with the exception of the Sunday and Monday football pullouts – has, as a proportion of the space allotted to athletic pursuits, declined. The problems they present – evening kick-offs, time differences, extra-time, laptop/mobile phone breakdown – make them a risk. Most major events take place during the nine-to-five slot; not the competitive arts. If it wasn't for sport, newspapers would be on the streets earlier, and cost a sight less to produce. Better, reasons the modern sports editor, to play safe and stuff the pages full of stories that can be done and dusted by 6pm, comfortably in time for first edition; computer design packages, helpfully, make substantive changes for subsequent editions immeasurably simpler and quicker than in the days of hot metal. Reports of the action remain a staple, naturally, but, courtesy of sport's increasingly broad visibility, equal billing is now bestowed on the by-products: the transfer/injury/disciplinary/tour/fixture/new boss/angry chairman/'Jones sucks says Smith' stories. Once the exclusive property of the Sunday papers and magazines, interpretation and behind-the-scenes burrowing (albeit not exclusively in the public interest) are now intrinsic to the daily diet, albeit less than they ought to be.

Sport is rare in that it has a foot in both the ancient entertainment industry and the newly-anointed infotainment business. For millions, as Tony Evans underlined, it is not a matter of desire or choice: we feel we *need* to know, for our general well-being, our team's latest result; and we watch that team because we want to be distracted, stirred and, ideally, uplifted. For the sports journalist, then, the priority was set in stone long ago: inform, then, if space and/or time permit, entertain. The weight of emphasis, if not completely reversed, has certainly altered.

SOCIAL CHANGES

As may already be apparent, the unfeasible optimism of the mid-1980s did not take long to dissolve. After all the wonders of that decade, a crash was on the cards; not that anyone truly suspected it would be quite as grotesque a pile-up as it was. As the century staggered to a close, there had, admittedly, been one or two hints that Nostradamus might well be proved correct. At the end of the 1985 cricket season the World Health Organization declared that AIDS had reached epidemic proportions. Four months earlier, 39 Italian lives had been lost in the Heysel Stadium disaster, at the European Cup final between Liverpool and Juventus: the most inglorious hour in the spit-and-spite-filled annals of hooliganism. Quite properly, English clubs were banned from European competition, for five years. Before the decade was out, 93 lives had been lost in the Hillsborough tragedy, originally blamed on the selfsame so-called 'English disease' but ultimately shown to be a result of the one-way relationship between clubs and supporters, which in essence amounted to all take and no give. The Taylor Report put an end to terraces, placing the accent, finally, on keeping the customers satisfied, for all that many still yearn for the era before prawn sandwiches and video screens.

Perhaps the most symbolic happening, though, came on the stock market, another field dominated by young men and their wild and lavish dreams. In Bible-belt USA and beyond, AIDS was widely viewed as divine punishment for homosexuality; the case for regarding 'Black

Monday' as divine punishment for greed was infinitely more credible. On 19 October, 1987, £50 billion was wiped off the value of publicly quoted companies in London; nobody escaped the fallout. The Hong Kong market closed; Wall Street endured the worst day in its history, the Dow-Jones index falling almost twice as far as it had at the nadir of the Great Crash of 1929 that had hastened the Depression, which in turn prepared the pitch for Adolf Hitler.

It was amid this climate that the Major League Baseball owners were not-so-secretly making a mockery of everything sport purportedly stood for. Corruption had reared its head most blatantly at the outset of the 1980s: Italy celebrated their third World Cup triumph in 1982 thanks largely to a striker, Paolo Rossi, who had freshly re-emerged after serving two years in jail for participating in a match-fixing scam. That, though, was but a split end by comparison with the GBH the baseball owners were inflicting on their constituents.

Stung by the advent of free agency in 1975, bent on reasserting their power in the face of a players' union that had won public support and all manner of belated financial concessions, George Steinbrenner and his cronies clubbed together in the mid-1980s and agreed not to bid for each other's free agents. Interviewed for Ken Burns's magnificent 1994 documentary history of the United States' most popular spectator sport, *Baseball*, Marvin Miller, the trailblazing union lawyer who had won the free agency battle on behalf of the Major League Baseball Players' Association and thus done endless favours for team players the world over, was adamant: since the owners were effectively telling supporters they had no interest in improving their teams, this amounted to the most cynical and widespread instance of match-fixing yet.

'During the next two seasons, player salaries grew at lower rates and high profile free agents routinely had difficulty finding anybody interested in their services,' related Michael Haupert of the University of Wisconsin.[6] The players duly charged the bosses with violating the 1981 agreement signed by owners and players which specifically forbade such collusion. Charges were eventually filed for each season from 1985 to 1987; the owners paid through the nose. 'The result,' wrote Haupert, 'was a return to unfettered free agency, a massive financial windfall for the impacted players [$280 million], a black eye for the owners, and the end of the line for Commissioner [Peter] Ueberroth.' It also marked the point of no return for sporting salaries, and the start of a far more perplexing development: the elevation of sports economics to back-page prominence.

Around the corner was the madness of Mike Tyson, a force and victim of nature the like of which even boxing had seldom glimpsed. Then there was drugs. Steroids and beta-blockers rather than nandrolene or testosterone were the boosters de jour, East German shot-putters and Russian hammer-throwers the usual suspects; the clouds gathered with renewed gloom at the Seoul Olympics of 1988 when sprinter Ben Johnson (a Canadian, note, rather than an American) lost his 100 metres gold medal after failing a drugs test: unavailingly did he accuse rivals of getting away with the same sinful practices but the whispers were gaining volume. All the old certainties were being swept away.

Bernard Levin, polymath, vaunted *Times* columnist and jack-of-most-trades, if assuredly no lover of the competitive arts, was driven to despair:

> *My words constitute an appeal to Heaven, begging whomever is in charge there to bring about, with the greatest possible despatch, the end of ALL international sporting events,*

> *productive as they now are of nothing but cheating, drug-taking, money-grubbing, racial hatred, political statements, advertising, hooliganism, envy, litter, selfishness, vanity, corruption, intolerance, defamation, sexual excess, robbery, drunkenness and, from time to time, murder. (And if I were to dwell on the spectators as well I would need to construct an entirely new thesaurus of condemnation).*[7]

What Levin did not see fit to add was that the world he was describing had much in common with the one in which he resided. Which is less a case of chicken-and-egg, I would humbly suggest, than egg-and-omelette.

Sales slashed by competition from the electronic media, newspapers themselves are now in turmoil. Witness the shrinking in England of what were once called broadsheets, the allegedly more serious-minded publications whose proprietors – with the exception of the *Daily* and *Sunday Telegraph* and the *Sunday Times* – finally disabused themselves of the notion that size is everything. 'The industry never had a proper discussion, post-tabloidisation, about quality journalism,' attested Martin Newland, a recent former editor of the *Daily Telegraph*, who took exception to *Independent* editor Simon Kelner's insistence that his paper remained a member of the so-called 'quality' sector rather than being a 'viewspaper' such as the *Daily Mail*. Kelner, he felt, consistently strayed into the latter territory with front-page headlines such as 'As Tony Blair laid a wreath at the Cenotaph, four more British soldiers laid down their lives in a wretched, futile war'[8] (however justified those of us opposed to the invasion of Iraq might have believed it to be). Newland continued:

> *It may well be that changing readership patterns and the digital age are redefining what is a quality newspaper, but if the confirmation of reader prejudices and the editorialising of headlines is now OK for the qualities, what are we doing excluding the middle market from the quality stable? . . . The only economically viable way forward for the quality press might be for them to steal middle-market tricks. But if this happens, the designation 'quality' should be more democratically applied.*[9]

This, then, is the context in which you are aiming to work.

CONTEMPORARY MORALITY

In many ways, the summer of 2006 was as ripe and demanding a time as there has ever been to be a sports journalist. Juventus, AC Milan, Lazio and Fiorentina were found guilty of pressurising referees for favours; the Tour de France winner was disqualified for failing two drug tests. Causes abounded, from equal pay for women at Wimbledon and the right of the less hairy sex to participate in golf's US Masters to the racist antics of Lazio FC supporters and the expansion of cricket in Afghanistan. Nor was there any shortage of unforgettable theatre. Was there ever a more controversial or equivocal climax to a major sporting event than the chest-butt for which Zinedine Zidane, the tournament's principal actor and, more importantly, an enduring symbol of tolerant, multiracial France at a time when Paris was struggling to live up to such high ideals, was sent off in the FIFA World Cup final? Damned universally one minute, the fact that he had been racially provoked by his Italian marker meant not even France's eventual defeat could stop the villain from being hailed a day or so later, by his own countrymen, as some kind of existential hero. That said, as Ed Smith reasoned in *The Times* once the dust had settled and the tubs had stopped being thumped, Zidane's failure to head the winning goal minutes earlier was surely the underlying cause of his temper-loss.

That the ultimate beneficiaries should be an Italian side chockful of players from clubs who, just days later, would be relegated and penalised points for their part in the aforementioned referee-fixing episode – though nobody could actually prove that money or even favours had changed hands, and the penalties were gradually, shamefully, reduced on appeal – did nothing to ease the complexity. How were we supposed to react, to all that? The function of the sports journalist is to steer us through these turbulent seas and find an island of understanding, even if that means conceding that there is no correct answer, no spiritually or morally correct response. Man likes to think definitive answers are always possible and that he has them (or knows a man who does); the wisdom of women lies in the fact that they are so painfully aware how wrong men are.

Much the same state of disconcertment arose when I conducted a survey of my BA Sport Journalism first year students for our webzine, *OverTime*. The question was straightforward: what, in their view, have been the sporting achievements most worthy of their awe? I primed them shamelessly, emphasising the feats of those they were (with one exception) far too young to have witnessed: Emil Zatopek's Olympic hat-trick of 5,000 metres, 10,000 metres and marathon; Don Bradman's Test average of 99.94; Jim Laker's 19 for 90; Bob Beamon's 29ft long-jump; Wilt Chamberlain's 100-point basketball game, and so forth. To my dismay, the winner was Lance Armstrong, for his seven successive Tours de France wins, a towering triumph rendered almost meaningless in many eyes by a complete lack of faith in the possibility that anyone might cross that particular line first *without* the aid of some sort of performance-enhancer. When I vented a modicum of my spleen, one especially promising student, Alexander Shaw, rapped back: 'Yeah, I know, but he beat cancer too.' For once, I paused before pressing the reply button.

Franklin Foer, the American political journalist, believes sport's global nature makes it possible to imagine, even construct, some form of global identity.[10] However, contends Raymond Boyle, 'the reality that he found on his travels around the world was a global cultural form that acted as a vehicle for the expression of conflict, tension and a range of deeply rooted local identities'.[11] Being an eternal optimist and hopeful romantic, I, too, prefer to emphasise the fruits.

Much, rightly, is still made of George Orwell's observation about sport being war minus the shooting; too little, scandalously, of its capacity for being politics minus the politicians. Think of the trailblazers and breakthroughs: Muhammad Ali, Basil D'Oliveira and Jackie Robinson, Billie-Jean King, Martina Navratilova and Cathy Freeman; Jesse Owens in Berlin and Makhaya Ntini in Johannesburg; Babe Didrikson on a men's tee; Belinda Clark running Australia's National Cricket Academy; India's cricketers competing peaceably with those of Pakistan. Never underestimate the reach of sport's tentacles.

At the same time, dangerous illusions can fester for decades. The team ethic, for instance, is not always ethical, or even moral. Images, furthermore, are thinner than an After Eight mint on a liquid diet. *Sports Illustrated*'s Tom Verducci summed up the reporter's dilemma in February 2005. His ire was triggered by the aftershock that followed the publication of

Jose Canseco's autobiography, wherein Major League Baseball's one-time home run champion, recently retired and long rumoured to be a user himself, accused his peers of taking steroids. While inclined to the unpopular view that there was probably something in Canseco's claims, Verducci was even keener to point a withering finger at Canseco's former boss at the Oakland As, the eminent Tony La Russa, a qualified lawyer and one of the most astute and successful sporting managers of the past 20 years (conducting the St Louis Cardinals in 2006, he became just the second man to manage World Series winners in both the National and American League). La Russa now claimed to have known all along that Canseco was partial to performance-enhancing drugs. Verducci charged,

> *Canseco lied, at least until he figured out how to goose the advance money for a book. Tony La Russa lied, at least until it fit him to fire back at Canseco. Only now does La Russa say Canseco would talk openly about his steroid use with the As while La Russa was manager. There was no condemnation then from La Russa, no effort that we know of to clean up Canseco and the oil spill that was about to spread over the game. Canseco could help him win championships. More important, it was 'his' guy, one of 'his' players, and the ancient code of the clubhouse has to be upheld: don't ask, don't tell. Especially don't tell.*

Protecting one's convictions, as a journalist, is far trickier, especially now news travels almost as fast as light. Another *Sports Illustrated* mainstay, Frank Deford, was handed a thankless task: try and make some sense of baseball's Kirby Puckett, whose undignified descent provided American sportswriters with the classic professional dilemma: how openly and adequately to report personal disillusionment.

Known fondly as 'The Puck', the Minnesota Twins' pneumatically built outfielder – one writer dubbed him 'a cantaloupe with legs' – was Major League Baseball's highest-paid player of the early 1990s. So undiluted was the warmth he generated, so untrammeled the affection, in the Twin Cities and beyond, he was on first-name terms with strangers. 'The state that had bequeathed us the original American sports hero, Paul Bunyan, finally had found the big fellow's 20th-century heir,' Deford reminisced.[12] When a local magazine ranked its '100 Best Things about the Twin Cities', Kirby, one of the inspirations behind Minnesota's 1991 World Series victory, was voted most popular resident and fifth overall, ahead of nationally loved cook Betty Crocker as well as the infinitely less mighty Mississippi. Elected to the World Sports Humanitarian Hall of Fame, he was variously described as 'a real-life Smurf', 'the eighth wonder of the world' and – the ultimate back-pat – 'everything that is good about baseball'.[13]

Then the Fates snarled. Upon awaking one spring morning in 1996, Kirby found he could not see properly out of one eye. Glaucoma was diagnosed. In due course came premature retirement and all the havoc that wreaks with an athlete's self-worth. 'Then he wasn't a ballplayer anymore, let alone a whale of one,' attested Deford, gallumphing along that slender line between compassion and chatty familiarity. 'Then he was just back to being fat little Kirby Puckett.'[14]

The clamour to be noticed, to find out how far he could push public adoration, grew rather than abated: urinating in a car park in full view of fellow shoppers was par for a sorry and seemingly pre-destined course. Kirby's mistress bore the brunt, though no-one knew so at the time – to the fans, and so far as the press presumed, he was the perfect spouse, an immaculate confection. Yet other women suffered too. In March 2003, a week before George W. Bush was due to forget the pressures of killing Iraqis and formally open the new baseball season, Kirby, cuddly Kirby, went on trial for alleged rape. Yolanda, his wife, was not overly surprised: according to her, he had committed domestic violence. As is the way of such things, an unseemly amount of revisionism and word-swallowing ensued, but the overriding response was disbelief. More stubborn than a pack of geriatric mules, blinder than a father defending his daughter's virginity, this was, of course, entirely in keeping with civilisation's appetite, in a largely Godless age, for visible-if-craven idols. Reasoned Deford:

> *We do cling hard to a belief in our athletes. Ours is an increasingly sedentary society, and we are beholden to technology – very little of which we comprehend – so the physical prowess of athletes is all the more appealing. Even with a war hanging over us, warriors, our most traditional heroes, are not so romantic anymore . . . Ah, but athletes: they who, as of yore, simply achieve physically, naturally (is there any sweeter phrase than natural athlete?), as human beings, flesh and blood.*[15]

The accompanying illustration depicted a jowly Puckett in glasses, the lenses reflecting images of his younger self, all guileless smile and generous, wide-eyed innocence. A tear creeps down his cheek. A tear for Kirby – and for those who cannot help Godding up those ball players.

THE CHALLENGE OF THE WRITTEN WORD

There can, however, be other purposes to all these loving labours. The written word may not be as fashionable as it was, but so far as sport is concerned, the printed or electronic page can still *entertain* in a manner, paradoxically, that television, the mass entertainer, cannot match. Because broadcasters invest so much money in sport, they tend to treat it more subjectively, protect it more jealously, buff its image more zealously and ignore its flaws more assiduously. If only because of the enormity of the audience, to criticise the Scotland rugby union captain live on air for failing to sing 'Flower of Scotland' with sufficient lustiness is considered a vastly more grievous crime than stating the same for consumption the following morning. The pressure of being expected to supply instant responses, furthermore, militates against commentators, who inevitably suffer, by and large, from what could be termed the GFT Syndrome: Great! Fantastic! Tragic! If reading this book persuades you to reconsider anything you might previously have believed about the practice of sportswriting, I fervently hope you decide that those three words should only be used when the context absolutely demands it, which should be only marginally more often than a Coca-Cola bottler demands a bit more fizz in their life.

The liberal, unthinking use of these three words encapsulates the difference between the written and the spoken word. 'Great night last night, eh?' is perfectly acceptable in everyday speech, but greatness, in the qualitative sense, is an accolade that can only be earned over time, and only bestowed after full consideration of what has gone before: to state in print that this goal or that try was 'great' is to expose yourself to ridicule from your readers, a goodly proportion of whom will know as much, if not more, about the history of that particular sport. 'Fantastic' is another word that has been castrated by everyday use: every time you are tempted to type it, ask yourself whether what you are describing truly is the stuff of fantasy. 'Tragic' is more confusing. Here is a word whose definitions have multiplied: after all, it is now freely used in reference to obsessives or those devoid of social skills. Its traditional translation, more pertinently, has been amplified by genuine tragedies such as tsunamis or the destruction of New Orleans. Nine point nine times out of ten, to use the word in a sporting context – much less ignore the fact, as many do, that a tragedy, in Shakespearian terms, means that an aspect of the victim's character has been instrumental in his demise – is to diminish true suffering.

If only because, I would contend, the written word is easier to follow, appreciate and remember than the spoken variety, and for all the homely eloquence of Bill McLaren or the pithy minimalist asides of Richie Benaud, there is more room on the page for graphic and vivid description, for lateral thinking and for what we in the trade call 'colour'. Again, it is all a matter of degree, taste and perspective, all of which have the unhelpful habit of changing with the passage of time. 'Ere the sun had set on McGraw's rash and presumptuous words, the Babe [Ruth] had flashed across the sky fiery portents which should have been sufficient to strike terror and conviction into the hearts of all infidels.' Thus did Heywood Broun, a revered and iconoclastic New York sportswriter, report during the 1923 World Series. The report began: 'The Ruth is mighty and shall prevail.'[16] To Nicholas Dawidoff, this was a 'classic lead'.[17] While good writing, like fine wine, can endure, what was once tolerated, even encouraged, might now prompt nothing but derisive snorts and swallowing difficulties.

Though perhaps demanding too much of those to whom an 800-word match report represents the peak of endurance, Hugh McIlvanney and Roger Angell, the most habitually lauded sportswriters of the past 50 years, are united by their exemplary judiciousness, contextual mastery and impeccable sense of balance and fair play, but also by an uncanny ability to construct monumental sentences and paragraphs, brick by solid brick, that never seem to meander and would, moreover, be worse off had so much as a conjunction or a comma been omitted. Angell first, writing in the weekly *New Yorker* on the contentious issue of whether Babe Ruth truly did, as myth has it, respond to the abuse of the Chicago Cubs fans during the 1932 World Series by pointing imperiously and presciently to the stands then duly hammering a home run – a 143-word sentence that might have been designed by Sir Christopher Wren:

> *A recent investigation of the microfilm files of the times seems to have cleared up the mystery, inasmuch as John Drebinger's story for that date makes no mention of the Ruthian story in its lead, or, indeed, until the thirty-fourth paragraph, when he hints that Ruth did gesture toward the bleachers ('in no mistaken motions the Babe notified the crowd that the nature of his retaliation would be a wallop right out of the confines of the park'), after taking some guff from the hometown rooters as he stepped up to the plate, but then Drebinger seems to veer toward the other interpretation, which is that Ruth's gesture was simply to show that he knew the count ('Ruth signalled with his fingers after each pitch to let the spectators know exactly how the situation stood. Then the mightiest blow of all fell').*[18]

As with Angell, McIlvanney's brief is less demanding than that of Red Smith or Cardus. The Scot has been a Sunday newspaperman for half a century and hence afforded the luxury of having longer to consider his verdicts. He made every moment count, often filing his meticulous copy on a Saturday afternoon yet doing more than anyone has ever done to invest that 'grubby vineyard' with dignity and stature. For a couple of years during the late 1990s, I was privileged to be considered his 'personal sub' at the *Sunday Times*. On a Saturday afternoon – just because Sunday papers come out once a week and like to put as many pages as possible 'to bed' that are not reserved for live reports and late stories, does not mean reporters are any less prone to flirt with deadlines – I would receive an article whose richness of language, elegantly plotted narrative, soft humour and warm nature buttressed writing of balance and perceptiveness. He would never be more than 20 or 30 words over the given wordage, and every omission/substitution I suggested, even a colon for a semi-colon, involved debate, however gentlemanly. More often than you might imagine, he would consent to my humble proposals, a triumph I regarded with more pride than you could imagine. He would also insist on being faxed a copy of the page, so that he could see the full context in which his work would appear: the headline, the pullout quotes and all the rest of what we call 'the furniture'. This would slow down the operation, preventing the sub from turning his attention to other stories and irritating the chief sub with a mounting in-tray, yet it seemed such a trifling price to pay.

Even in the twilight of his career, McIlvanney could still make you want to read out his observations in a melodious Scottish accent. Try this sentence about Britain's latest Great White Tennis Hope, Andrew Murray:

> *Not only did the prodigy from Dunblane halt a wave of sporting genocide in SW19 by refusing to figure in the otherwise total extermination of British challenges by the fourth day (including, of course, Tim Henman's); more importantly, he demonstrated the genuineness under pressure of an armoury of skills and natural attributes sufficiently remarkable to permit serious optimism about his chances of progressing into the upper echelons of tennis.*[19]

THE SPORTSWRITER AS PSYCHOLOGIST

The sportswriter-as-psychologist breed is a comparatively recent development, dating, arguably, back to the explosion of televised sport in the 1980s and 1990s. 'It was lurking there,' Simon Barnes elaborates.

> *Rex Bellamy [Times tennis correspondent] and Geoffrey Green [Times football correspondent] looked at what made players tick in the Sixties but perhaps only since the amount of space devoted to sport in newspapers has increased has there been real scope to do so. Now, thanks to TV, we see sportsmen in close-up, people under colossal stress and clearly not enjoying themselves.*[20]

This strain of journalism is exemplified by a pair of Westcountrymen: the coolly analytical Peter Roebuck, former captain of Somerset County Cricket Club, and the lyrically compassionate David Foot, chronicler-in-chief of the club and its greatest players, including Harold

Gimblett, who committed suicide. Both responded thoughtfully to one of the most depressing cautionary tales of recent times: the sudden, saddening withdrawal from the 2006–07 Ashes tour of the Somerset batsman Marcus Trescothick – a 'mystery virus' was the official verdict but stress-induced depression appeared the likeliest cause, fuelling some justly caustic columns about overloaded fixture lists and administrative greed. Perhaps because of the sheer amount of time they spend earning a living in a hermetically sealed, boys-only universe where individual and collective concerns are so often at odds, and life after the ball can be so lonely, cricket is said to have a higher suicide rate than any other sport. It is certainly the only one I am aware of that has inspired a book – David Frith's supremely researched *By His Own Hand*, retitled *Silence of the Heart* in subsequent editions. 'The line I took on Trescothick,' says Barnes, 'was that it was a very human story, that we've changed, in society, in how we see mental problems, and those of sportsmen in particular. We're more sensitive.'[21]

Roebuck wrote:

> *Last winter Trescothick began to feel the seeds of unhappiness. Even beyond sport it is possible to go to sleep and wake up more tired. Strength seeps away, the will is slowly defeated. Once this mental cancer takes hold it is the devil's own work to stop it. Trescothick went home from India, started the next campaign afresh then slowly faded . . . Every cricketer, and every Australian, will wish Trescothick well in the next few months. His friends will advise him to put cricket aside, and remind him that life has many more things to offer a capable young man than the scoring of runs and the winning of matches.*[22]

Unlike Roebuck, Foot, now more or less retired, was far from the action. Not that you would have known it, other than the absence of an 'in Sydney' next to his byline. Having known Trescothick since his teenage days as a hefty hopeful with a rustic outlook and penchant for sausages, he had the priceless advantage of local knowledge and personal insight. Drawing on a lifetime of observing and talking to sportsfolk as they wrestled with their opponents, external and internal, he delivered a matchless overview:

> *[Trescothick] is a big man, physically, with a surprisingly fragile mental strength. He is at his best – and then it does show on that normally dour expression of his – when he is standing distinctively upright and challenging at the crease. But more recently that more engaging confidence has been elusive. There is no lustre in the big countryman's eyes.*
>
> *His England team-mates have noticed it, exchanging glances and sensing the torment which he mostly keeps to himself. Again, on this visit to Australia, he has appeared, at least to the more perceptive, as a painfully lonely figure: missing especially his family, the jokey, uplifting West Country accents, and inwardly recoiling from the rigid disciplines demanded of Test cricketers.*

The summation was worthy of the most sagacious judge:

> *First-class cricketers are a melancholy breed. Whatever their facade they are acutely sensitive, and not just about their form. For the Test players it is worse. Their tour*

> *cricket makes deep, disruptive inroads for weeks at a time into their family life. Training is onerous and repetitive. They occasionally get on one another's nerves. Some crack up.*[23]

Thomas Boswell does something neither Angell nor McIlvanney would ever do: even though he has long worked for one of the planet's posher papers, the *Washington Post*, he has never been shy of employing those tabloid staples – short, crisp, one-sentence paragraphs. As in 'And probably always will be.' By the same token, he speaks directly to the reader with a certainty and matiness that many strive for and few attain. 'You must ignore the cold mist in your hair,' he wrote in the same article, playing therapist-hypnotist to every Boston Red Sox fan contemplating renouncing their support in the wake of that improbable last-gasp loss to the New York Mets in the 1986 World Series, extending as it did the club's allegedly cursed sequence to 68 winless autumns. 'You must concentrate very hard. You must think of nothing. You must forget. Then, come spring, you must forgive them again. And although it does not seem possible, love them – as you would blood kin – just a little more.'[24]

PERFORMANCE-ENHANCING DRUGS

There can be no doubt that the thorniest, most taxing question faced by contemporary sportswriters is performance-enhancing drugs: fair or foul? Unless, that is, you believe corruption has the edge in loathsomeness. My *bête noir* is match-fixing. Spectators at sporting events now pay fairly close to a king's ransom for a ticket, especially in an era of booking fees and eBay; nor is it all that much cheaper a thrill for those who get their kicks secondhand, via television. To fix the result of a match is to cheat them, not to mention betray the principles and obliterate the very foundations of sport. To do so when your chosen sport already rewards you handsomely, as South Africa's captain Hansie Cronje did when accepting bribes from a bookmaker to manipulate events on the cricket field, is surely beneath contempt. To do so while dragging two inexperienced and insecure colleagues into the conspiracy, as Cronje did, is assuredly beyond words. There is, happily, a straightforward route to minimising this perennial, insidious threat: life suspensions. Meted out to the Chicago 'Black' Sox but precious few of their successors, it is doubly unfortunate, therefore, that authorities have been so reluctant to impose such a punishment. The only excuse I can offer on the administrators' behalf is that this is almost certainly attributable to fear of lawsuits and the emphasis placed on fighting the drug-takers.

The notion that the war on drugs is not only unwinnable but pointless is more widespread than I had imagined. Over the past five years, discussions and debates with students at both the University of Brighton and University College Falmouth have revealed an ambivalence that huge swathes of my generation would regard with rather more shock than awe. Indeed, when I mentioned this to one leading sportswriter, it drove him to such heights of apoplexy he not only wrote a column on the sins of drug-use a few days later, he volunteered his services to come and deliver a lecture and 'sort those students out for you'.

I was torn for a long time. Then, in 2005, I read Howard Bryant's *Juicing the Game*, a collection of a series of newspaper articles by a Boston sportswriter tracing and analysing the drug problems that have infested baseball over the past decade. His conclusion was alarming enough: until 2004, this was wilfully ignored by the game's administrators, who were not ill-disposed to the impact on attendances and income of improbably musclebound hitters swatting ever-longer home runs. My Damascene moment came when Bryant related the story of two ambitious college ballplayers who committed suicide: the drugs enhanced their performance but triggered depression.

For all the passions the subject promotes, this is assuredly no black-and-white matter. The chief difficulty now, as Geoffrey Goldspink, Emeritus Professor of Surgery at University College London, told Matthew Syed, lies with advances in gene therapy. While offering relief and potential cure to those suffering from diseases and horrendous physical conditions, these developments cannot but aid the cause of faster, further and better. It was Goldspink who developed Mechano Growth Factor (MGF), an injection that in the space of three weeks can apparently increase muscle mass in mice by 25 per cent, bringing hope to those incapacitated by muscular dystrophy. When he made this discovery, however, he was painfully aware of the temptations that would inevitably follow. '[MGF] is currently being produced in California and China,' he apprised Syed, 'and I would not be surprised if it were already being used by sportsmen.' By way of affirmation, wrote Syed, 'a court case in Germany in February [2006] revealed that coaches are jockeying to get their hands on gene doping technology.'[25]

Nor do the complexities stop there. Gene doping may be banned by the World Anti-Drug Agency but it is exceedingly hard to detect, although Professor Colin Creaser of Nottingham Trent University is optimistic that a form of diagnostic testing will make it possible to do so by 2012. Yet although scientific evidence of the benefits of cryotherapy and hypoxic chambers is anything but conclusive, neither is on the World Anti-Doping Agency (WADA) unwanted list. 'Sport,' concluded Syed, 'is caught in a deadly pincer movement, with scientific progress on one flank and ill-advised responses to it on the other. The stakes could not be higher.'[26]

But how would the devil's advocate counter-punch? Possibly along pragmatic rather than emotional lines. In many eyes, to compete as an elite sportsman or sportswoman in the early twewnty-first century is to feel obliged to take whatever aids are available, and if that results in self-harm, well, quite frankly, that is the individual's risk. Why condemn athletes for trying to give us more thrills for our pounds (is it really *so* wrong to want to see a woman run the 100 metres in 9.5 seconds?), when we laud musicians and writers whose best work has been fuelled by chemical abuse? In fact, bearing in mind the costs of policing drug use, the inability of the testers to keep up with the chemists, and the fact that that money would perhaps be better spent on helping the casualties, let alone that performance-enhancers do not guarantee victory, why not a free-for-all?

Under these circumstances, prone as we are to being asked to render instant judgments, the journalist's enemies are anger and dogmatism. Nothing is more likely to incite indignant and irresponsible reporting or editorialising than the announcement that X has failed a drugs test, or forgotten to turn up for one. Guilt is assumed. Discovering that X's distinguished career may have been a sham sits even less well with those who have hitherto been faithfully, and admiringly, relating their dynamic deeds. The sense of betrayal is incalculable. And seldom in recent years has the media's innate incaution been exposed quite so nakedly as it was when, in the late summer of 2006, Marion Jones, a former Olympic sprint champion, was apparently caught redhanded. All those pious leaders and woe-is-she lamentations were made to look a trifle premature a few days later when a second test found no trace of anything untoward. Jones was cleared.

THE ADMINISTRATORS

Exposing cheating, corruption, injustice or even plain rotten governance *can* make a difference. At the very least, you can be a filter, observing and recording others making a difference, and hence legitimately claim a role in the process, which is, realistically speaking, the zenith to which any journalist can aspire. Which, more often than not, means regarding governing bodies and administrators – the primary purseholders – as the baddies. Indeed, curious as it might seem to some, sport's once-silent partners – chairmen, presidents, directors, owners, secretaries – are now as sought-after for news and comment as the players. The key to unlocking most stories is knowing who holds the reins. Or the purse-strings. They are usually one and the same.

Once upon a time, before the players demanded something akin to a commensurate recompense for their labours, and multinational and local companies alike were persuaded, through television, that it was worth having one's name associated with sportspeople or sporting events, administrators would administrate strictly for love and ego. These days, because of the extreme sums their product often fetches, their jobs are full-time; these days club secretaries, for more than a century the lifeblood of any sporting concern, give themselves airs – if not graces – by calling themselves chief executives. As such, these positions now attract large salaries and those to whom bottom lines are more important than the good of the game.

Furthermore, for all the progress made in baseball and other American sports, players' unions are still relatively toothless, administrative powers appear to be ever-expanding, the players' burden ever heavier, the threat of burn-out, as embodied by Trescothick, ever more acute. Much the same, correspondingly, can be said of the temptations. For now at least, the supply, of top-quality sport, cannot hope to meet demand. More than ever, given the global impact of their decisions, the men (now there's a clue) running sport are forever fluctuating between defying governmental interference and being guided, subsidised and generally mollycoddled by a higher authority that carries every can and can thus safely be blamed for any subsequent troubles. Which is partly what makes these besuited types so fascinating. Besides, power is a journalistic aphrodisiac: the taller the poppy, the more brutal the swipe.

JOURNALISTS' VIEWS OF THE IMPACT OF TECHNOLOGICAL CHANGE

As a TV and radio broadcaster, newspaper correspondent and magazine editor, Christopher Martin-Jenkins has done it all. If, among English sports journalists, he is the most respected all-rounder of his generation, Matthew Engel is probably the most respected scribe. In good part because of his passion for the game of cricket and unfailing fairness, the former, I would hazard, has the best contacts of any specialist correspondent; the latter quietly revolutionised his trade in England with a blend of ardour, proportion, authority and humour worthy of Red Smith himself. Few, if any, did more to cremate the myth that sport and politics are mutually exclusive; even fewer have so ably heeded the famous admonition of that noble Trinidadian Marxist C.L.R. James, 'What do they know that only cricket know?' Indeed, he has also covered General Elections and party conferences. Chapter 13 contains responses to a questionnaire I circulated among two dozen leading sports journalists; I make no apologies for singling this dynamic duo out for the following sneak preview.

When and why did you become a sports journalist?

CMJ: 'I joined *The Cricketer* in 1967 after some freelance work for *The Cambridge News* and the student publication, *Granta*. I had been offered training with the Kent Messenger group but was advised to aim higher. It had been a vague ambition to become a cricket commentator since childhood days when I played cricket in the garden or on beaches with my brothers and always commentated on what was happening – a la Swanton, Johnston or Arlott, either in my head or out loud. Curiously enough, although I possibly had the ability to have played cricket professionally I never saw any path towards doing so. Most people, I think, have to plan a career in order to get the mindset right.'

ME: 'When I was 21. I didn't have any other skills, except a vague facility for pinball. Pub quiz machines had not yet been invented. I wanted to cover Northamptonshire for the *Northampton Chronicle and Echo*. I achieved this with great speed, owing to remarkable luck and what some describe as a ruthless streak.'

What have been the most significant changes in the practice of journalism during your career and why?

CMJ: 'Cor! Where do you start? In magazine publishing I started by making edits on the stone – hot metal – at the printers. Desktop publishing and new printing methods changed that. In daily newspapers the switch from typewriter to laptop – starting with the lovely, simple, neat little Tandy – preceded the other great change, the availability of information on the Web. In broadcasting the biggest change has been the ease of making broadcasts on the hoof rather than needing to go to a studio to get on the air. Telephone broadcasts were deemed never to be of sufficient quality in my early days at the BBC.'

ME: 'Technological change; the dramatic alteration in the nature of "quality" paper journalism.'

Would you have preferred to have worked in journalism before television changed the rules?

CMJ: 'Yes. Much easier, for example, to write a report of a match if you knew that your readers were not aware of anything more than the result of the match or the approximate outcome of the day's play.'

ME: 'Yes – but not for that reason. I think the older generation had more fun.'

What have been the most beneficial and counter-productive aspects of television in terms of sports journalism?

CMJ: 'The negative aspect has been a loss of perspective. Everything tends to be seen from the viewpoint of the players. At the same time, coverage of sport in close-up and from all angles has brought much greater insight. It has also magnified both the mistakes and the immense skill of professional sports folk.'

ME: 'Good: TV severely limited the capacity for fictional sports reporting in newspapers. It also heightened public interest and – contrary to what everyone expected – made them want to go to major events (though not second-rate ones) for real. Bad: It made everyone take sport far too seriously.'

Has the technological boom (post-Tandy) been a boon or a disadvantage, and why?

CMJ: 'Technology is amazing but, when it does not work, immensely frustrating too. Moments of panic and lost work have taken a few years off my life.'

ME: 'Yes – Production standards are far higher. Journalists have far more control over their words without being dependent on copy-takers, print unions, etc. Photographic standards in particular are infinitely higher.'

How does Web journalism differ from print journalism?

CMJ: 'It is, generally, glibber.'

ME: 'Web journalism remains highly derivative. The next phase must surely involve the pursuit of excellence, but this seems improbable unless web-users are prepared to pay for content.'

Which sports journalist(s) do you most respect and why?

CMJ: 'I respect all my fellow correspondents in cricket press boxes and my successor as BBC cricket correspondent, Jonathan Agnew, who combines astute journalism with apparently effortless communicative skills. I also particularly admire Scyld Berry's original mind and his ability to travel down paths that others ignore; and Simon Barnes's lucidity, erudition and humane judgement.'

ME: 'Frank Keating (originality); Simon Barnes (productivity); John Woodcock (authority); Greg Wood and James Willoughby (high standards in an area of sport where standards aren't always high); David Conn (hard work); Clement Freud and Michael Parkinson (distinctiveness); Martin Samuel (for versatility) and Pat Collins (for humanity); Gideon Haigh, Scyld Berry, Simon Kuper . . . dozens more.'

What article are you most proud of and why?

CMJ: 'They all involved a ridiculous amount of sweat and mental anguish at the time. Now they are recycled paper.'

ME: 'One of my first pieces for the *Guardian* was on the European tiddlywinks championship. The copy-taker was so appalled she thought I was an imposter and put the phone down to complain to the news desk. It was used on page one.'

Is the *Daily Telegraph* right to proclaim that it offers world-class *opinion* rather than reporting?

CMJ: 'Well, I can see their point if TV, radio and the Web have cornered the instant news, but newspapers must still record facts as well as analyse them.'

ME: 'Yeah, newspapers can't just offer news these days.'

Curiously – possibly because the way the questions were phrased, possibly because they felt it went without saying – both omitted to mention one indispensable aspect of the journalist's craft, namely the need to keep news uppermost in mind. For all the difficulties it now involves, the need to break fresh stories, stories that reveal something of value rather than stroke and caress egos, cannot be, should *never* be, underestimated. Now more than ever, this is the chief function of the sports reporter, as distinct from the commentator, columnist, presenter or pundit: as supporter-promoter-critics, we are the true guardians of the game, however sceptical, at times cynical and, yes, lazy we have become (it's all that nasty electronic media's fault for saving us all that precious time and energy). When I asked him whether print journalism has benefited from the flood tide of television, David Hopps, author and award-winning sportswriter with the *Guardian* for the past 20 years, pulled no punches:

> *There haven't been any benefits. Mass coverage has made writers, performers and their audience stale and, at worst, cynical. Journalism is so much froth these days. I guess that 75 percent of media studies graduates think they want to be journalists when actually they really want to be TV personalities. The obsession with celebrity is a canker on society and is TV-driven. It is the job of people like [the author] to change this!*[27]

Reviewing Raymond Boyle's *Sports Journalism – Context and Issues*, my friend and colleague Steve Redhead, Professor of Cultural and Media Studies at the University of Brighton, alights on what he calls the 're-professionalisation' of sport journalism, tracing it back to the British fanzines of the 1970s and 1980s.

> *The fanzine culture which grew up then, particularly around sport, and even more especially football, was broadly dedicated to democratising journalistic writing on cultural industries in the face of a profession which had lost touch with its own object of desire, or else had become too close to it to be properly independent and critical. In some cases (Stan Hey who wrote for* Foul, *Mike Ticher who started* When Saturday Comes*) fanzine writers grasped their fifteen minutes of fame and became professional sport journalists, democratising the sport journalist's subculture from within. The perceived democratisation from this era has recently become even more widespread with the fast changing new technologies of the internet and the world wide web: e-zines, websites and weblogs have globalised and digitised the ironic and sardonic fandom of fanzine culture. The reaction to this democratisation over a three-decade period has been to professionalise (again) the sport journalist's training and practice. Hence the upsurge in university courses in sport journalism and the quest for professional accreditation. Part of the reason for this is that the democratisation process was actually a failed and flawed process. It was more a post-modernisation – a flattening of the previous hierarchies and anti-elitist populism. An increasing lack of the critical edge in fanzine culture, which as far as sport is concerned became as establishment and conservative as the culture it once so successfully criticised and lampooned, has led to an acceptance of the need for an investigative and professionally written sport journalism. The fanzine writer now takes his or her place on university courses on sport journalism alongside the gonzo journalism of Hunter S. Thompson. But as historical context rather than as role model.*[28]

Some editors, albeit a waning number, still regard sport as the toy department rather than a joy division with social and political implications. 'The mindset is wrong,' affirmed Evan Weiner.

General Electric is spending billions of dollars so that its NBC TV network can broadcast the 2008 and 2012 Olympics. Communities all over America have created special tax districts; raised hotel, motel, rent-a-car, restaurant, cigarette, and beer taxes to fund stadiums and arenas. Congress may take up discrimination legislation against men-only member golf courses, change tax exemption laws as they apply to companies that are Olympic sponsors, and legislate the boxing industry.[29]

Since the public is entitled to be aware of how governments influence the sporting industry and agenda, journalists must intercede on their behalf. Without the change in the 1986 US Tax Code, Weiner stresses, new stadiums would not have been constructed, forestalling the mass renewal of the 1980s and 1990s that aided baseball's box-office renaissance. This tax change allowed municipalities to become closely involved in public–private sponsorship. With players' unions and associations mushrooming, the public also deserve to know how such negotiations are conducted, and whether they are done so in the audience's best interests. Sport, Weiner sums up, 'is dependent on government funding for facilities, for cable TV regulation or deregulation, and tax breaks for corporations who buy tickets as a business expense and write-off' – hence the pressing need for vigilant watchdogs. 'Just about every American citizen has some money directly or indirectly invested in the sports industry,' she concluded. 'That's why we need more competent journalists taking a closer look. It's great to watch a game and report on it, but the democracy deserves more than a box score when it comes to scrutinising the business of sports.'[30]

Andrew Jennings, too, has forthright views to contribute.

Sports reporters – and I'm generalising here – report matches. When I speak to editors, I say 'I know nothing about sport but I've got some documents here that prove [Sepp] Blatter did it.'

I'm 63 now and I've been around. I've been a sub on the populars – what we used to call the red-tops – and that's where I learned to do TV and radio because it was all about tight links and signposting people. They were the rigid, horrible days when the back bench would scream at reporters and we had to complain to the NUJ to get anything done about it. But those editors and subs taught you how to write well and clearly. There was no ideology, no politics about it, just good writing. Now newspapers are talking about cutting their freelance rates and taking even more wire service stuff. More and more and more Internet news sources are just bland, cautious wire service stuff. It's not good enough and in this tepid lagoon stands out islands of investigative journalism.

Investigative journalism, in whatever branch of the media, is the future, but the newspaper industry is overstaffed with people who simply recycle agency reports – and not just in sport either. This is particularly true of the broadsheets. What the Daily Telegraph *is doing [cutting staff, multi-tasking] is good – if they really make space for creative reporting and don't expect more work from less staff. As a radio and TV pro I watch some of the video and podcasting that print reporters are being hustled into producing with deep embarrassment. We are all too busy to watch and listen unless it's cracking material, professional or whimsically, idiosyncratically delivered.*

I've held a lot of sportswriters in ill-repute. They're lazy, uninspired. One function of a newspaper reporter is to fill the space between the ads that pay the rent – that's not what many of us got into it for. We didn't even notice the ads. Those who won't take the internet opportunity to get with the fans will be very lonely and then redundant. Too many in my generation of oldies have passed on the message that it is more important to be liked by the editor and the readers/viewers/fans don't matter. It's going to be the reverse. The kids will jump sites that are lazy and not disclosing anything – the advertisers will see the hits figures and career death will follow fast for the lazy editor and the uninspired reporter who isn't giving the readers what they want. A few well-crafted blogs could kill most current sports sections in the new world. The advertisers will follow the fans' wishes. It could happen very fast.[31]

All that said, Jennings' enthusiasm for journalism remains undimmed. 'It's THE most exciting job in the world – and you don't have to get re-elected or kiss babies, and – if you know your stuff well enough – you can even tell the lawyers to eff off.'[32]

The message? Cultivate those contacts as your mother might a prize begonia, sharpen that nose, resist easy conclusions, don't follow the crowd or submit to idleness, be profoundly suspicious of authority and never, ever, sit back for more than five minutes and imagine that you are, can ever be, a master of this particular domain. Demand answers, and don't give up until you get them. And if you can't do that, make us laugh. Or cry. Or, best of all, persuade us to re-examine our most jealously guarded prejudices. You are, to coin a phrase, an infotainer: but never forget which half-word comes first.

Chapter 4

The knowledge

The countless Armenian dead [from the genocide in Turkey between 1915 and 1917] are testimony to the danger of forgetting, and how the past cannot be ignored or covered up. Equally we should remember that Nicolas Sarkozy's great-grandparents were also citizens of the Ottoman empire, living a few streets away from Ataturk in Salonika, both comfortable members of the Islamo-Judeo elite. That is not a combination of words we see often now. What we forget in a few generations.

(Fiachra Gibbons, Guardian, *13 October, 2006)*

Upon moving home during the course of writing this book, I found myself gazing at my bookcases, the newly restored contents of which – it may not astonish you to learn that a substantial majority are sportily inclined – comprised more than half the vanload. Casting my eyes wearily over the endless shelves and Eiffel-esque piles of newspapers, I asked myself a question I had resisted for nearly a decade: do you *really* need all this? A goodly portion, after all, duplicated information easily retrieved on the Internet in less time than it takes to pluck out a tome or a *Guardian*, blow off the cobwebs, check the index or flick the pages. Closer inspection, however, revealed that the vast majority of those publications focused less on two-dimensional scores and records than the three-dimensional stories behind them: histories, biographies (auto- and otherwise), memoirs and treatises; tourbooks, yearbooks and annuals; match reports, interviews and ghosted columns; quotes books, rulebooks, chronicles and encyclopaedias. On the other hand, how many times a decade would I actually relieve *The Glory Game* or the December 1979 issue of *Wisden Cricket Monthly* of dust? The conclusion, to steal shamelessly from Talking Heads, was the same as it ever was: those shelves are my security blanket. Phonelines may go awry, fuseboxes may blow, but a collection of cardboard and paper will never let you down. Should you follow my lead? Provided your significant other does not put up too much of a struggle, absolutely.

In theory, this ought to be the longest chapter of this book. There is, after all, no limit – or at least no statutory or even officially sanctioned limit – to the depth of knowledge a sports journalist requires. In practice, I propose to keep it as short and sweet as possible, if only because that depth of knowledge should almost certainly be more than you could ever live long enough to impart in its entirety.

Received wisdom is the enemy. Scyld Berry's latest book, *Cricket's Burning Passion: Ivo Bligh and the Birth of The Ashes* (Methuen 2006), written in conjunction with Bligh's great-grandson Rupert Peploe, reaffirms that, contrary to most of the hand-wringing reactions at the time, the crisis over betting and match-fixing that ripped cricket apart in the late 1990s was nothing new. In 1881–82, Berry records, 'the English professionals backed themselves at 30–1 to win the match against Victoria when they were on the verge of losing. They won both the match and their money, while other rumours abounded,' including the claim that one pair had tried to lose a game for a bet, and beat up a third tourist player who ratted on them.

BEST, WORST, FIRST

Keen as sportsmen and sports journalists are on perpetuating myths, most of them self-serving, their forte is encouraging unresolveable arguments and unproveable comparisons. Does any other subject provoke such intense speculation about bests, worsts and firsts? Is David Beckham the best footballer ever to represent England or was Stan Matthews? Was Graham Taylor the worst national manager or will Steve McClaren prove the prize turnip? Has there ever been a better Formula 1 driver than Michael Schumacher? A finer tennis player than Roger Federer? A more remarkable golfer than Tiger Woods? A more stupendous feat than Lance Armstrong's seven Tours de France on the trot? One of the many wondrous, tantalising, unique facets of sport is that there are record books that appear to settle some of these arguments conclusively, yet are nonetheless distrusted with all the vehemence normally inspired by a ministerial statement about an extramarital affair. Again, it is all about context, about knowing the subject in sufficient depth. What constitutes 'sufficient' might strike some as a somewhat elastic concept, but 'all you can glean within the bounds of practicability and sanity' strikes me as the safest place to start.

Comparing sporting masters of different eras is a timeless pub debate publishers are more than happy to keep stoking. Such arguments, though, are fraught with difficulty. Sport evolves with the society that sired it; conditions and environments change, impacting on opportunity. African-American baseball players were kept out of the major leagues for most of the first half of the twentieth century (by ungentlemanly agreement between racist franchise owners rather than by anything so blatant and actionable as a formal decree), yet those who saw Satchel Paige and Josh Gibson, the leading lights of the so-called Negro Leagues, hold them to be every bit as good, if not better, than their Caucasian peers. (Trivia alert: Woody Allen named one of his sons Satchel.) Indeed, in more than 400 encounters between teams representing the two leagues, the major leaguers, much the better-paid, were beaten twice as many times as they won. And once the doors did open – courtesy of Branch Rickey, general manager of the Brooklyn Dodgers, and Jackie Robinson, an impossibly brave and inspirational man to whose memory all sporting pioneers must kneel – African-Americans were soon cleaning up the MVP awards. In other words, to state without qualification or fear of contradiction, as many of the game's chroniclers do, that Sandy Koufax is the game's greatest pitcher, or Johnny Bench its foremost catcher, is to be ignorant or contrary.

And if social conditions change, so do rules and equipment, techniques and fitness levels, standards and outlooks. Would Federer have beaten Rod Laver had his racket been as wooden as the Australian's? Would Schumacher have bested Ayrton Senna or Juan-Manuel Fangio in the days when tracks were more hazardous, cars less reliable and computerised assistance unavailable? Don Bradman, statistically the greatest of all batsmen by an enormous distance, is hailed as the one sporting untouchable, but would he have been half as successful on less amiable pitches, or against the brutally efficient and highly athletic West Indies pace squadrons of the 1980s? The beauty is that there are no definitive answers to such questions, merely well- and not so well-informed opinions. A sports journalist, it goes without saying, is obliged to err massively towards the former, primarily because the audience, or a hefty chunk of it, is so knowledgeable. And the audience is so knowledgeable (does any branch of culture attract, and keep, so many mildly and fervently potty aficionados?) because they have invested their emotions as well as their wallets.

BUILDING KNOWLEDGE, ENSURING ACCURACY

During my maiden Induction Week at the University of Brighton, I was asked to liven up the ennui of registration by means of what was announced, by my effervescent course leader, Jackie Errigo, as a 'pub quiz'. Anticipating, predictably and correctly, that football was the commonest denominator, I weighted the topics accordingly. A tiny coterie took almost everything I could throw at them with enviable aplomb, but I would be fibbing if I said that the overall level of ignorance was not depressing. When I reported this to contemporaries that evening, memories were consistent: when we initially fell in love with a sport, one of the first imperatives was to find out as much about its foremost performers and history as quickly as was humanly possible. We were thirsty: not just to know who, what, where and when, but how, and, most fascinating of all, why. I can only surmise that the seemingly infinite tonnage of sport now hurled at us from all directions by the media is apt to de-parch the driest throat. I sympathise. Keeping up is trying enough.

That sobering experience reinforced my decision to ground students in the bare necessities. During the first semester the previous year, I had conducted team-based quizzes on individual sports and themes. Having made the point that not everyone can be a football reporter and that versatility is imperative, I tried to cover as many major sports as possible and hence compile an end-of-year examination featuring two or three questions on each (see Exercise below). Given where we started from – something perilously close to zero in the majority of cases beyond football – the results were extremely gratifying: nobody failed, many excelled. I trust they will one day decide that their boring old fart of an editor had not mislaid quite every marble in his limited collection.

As a sports journalist, as any journalist worth a grain of salt, you need to have facts not merely at your fingertips but under your nails: facts that occasionally need refreshing because they have been superseded, yes, but mostly facts that are logged in a memory bank whose hard drive happens to be your heartbeat. I am not sure whether I should be proud, falsely modest or embarrassed by this, but when I embarked on my journalistic career I could cite the home ground of all 92 Football League clubs, the score in every postwar FA Cup final and the result of every Test series in England since the end of the 1920s. Mind you, I could also recite the line of succession from William the Conqueror to Elizabeth II, the dates of most of the major land battles on British soil and every hit, in order, by The Beatles, which to some, not unreasonably, might sound more than a bit sad.

These facts, these contextual crutches, should underpin everything you do – which is why, no matter how highly you rate your memory, always double-check. They may be current or recent facts – the name of a club's manager/chairman/ground, the state of its injury list, identity of suspended players, position in the league, progress in the cups. In football, club secretaries and slowly expanding match programmes were long the primary source for such information, yet newspapers and magazines, annuals, Ceefax and the Web have proved almost equally reliable. Similarly, there is no shortage of sources for historical records. Even if you are unable to deposit too many in that memory bank, ensure dependable sources are always at hand (and no, Wikipedia is not always dependable). The Internet, indeed, has theoretically relieved the reporter of the tiresome task of traipsing around the world schlepping a case misshapen by crammed-in reference books, though I know of few who do not back up those sometimes dodgy Broadband connections by schlepping anyway. The point, though, is that your audience can draw from those same sources, and thus expects more of you. Never has there been less excuse for getting these facts wrong.

As a specialist correspondent, this responsibility is more onerous. Nor is it a case simply of knowing the fixture list a month ahead. For one thing, with fixtures and tours more frequent, you need to be on top of your game at all times, thinking ahead and planning. The angel is in the details, not the devil. A cricket correspondent, for instance, will know when and where the next three World Cups are being staged (the Caribbean in 2007, South Asia in 2011, Australasia in 2015), the frequency of Ashes series (three every four years) and, in some cases, even that 2013–14 will bring the centenary of the most egregious bowling performance in a Test series – S.F. Barnes's 49 South African wickets in four matches. If a team or individual is in the running for a seventh consecutive title or gold medal, a journalist covering that sport will be aware of the precedents, if any. If a driver crashes in 12 successive grands prix, ditto. Likewise if a coach or manager is sacked for a sexual indiscretion, or the leading horse in the Grand National pulls up with yards to go, or a season has to be shut down by bad weather or foot-and-mouth disease. It may be a stretch to concur with that ancient adage about there never being anything new under the sun, but sport has been played for long enough, and chronicled for long enough, for there to be precious few rock-solid exceptions.

I reiterate – and almost certainly not for the last time: perspective is all. Take the makeup of the England cricket team, and in particular the hostility encountered by Kevin Pietersen. For a reporter to imagine that the South African is the first such player to stir equivocal reactions in what John Woodcock once termed 'the unequivocal Englishman' is to fail in one of your obligations to your readers or audience. During the apartheid era, starting with Basil D'Oliveira in 1966, several South Africans, denied the opportunity to represent their country, played for England (and, in one case, Australia). Three illustrious Indians, moreover, did so between 1896 and World War II. But you have to delve even further back, to Billy Midwinter in the winter of 1881–82, to find the first of many Australians who turned out on behalf of St George.

Similarly, to quote the most frequently spotted error of sporting fact, Jackie Robinson was not the first black player permitted to make the grade in Major League Baseball, merely the first in the twentieth century.

The greatest peril faces those who fail to keep abreast of developments, notably the smashing of those hard-boiled myths. It is now accepted that there is no evidence, for example, that, on the steps of the court during the trial of eight Chicago White Sox players for intentionally losing the 1919 World Series, a disillusioned boy ever pleaded 'Say it ain't so, Joe' to one of the eight, 'Shoeless' Joe Jackson. For nearly nine decades this story has been routinely and unthinkingly trotted out. Nor, even more culpably, is there any evidence whatsoever to perpetuate the oft-printed and widely accepted claim that General Abner Doubleday invented baseball. Not the least impressive book I have read of late, and much the most impressive title I have come across, is Bob Carroll's *Baseball Between the Lies*, the title a play on the name of innumerable sporting tomes and headlines, though the subtitle is even more admirable in its frankness: *The Hype, Hokum, and Humbug of America's Favourite Pastime.*

APPLYING YOUR KNOWLEDGE

How best to invest all that information is the next step. Especially when celebrating an anniversary – ideally a round number such as 10 years or perhaps five, 15 or 25 – feel free to show off that knowledge so long as it heightens the reader's appreciation: don't slide down the road to obscurity or self-indulgence. Challenge the reader by all means, but the background must serve the foreground, the past illustrate or ground the present. In features and columns, today's bungs inquiry or last week's cheating allegations may prompt reflection and reminiscence, contextualising the story, proving there really is nothing new under the sun, but the conclusion should thrust the reader back into the here and now. What do all our yesterdays teach us? Do they enhance our understanding of the current dilemma? Do they facilitate a sense of proportion? How do they point the way ahead?

Then there is the small matter of metaphor, reference and allusion. You may know more about Woody Allen and Steely Dan (my own favourite non-sporty reference points) than they know about themselves but, before taking the plunge, ask yourself what percentage of your readers are likely to be on the same wavelength or carry the same cultural baggage? It is a matter of risk assessment, of knowing your audience – or at least having a reasonable grasp of what the focus groups and customer surveys say about who they are and what turns them on – or, no less pertinently, off. And to all intents and purposes, the subs, revise subs and editors are your audience and jury (think of letters to the editor as the Court of Appeal). Needled and mildly nauseated by the constant references in cricket and soccer reports to Shakespeare, Tennyson and Homer, even in the 1980s, I felt it my duty to add balance, to drop in a spot of pop culture whenever appropriate, to emphasise that the world had moved on, that sport existed in the now as well as the then. I would estimate my initial success ratio, in terms of gaining the subs' approval, at around 85 per cent, so I persisted. In 2000, introducing an interview with Graham Thorpe for the *Sunday Telegraph*, I quoted the first verse of a track, *What A Shame About Me*, from a new Steely Dan CD, the first in 20 years: the lyrics were remarkably apposite: both acts were making a comeback. It was a calculated risk: the then cricket editor, Peter Mitchell, is another musical anorak with almost impeccable taste. The sub saddled with conceiving a headline, better yet, had the exemplary presence of mind to plant a reference to an old hit by the selfsame musicians. I always did rather fancy being known as the first rock 'n' roll cricket writer.

Simon Barnes mentioned the long-gone Hollywood producer Sam Goldwyn in one recent article without feeling compelled to explain who he was. I had been prepared to bet my right arm that at least one member of *The Times* sports desk had stared quizzically at that name, and proposed that 'the legendary Hollywood producer' be inserted. Barnes insists not. That the sentence was apparently left untouched underlined the perceived difference between the readerships of the *Sun* and *The Times*, for all that they are owned by the same man and produced under the same roof. After the former ran the headline 'Louie, Louie' over a story about Manchester United's Louis Saha missing a penalty, three of my 58 first-years recognised it as a nod to a 1960s pop hit.[1] Assessing such things is not, of course, an exact science, more a gut instinct.

Barnes admits:

> *It's a hard balance to strike. Occasionally people on the desk will ask me to explain, but not on this occasion. If you didn't know who Goldwyn was, it's still a funny line and the reader goes and finds out who he was. Like any form of journalism, it's a constant series of decision-making. I like a broad frame of reference but occasionally you can lose people. On an instinctive basis I suppose do calculate the likelihood of a certain percentage of readers 'getting it'. I recently mentioned Lenny the Lion in a piece and felt obliged to explain that he was a 1960s TV character, but if it's obscure, you don't necessarily have to explain who the person is that you're referring to: you can glory in the obscurity of it.*[2]

THE OBITUARY

The fruits of an inquiring mind, a multi-gigabyte memory, a relish for research and a well-stocked library can be plentiful. Writing your own books becomes an option, which in turn might see you perceived as an expert ripe for plucking by broadcasters hungry for even vaguely authoritative talking heads. Then there are obituaries, aka obits. These take up one or two full pages in the national daily heavies (their Sunday brethren go to press too early to provide a worthwhile service); sport is seen as an extensive and fertile field. For journalists in particular, they can be a source of useful information and are hence worth reading as well as writing.

In September 2006, the *Guardian* commissioned an obit for Wasim Raja, a revered but less than widely known Pakistani cricketer. That I was asked for as many as 700 words might suggest it was a slow day on the mortality front. That I had barely an hour at my disposal (younger daughter's sports day) and still accepted the commission testifies to the fact that a) obits pay well, and b) I was confident enough in my command of the subject and range of close-at-hand sources to believe I could adequately fulfil the brief. With precious few exceptions, the only obits that appear in newspapers the day after the subject's death are those of the extremely famous (monarchs, presidents and prime ministers, cultural icons, genocidal maniacs): these are commissioned well in advance and kept on file for the inevitable day, and updated periodically. Those lauding less prominent mortals, notably those from foreign climes, might not appear for three weeks.

One exception cropped up when I received a surprise Sunday morning phone call from Nigel Fountain on the obits desk at the *Guardian*. 'Are you well?' he asked with typical good cheer: he had been my editor at *City Limits* 23 years earlier when I took my first tentative steps under pseudonyms such as Osgood Peters, Barry Kennington, Teddy Waring and Jean-Pierre Rivets, the better to disguise the fact that I was writing an inordinate share of the sports section. I told him I was indeed well, to which he responded in typically deadpan fashion: 'You know, of course, that this call means that some poor bugger isn't.'

That somebody was Trevor Berbick, the Jamaican-born heavyweight who terminated Muhammad Ali's career then became Mike Tyson's passport to notoriety. Having returned to his homeland after a brain scan impelled him to retire at 46, he had become a preacher and boxing trainer. Police had found him in a church the previous day, the apparent victim of a gruesome murder. Despite having had next to nothing to do with boxing since completing my biography of Sonny Liston, I was sufficiently aware of Berbick to accept the commission, albeit warning Nigel that, since I had to take my children to the airport, I would not be able to start researching until two hours before the 3.30pm deadline. Undeterred – I strongly suspect I was his last resort – Nigel emailed the Associated Press news story and, upon my return, I scoured my bookshelves and the Internet in my pursuit of instant experthood. Journalists are nothing if not jackdaws: one Fleet Street column in the 1980s went under the pseudonymous byline Jack Dawe.

The estimable Mike Lewis's report in the *Sunday Telegraph* fleshed out the AP report, reminding me of Berbick's conviction for rape and deportation from the US; an online boxing encyclopaedia (which I double-checked, albeit not through Wikipedia) supplied the key bones – date of birth, overall professional record and bout-by-bout minutiae; Thomas Hauser's Biblically-proportioned biography of Ali was a boon, highlighting Berbick's relationship with that arch-promoter Don King and reminding me that the Berbick–Ali 'Drama in the Bahamas' fight had been the only one Muhammad's daughter had ever wanted him to lose; handy, too, was Jeffrey T. Sammonds' academic tome *Beyond the Ring – The Role of Boxing in American Society*. Seven hundred words in the bag, I was about to press 'send' when I found one final source: a profile of Berbick by one Neil Hunter, published on *JamaicanPride.com*. I assumed, mistakenly perhaps, that the author was Jamaican himself and hence could be relied upon for a more objective view. What cemented that trust was his assertion, early in the piece, that Berbick had been born in August 1955 and not, as widely believed, the previous year. Relieved to have discovered this, I read on: while it offered confirmation of what I had read elsewhere, I did reproduce his final phrase – characterising Berbick as 'a Jamaican hero' – along with a full attribution.

The following day an email from Hunter was forwarded to me by Phil Osborne, the *Guardian*'s obituaries editor, pointing out one or two factual inaccuracies, complaining that I had plundered his biography of Berbick (until that moment I was unaware of it) and threatening to report me to the Press Complaints Commission. What particularly vexed him was my use of that characterisation of Berbick as 'a Jamaican hero': he felt I had been 'sarky'. I wrote back, explaining: 'I deliberately quoted your reference to Berbick as "a Jamaican hero" at the end as a means of balancing the litany of unheroic behaviour. I am sorry you construed this as "sarky" but that was never my intention. If you were not mitigating Berbick's crimes with that comment, I can only assume you were being sarcastic when you made it. I did not get that impression, however, hence my using it as a means of balance.' To date, I have yet to receive a reply.

THE PREVIEW

The unification of tenses in the context of sports journalism is never more apparent than when previewing an event. This is where your in-depth knowledge is used to guide the reader, to advise them whether Marks or Spencer is likely to win, and why. It is also where the alleged permanence of the past and the purported certainty of the present meet on the treacherous turf of conjecture. The ingredients are countless: current form, recent encounters and historical patterns; the type and quality of surface; the impact of weather and home advantage; injuries and suspensions; team changes; the influence of rule changes, of fatigue and mental health, of families, chairmen and economics; right down to odds, omens and gut feelings. You will never have enough space to mention all the constituent factors that can determine the outcome, so be selective. And be wary. Current form can be deceptive if results are studied in isolation; beyond longstanding rivalries and their inbuilt pressures, the fact that teams are in such a constant state of flux means that historical patterns are largely irrelevant.

Over the past 20 years or so, the preview has been given something of a makeover. Once a dry, orderly recitation of pertinent facts, culminating in an almost habitually safe forecast – a function now often fulfilled by a betting column – it is now regarded as an appetiser. And if there is one area in which print journalists can steal a march on their electronic rivals it is in setting scenes. This is not to say that the rugby union or tennis correspondent will not preview in the traditional manner, just that they will often be supported by one or more interviews, either with a participant (sometimes one from each side if the occasion demands) or someone who did something memorable in a previous match between the protagonists. Their views on the likely outcome are of interest, yes, but what counts is the depth of background detail and the resonance of the reminiscences.

Above all, effective previewing – by which I mean giving the reader a good idea what to expect from a match or race rather than simply being an astute and reliable tipper – also means learning to love the conditional. In other words, be circumspect and judicious, pragmatic even. Would, should, could; ought, may and might: these are your most flexible friends. Failure to use them leaves you open to mistrust and ridicule. No editor, moreover, will persist for long with a correspondent who consistently gets it wrong by sticking their neck out recklessly. Ridicule, as Adam Ant adamantly noted, is assuredly nothing to be scared of, but neither is it always a backhanded compliment. Remember, too, that today's first edition is not so much tomorrow's fish-and-chip paper as next month's computer printout. Mistakes are harder to banish than they were.

Even more so than with other journalistic articles, the outro or payoff is crucial to a preview, leaving the reader with a clear verdict, however much bets are hedged. Yet this does not necessarily mean going out with an obvious bang. As he mulled over Australia's squad announcement for the opening Test of the 2006–07 Ashes, effectively a preview of hostilities masquerading as a news story, Gideon Haigh, reporting from Melbourne, captured the essence of the understated but pointed climax with the help of a salient fact: with the premature departure of Marcus Trescothick earlier that week, not one of the touring batsmen had played a Test in Australia. 'For Australia, reducing three in-form pace bowlers to one is, to delve more deeply into the Code of Cliché, "not a bad problem to have". The questions concerning England's final formation, now lacking any batsman with prior Test experience here, are of a more fundamental kind.'[3]

One example of how hindsight makes fools of even the canniest judges came at the outset of the so-called 'Packer Crisis' that enveloped cricket in the late 1970s, wherein an Australian media magnate named Kerry Packer signed up most of the world's best players, a notoriously underpaid breed, persuading them to reject their paymasters and help boost his TV ratings: hoisting their wages to realistic levels, he trounced the game's trade-restraining, anti-progressive mandarins in the High Court and ultimately dragged the game kicking and screaming into the twentieth century. Writing in the *Sunday Times* shortly after Packer announced his intention to launch a rival product in May 1977, the paper's widely respected, prolific maverick of a cricket correspondent Robin Marlar left no room for doubt as to how he envisaged the outcome: 'Packer thinks he will win, and that eventually world cricket will have to treat with him. "The fact of giving it up is not a possibility," he told me. But in the end he will lose.'[4] Packer won; so did cricketers. Nor did cricket emerge too shabbily: it was Packer's introduction of floodlit matches that finally brought the game within reach of those unfortunate enough to be working nine to five. The fact that such a time-consuming, anti-social game has any future at all can be directly traced to Packer's intervention. A little knowledge and a wealth of prejudices always was a dangerous combination.

EXERCISE

What follows is a two-and-a-half-hour sports history exam I set in the summer of 2006: I like to think it covers a broad spectrum of essential and/or useful knowledge as well as offering the opportunity to deploy that knowledge in a discursive, analytical manner suitable to a newspaper or magazine feature. I make no apology whatsoever for failing to supply the answers: this is a research exercise.

Section 1

Question (marks)

1 Name two Scots who have won the F1 title. **(2 marks)**
2 What was unique about Jochen Rindt? **(2 marks)**
3 Name the five English 'Classic' horse races and the year each was first run. **(10 marks)**
4 Which horse-and-jockey team won the 1953 Derby, and why was the occasion so cherished by the English? **(3 marks)**

5 Which American competitor is most closely associated with the 1972 Olympics and why? **(3 marks)**
6 Why do you imagine a panel of distinguished US sportswriters named Jim Thorpe, who drew worldwide acclaim at the 1912 Olympics, as the greatest sportsman of the first half of the twentieth century? **(6 marks)**
7 Which man has won the most professional tennis titles in the Open era, and how many has he won? **(3 marks)**
8 Who was the last Briton to win the Wimbledon women's singles title and when? **(2 marks)**
9 Who is the odd man out, and why: Arnold Palmer, Gay Brewer, Jack Nicklaus, Gary Player, Tiger Woods? **(2 marks)**
10 Who was the first golfer to achieve a Grand Slam, and when? **(3 marks)**
11 Name all 11 members of England's Ashes-winning XI at The Oval in 2005. **(11 marks)**
12 What is the highest team score attained in Ashes history, by whom, where and when? **(4 marks)**
13 What is the best match bowling analysis in Ashes history, by whom, where and when – and what made it even more special? **(5 marks)**
14 The Test record stand for the sixth wicket is 346 by Don Bradman and Jack Fingleton against England in the 1936–37 Ashes series. What were the unusual circumstances? **(2 marks)**
15 Name England's 1966 Football World Cup-winning XI. **(11 marks)**
16 When did England first compete in a FIFA World Cup? **(1 mark)**
17 What links the only scorer of a World Cup final hat-trick to the first man to captain a club to the League Cup double in the twentieth century? **(3 marks)**
18 How many World Cup finals, respectively, have Brazil and West Germany/Germany played in? **(2 marks)**
19 Who is the odd man out and why: Phil Bennett, Gareth Edwards, Barry John, Rob Andrew and Jonny Wilkinson? **(2 marks)**
20 What is the biggest live attendance for a boxing title fight, and where, when, and who were the combatants? **(6 marks)**
21 Who was the first black heavyweight champion, and when and how did he further arouse the wrath of white America? **(5 marks)**
22 Who am I? **(6 marks)**

Clues:

(a) My nickname stemmed from the day I hit five home runs in a baseball game.
(b) I divorced my husband when I discovered he was gay.
(c) I won Olympic medals for javelin, 80m hurdles and high jump.
(d) I was the first woman to play in a men's PGA golf event.
(e) Katherine Hepburn played a character based on me in the film Pat and Mike.

23 Who am I? **(6 marks)**

Clues:

(a) Many people say that, but for injury, I might have been the best women's tennis player who ever lived.

(b) I was at my peak around the time Elizabeth Windsor began organising the shopping at Buckingham Palace.
(c) I was known as 'Little Mo'.
(d) I was American.
(e) I fell off a horse and retired young.

Section 2

Please write an 800-word reflective feature addressing one of the following:

1 During cricket's match-fixing crisis of the late 1990s, the names Dennis Lillee and Rod Marsh, two members of the Australian side that lost the 1981 Headingley Ashes Test, were widely invoked by reporters. Discuss the reasons for this.

2 In the long term, the triumph of Alf Ramsey's 'Wingless Wonders' at the 1966 World Cup did English football more harm than good. Discuss the reasons why you agree or disagree with this statement.

3 Bob Beamon's gold medal-winning long jump at the 1968 Olympic Games was the greatest Olympic feat of modern times. Discuss the reasons why you agree or disagree with this statement.

NB: There are no correct answers to Section 2. I was looking for facts and context embedded in a well-argued response. In the case of the second option, I confess, a degree of subjectivity crept in: I penalised anyone who overlooked the 'Wingless Wonders' clue and omitted to mention the defensive mindset of successive England managers under whom the national team failed to qualify for World Cup finals in either 1974 or 1978. Which, in this case, constitutes something of a giveaway . . .

Chapter 5

Then, in the final minute ...

The match report

Italy substituted Juliano for Bertini, Rivera inexplicably for Boninsegna, but it made no difference, other than to diminish their threat up front. Three minutes from time, another finely articulated Brazilian movement concluded with Carlos Alberto to come thundering in to score his captain's goal. It was, all in all, a fine day for football.

(Brian Glanville, World Football Handbook 1971, *Mayflower 1970)*

The match report is both the essence of sportswriting and its area of sorest neglect. After all, so much sportswriting now revolves *around* the match – the preview, the post-mortem, the follow-up story, the transfer story, the injury story, the discipline story, the Jose-slags-off-Arsene story, the corruption story, the drugs story, the sex-scandal story, the Bloggs-has-a-book-to-sell-so-he'll-say-anything story.

More than that, the nature and perception of the job has changed with the intrusion of live television coverage, the Internet and the mobile phone that can do everything bar shed those extra pounds for you. By the time most newspaper reports are read, the essential facts of the match – at the very least – will be familiar to most if not all readers. Yet with fixture lists bulging as never before, and international events proliferating like hyperactive rabbits, the perceived obligation to cover as many major happenings as possible remains. As a consequence of this, to take but one pertinent development, *The Times* recently appointed Richard Hobson as its 'One-Day Cricket Correspondent', allowing Christopher Martin-Jenkins, some 20 years his senior, to concentrate on the longer variety and hence maintain his appetite.

So why do newspapers and magazines still bother sending reporters at sometimes lavish – and always appreciable – expense to cover sporting contests when they are invariably last to the punch? Let us count the ways.

For one thing, finances permitting, publications want to be at every event that matters to their readers: it is a matter of being seen to be there, of representing those readers, of pride, principle and professionalism. There is an unwritten contract between publication and reader that echoes the sentiments of the *Friends* theme song: don't worry if you cannot purchase a ticket, or fail to get home in time to watch the game on the box, or a power surge knocks your electricity out – we'll be there for you. For another, even a four-paragraph, 200-word match report permits more depth of detail and scope for insight than a 30-second summary for television or radio. It is also a question of broadening horizons and refining focus. A single match might offer any number of different angles, which is why, while at Hayters, I would frequently file five different reports for five different titles: a national paper or two that had not felt it worthwhile sending a staff reporter or byelined freelance; the local/regional papers for each side when the expenses of a trip to London were deemed too steep for the staff man to attend; a title such as the *Belfast Telegraph* that wanted a watching brief on a player due to be playing for Northern Ireland the following week; perhaps even an Anglophilic and/or English-language paper such as the *South China Morning Post*. In almost every case, the perspective would be different. Varying between 150 and 400 words, each report had to be completed and filed within 20 minutes of the final whistle, some as running copy. On occasion, if I was lucky, I would be granted the services of a phone assistant who would somehow decipher my scrawl and dictate the right copy to the correct paper (embarrassing mix-ups and panicky re-dictations were not unheard-of). Even with that luxury, it was the most demanding work I have ever done, with the possible exception of a midnight-to-five shift at a kibbutz creating polystyrene containers at the rate of one every 20 seconds. I lasted a week in that particular business; the match reporter in me had marginally more staying power.

Whoever you are writing for, the principles involved differ only in geographical terms. The vast rump of match reports are written for local and regional newspapers and hence are at least slightly biased. In theory at least, a national paper will adopt a neutral approach to domestic fixtures and a nationalistic – if not uncritical – stance for international engagements.

Then there is the time factor. For a national daily, it is not simply a case of running reports of the previous day's games; on the basis that not everybody buys a Sunday paper, Monday editions not only cover Saturday's fixtures but sometimes – as with the 2006 World Series – even those that took place late on the previous Friday night. These differ from Sunday paper accounts on two levels: they are written many hours later, when the adrenalin has ceased pumping and critical faculties are clearer; they also project forward instead of dwelling primarily on the run of play. A local weekly paper, meanwhile, may not run its report of Saturday's game until five days after the fact, but even if it has already been covered by the nationals, readers still desire an account wherein their team, win, lose or draw, are unashamedly to the fore. Match programmes and club newspapers hold the same allure. An evening or morning regional title such as the *Evening Standard* or the *Yorkshire Post* bridges the gap between national and local interest, openly favouring representatives from the area and highlighting their contributions at national and international level, sometimes at the expense of the national cause, albeit increasingly less so. A weekly magazine such as *Sports Illustrated* might home in on a leading protagonist and build its coverage around them, while simultaneously supplying the sort of analytical dissection prohibited by the space restrictions and tighter deadlines of the dailies. Monthly publications also promise critical distance: *The Wisden Cricketer* and *World Soccer*, for instance, can report a Test or a tournament in toto, unconstrained by the narrow lens of the daily deadline. An annual perennial such as *Wisden Cricketers' Almanack* might not publish a report of a dramatic Test until a year later; all the more reason to trust its veracity.

In addition, of course, a goodly portion of the fun in watching and participating in sport, at however remote a remove, lies with the potential it offers for a rousing argument. To say that those on the spot have a better view than the audience in pubs and on couches is no longer tenable. Shouting at the television commentary – or, better yet, muting it – is one highly satisfying method of venting one's displeasure; grouching and growling over one's corn flakes while reading a report that contradicts your every instinct and observation is no less rewarding. During the 2006 Champions Trophy match between West Indies and England in the Indian city of Ahmedabad, that buccaneering all-rounder Dwayne Bravo was quite happy to see Michael Yardy trudge from the crease after appearing to take a catch in the deep. When the TV replays showed beyond any doubt whatsoever that the ball had bounced before being caught, my armchair-confined fury knew few bounds: although the fielder did not celebrate, and not a single appeal rent the air, Yardy had taken Bravo's languid body language as a sign that he had taken the catch cleanly. In the heat of the moment, it was hard not to conclude that the latter had cheated. Both umpires expressed their unhappiness with what they, too, perceived as conduct unbecoming, but the match referee, Mike Procter, took Bravo at his word, as one always suspected he would. Cricket, after all, likes to imagine itself the most principled of games, and self-image comes before all else. When the incident received but a cursory mention in the English press the following morning – the Agence France-Presse match report ignored it completely – I felt cheated. I had to wait three weeks, until the November edition of *The Wisden Cricketer*, for Kevin Mitchell to deliver the sceptical sermon I'd craved, under the headline 'Cheating?! In cricket? Unthinkable'.

It used to be so much easier. When I started out in the early 1980s, reporting the action, as it happened, was the most exciting aspect of the job. The incessant noise of the crowd; the pressure to find enough to say; the constant shadow cast by the deadline; the claustrophobic and sometimes cockle-chilling working conditions; the need to shout out every letter and syllable of your carefully hewn words down a fuzzy phone line while others were doing likewise (or worse, dictating solo to the merriment of all); the possibility that your match might provide the story of the day, pumping up your wordage from a puny 200 to a War-and-Peace-esque 800. You also felt as if you were supplying an important, not to say unique, service. All these factors combined to set the adrenalin racing like Michael Schumacher after one too many cups of coffee. Whether your canvas was a typewriter or notebook, filing copy was a lengthy and arduous process, but part of the rush: one of the advantages of dictating copy is that you can ad-lib changes according to how the game was progressing in front of you, an extremely useful option when it's 4.45 on a Saturday afternoon, you're at Lord's for a Test match, and someone has taken a hat-trick since you began dictating.

Then again, there are those who go to the other extreme. Perhaps the best, and certainly the most oft-quoted, cautionary tale was furnished by a county cricket match between Surrey and Essex 20-odd years ago. Henry Blofeld, better known as a radio commentator with a curious obsession for double-decker buses and pigeons, was covering the game for the *Guardian*. He had a pressing engagement so bade his leave after the Essex innings ended, there only being time, he rightly reasoned, for a smattering of overs. A couple of hours later he made a check-call to the sports desk: 'Everything OK old boy? I'm sure you can just drop in the

Surrey score – what was it? Ten for no wicket?' The answer, which the sub-editor in question, displaying a genuine talent for sadism, delighted in dragging out, was 14 – all out! Blofeld had missed one of the lowest scores ever achieved in a professional cricket match.

In a memoir of his formative years as a journalist in the Birmingham of the 1950s *Copy! Boy! A 'Black' from Brum*, Peter Deeley quotes an even less admirable example of liberty-taking: 'John Cooper recalls a game at Villa Park when Desmond Hackett did not arrive until half-time. "I was phoning the copy and he came late, yet his report on the Monday was the most graphic account of the whole game."' Fellow reporters, acutely aware that the same might happen to them one day, doubtless helped fill in the blanks. When I started out, I ensured I was always present and correct at least half an hour before the start of play or kick-off, primarily because there was always the chance of bumping into a player/manager/coach and perhaps grabbing a word, but also out of undiluted paranoia. Partly out of a sense of camaraderie and empathy, but also because our positions might one day be reversed, I was always quite happy to fill latecomers in with salient details. Payback arrived when I moved to Cornwall and getting to Manchester or Durham by 11am sharp did not always prove feasible. That said, even now, I still have a recurring nightmare that finds me fetching up late *and* at the wrong match.

In the mid-1980s came the Tandy, a precursor to the laptop that liked nothing better than meticulously erasing your carefully carved copy just as you were about to press 'send' (a process that might take half an hour rather than half a second to complete). Personally, I never trusted the thing. I preferred the freedom of dictated copy, even though it might take 20 minutes to dictate a 900-word report, accentuating the pressure to get the words down in time. That said, one or two gifted souls had the wherewithal to file without writing a word. One of these is a cricket writer of whom I am extremely fond, who once dictated a feature down a foggy phone line from Zimbabwe to London without recourse to notes. The only problem was that this particular piece was written under the dual influence of alcohol and bile, the upshot a migraine for the *Sunday Times* legal department.

I was something of a Luddite. When it comes to technological advances, because their very essence is communication, journalists must always be up to speed, even ahead of the game. Yet although I am fairly confident I was one of the first national paper reporters to use email (I can only ascribe my speed off the mark to a freelancer's fear of falling behind and to a new parent's desire to spend as much time at home as possible), I was also one of the last to cling to notebook and pen, which regularly drew strange glances. I was clinging to the memory of that Saturday ritual, when I would ask the copytaker to start again and ignore the par I had just completed with such careful, perfectly enunciated deliberation ('Lineker – l for lovely, i for idiot, n for nobody, e for Edward, k for kosher, e for Edward, r for rubbish'). Even now, I dictate my address to credit card companies and the like as if a copytaker is at the other end.

Suffice to say I finally saw the error of my ways during the cricket and rugby union World Cups of 1999, when the pitfalls of prehistoric mobile telecommunications became horribly apparent. In fact, so accustomed as am I now to having the extra time email affords, I can no longer imagine dictating copy. Filing by laptop may mean placing an inordinate amount of faith in the availability of a decent phone line and Internet connection but, provided you test it before kick-off – send over the team details – the advantages are eminently worthwhile. Besides, this is the age of Bluetooth and wirelessness, so excuses are fast expiring.

Of the 30-odd journalists I polled for this book (see Chapter 13), all but a couple worked in the pre-PC age: not one contested the notion that filing copy by electronic means has been a decided boon. That said, the commensurate increase in deadline pressure supports a more insidious agenda. 'My reservation about technology,' as Gideon Haigh, a respected contemporary business journalist as well as Australia's pre-eminent cricket writer, puts it, 'is that each new version seems to bring deadlines forward, because it is dedicated to the priorities of the publisher, who wants bigger newspapers, rather than the journalist, who wants better.'

A laptop *should* ensure that there are no spelling or factual errors that might be (and often are) blamed on the poor unsuspecting copytaker. I have only done this once, so far as I can recall – I once blamed a copytaker for sending 'enervating' instead of 'elevating', strictly to cover my own ignorance of the true meaning of the word 'enervating': I genuinely believed it meant 'uplifting'. Not that I am suggesting for a second that you place your trust in your computer's spellcheck. For a start, it will almost certainly check for American English, and hence turn your –ises into –izes and your flavour into flavor. For another, only place your trust in a dictionary, an up-to-date one at that, probably the *Collins*, if only because of its popularity on the desks that matter.

Copytakers still exist, but numbers have been pared back considerably since Mr Gates and Mr Jobs started taking turns to connect the planet. In September 2006 I received an email from the admirable and gentlemanly Charles Morris, sports editor at the *Financial Times*, informing staffers and freelance contributors that, from the 29th of the month, as part of ongoing cost-cutting measures, the paper would no longer be employing copytakers, or even a remotely based copytaking service. The words were gutfelt: 'This, alas, removes the safety net we have all benefited from when technology fails us.'

THE PRESS BOX

Unlike most other reporters, sportswriters have their own office. The sheer number of publications wanting to cover games and events has long since made the press box an integral component of major and even minor venues. Nourished by testosterone and visions of eternal youth, the atmosphere is unique. Some sports desks would love to imagine that, inside those sacred, almost invariably cheery confines, we are all at each other's throats, sneaking around doing underhand tricks, slipping drugs into our neighbour's pint, peeking over his or her shoulder, sending them emails brimming with lethal viruses – doing anything, in short, to beat the competition. Most know better.

The camaraderie of a cricket press box makes it the most pleasant office I have sampled. We all know we are slightly potty in being so stricken by as superficially slow a game, and that sitting around for months on end watching ball games is not to be confused with hard labour. Football and rugby boxes, playing host as they do to those in a perpetual rush, are no match for the cricketing variant. David Foot told me that the first question his wife, Anne, would ask whenever he returned from a day's reporting, was 'What was the box like?' In other words, how was the company? Having to spend so much time together does not necessarily mean that everybody gets on all the time, but evenness of temper and boyishness of outlook are common traits. Cricket writers are among my favourite species. I could not say the same of any of the estate agents, accountants, bankers or record-shop salesmen I have worked alongside.

My most cherished moment in a press box was the cuticle-crunching climax of that aforementioned World Cup semi-final between Australia and South Africa at Edgbaston in 1999. All over the world, deadlines were being stretched and defied. Tensions were running high, tempers fraying, chills scampering up and down the backs of 50-odd necks. Though the

PRESSBOX PROTOCOL

For newcomers, protocol, though strictly informal and unsaid, is fairly straightforward:

1. Try not to ask your elders and alleged betters for information until you are known and established. Doing so runs the considerable risk of a patronising comment at best and, at worst, being pigeonholed as a slacker – i.e. not doing sufficient research. And once you are pigeonholed, perceptions take a great deal of time to change.
2. On the other hand, do pump those elders and alleged betters for reminiscences – 'What was it like interviewing George Best?' might be a decent opening gambit. Listening and heeding is part of your education.
3. Don't be fearful of expressing yourself, but be wary of being too loud, or too forceful: the right to eccentricity has to be earned.
4. Take copious notes. As with research, yours should be more thorough than anyone's; again, this will enable you, once you have completed this informal apprenticeship, to nudge your grizzled neighbour if you miss a goal or a wicket.
5. Bring as many reference books as your bag will hold and your back can take: furnishing colleagues with information they cannot easily obtain from the Internet is the first way to their hearts.
6. Don't sit in the corner glued to your seat. If you are sent on an assignment outside your patch, approach the local reporter who regularly covers the home team and instigate an exchange of information, however informally or casually. The key is to give first: in time, they will be only too happy to hand over titbits they might be reluctant to pass on to others. Similarly, cultivate overseas reporters if you are covering an international contest – they will appreciate the contact as well as the chance to exchange news and views. And be consistent. Always be amiable and genial, not solely when you want something.
7. Don't be afraid to approach scorers, statisticians or media relations folk for assistance: it is their job to help you, so don't let them sneer you into going away. By the same token, do make them feel as if they are doing you a huge favour.

box was densely populated by a sweaty mixture of Englishmen, Australians, South Africans, Pakistanis and Indians as well as a sprinkling of Sri Lankans, New Zealanders and Jamaicans, the warm grins and raised eyebrows spoke of a bond that drove a coach and horses through notions of national identity. United by our appreciation of the game, these were gestures of gratitude. We were sharing the same sensation, the same instant awareness that you had been a part, in however remote a way, of something utterly unforgettable. Years later, we would be able to bump into each other and smile knowingly: 'Remember Edgbaston?'

Yet those who inhabit these dens of largely boys-only-iniquity can also be the most duplicitous of rivals. Keeping an exclusive to yourself in such a matey environment can be a devil of a job – and exclusives, after all, are what your editor values and prizes most highly, however scarce they may be. More importantly, you dare not miss the story everyone else has. Leaving that comfort zone to go the extra mile carries inherent risks. Striking a balance is not easy.

During a Test match at Headingley a few seasons back, a nervy young reporter from the *Mirror* was set up by the press box police. Word had spread: he had been peering over shoulders and stealing material from other reporters' laptops. By way of slapping his wrists, somebody tapped out a fake story. It was about that cricket aficionado Mick Jagger, who, if memory serves, was said to be contemplating buying a controlling interest in Yorkshire County Cricket Club. Only after the story duly appeared in the *Mirror* the next morning did the shamefaced youth learn he had been duped. Having once fallen prey to a similar wheeze, albeit a good deal more innocently, I felt for him.

Your task will be rendered a good deal easier by the support of those in the office. Time was when all that would accompany a match report would be the headline – which tended to give the game away – the scoreline and the name of the reporter (and not always the last). These days, the process is a great deal more collective. For example, in the *Guardian*'s expanded Monday sports pullout, if a major football, rugby union or cricket game has been played the previous day, the report of the action is often accompanied by what is best depicted as a highlights package, wherein the major events of the game are briefly chronicled and buttressed by photographs. This can be done from the office by a sub-editor watching the game unfold on television, who will also do what he or she always does and add the details at the top and bottom of the report – score/scorecard, teams, venue, attendance, half-time score, bowling figures, scorers, goaltimes, substitutes, red and yellow cards and so forth. There might also be room for columns of player ratings, as judged, more often than not, by the second reporter on duty at the game (though when I did this for the *People*, the paper that introduced star ratings, it was strictly a one-man show). In 1970, the only matches that warranted this sort of approach were FA Cup finals. As the practice of sending more than one reporter to a game took root in the 1980s – in response to ever-multiplying sports pages and the march of television – so the possibilities for teamwork expanded. Thus is the match reporter now freed to write a critical analysis without dwelling excessively on whether Jones scored in the 36th or 37th minute.

This does not mean, though, that you should waste words. While the game considered the most important or dramatic might be allotted 900 words or more, most national paper match reports run between 200 and 400 words, so economy of expression is crucial. That you can take a certain degree of knowledge on trust is beneficial in this respect. Take the following description of a strictly imaginary goal: 'Moving on to a good, accurate cross from the right foot of his capable right-winger, Wayne Rooney leapt high to meet it and head firmly past the keeper's vain dive and into the left-hand corner of the net.' This can just as easily – and far more efficiently – be expressed thus: 'Rooney leapt to nod home a fine right-wing cross.' A saving of no fewer than 30 words. We don't really need to know which corner the ball flew into, nor that the winger was right-footed: if he was left-footed, which is decidedly more unusual, then we might. Nor do we need to know that Rooney leapt high; the word 'leap' infers as much. Nor do we really need to know that he connected – we assume this. Nor that he did so with firmness: unless the header was weak, we take this as read. And we certainly don't need to be told that the keeper dived in vain. Had he remained statuesque, or propelled himself the wrong way, that would have been worth recording. Similarly, try not to duplicate information obtainable elsewhere (the score above all) unless it is to make a wider point. Don't fritter away words on the norm.

The aim is to strike a balance between necessary information and vivid descriptions that enhance it. If you are accustomed to writing short reports, then suddenly find yourself with room to breathe, the temptation is always to substitute adjectives for the more detailed analysis that space permits. Resist. True, there is no reason, if an incident demands more graphic exposition, why 'a 20-yard drive' shouldn't become 'a vicious, dipping, swerving, brute of a shot that threatened to forcibly divorce the goalkeeper from his hands', but a comment about the defence's culpability is often more valuable. Besides, in my experience, newspaper sub-editors, by and large, have as much fondness for adjectives and purple prose as they do for malicious viruses. Times have moved on. Or should that be back? Where lengthy descriptions of a batsman's forward-defensive or a fly-half's dummies were once written safe in the knowledge that the reporter's say-so was the reader's sole passport to enlightenment, they are now back in fashion because they can do what those harassed, time-poor broadcasters cannot, or at least seldom do as well. The point is: be sparing. Keep your powder dry.

RESEARCH

Your ability to write a good match report stands or falls according to the research you have done beforehand. This will enable you to place the game in its full context, which in turn means that you will have a full grasp of the game's newsworthiness, and hence the wherewithal to request extra space should the story develop in an unexpected manner.

The following are the main areas of research you should carry out prior to any match reporting assignment:

1 Take more heed of form than the history of meetings between the opponents in question, albeit not unthinkingly. With some matches – such as England–Wales at rugby, England–Australia at cricket or a local derby, it is that sense of history being prolonged and developed that gives the match its intensity and newsworthiness. On the other hand, turnover in team personnel is high, so not too much need be read into the overall pattern of results. Unless, that is, a hoodoo is involved. For the best part of 70 years, for instance, journalists reporting Tottenham's visits to Anfield were obliged to mention that the visitors had not won there since The Titanic sank. Nor were those covering the 2006–07

Ashes tour shy of reminding readers that England had not won in Australia for 20 years – or, by way of more meaningful variation, since the fall of the Berlin Wall. Or even, to be more precise, since the 1987 release of the box-office smash *Crocodile Dundee*, the movie which defined for countless millions of outsiders the purported indefatigability of the Australian male.

2 Apprise yourself of the most newsworthy recent developments concerning the protagonists: Is Roger Federer's decline attributable to that rumoured wrist injury? Has his manager/coach resigned? Is he embroiled in a paternity suit? As with so many areas of research, do not rely on official websites – too subjective and biased – or on the Internet in general: pick up the phone or go to a training session and chat to somebody with the authority to say something significant. And what lies ahead? Does Team A have a big Euro tie the following week? Are its directors due to meet the liquidators? Is X about to begin a suspension? Is Y due to make his debut in the next game? Is Z going to get the vacant manager's job? The subtext may be more subtle and personal. The 2006 World Series, for instance, pitted Tony La Russa, manager of the St Louis Cardinals, against Jim Leyland, his Detroit Tigers counterpart, who not only happen to be best friends but who had worked together in St Louis for the previous four seasons, giving reporters a thread to die for. The trick is to think as a fan. Try and find out what you would want to know if you were reading the article.

3 Statistics, of course, are the sports journalist's most reliable and frequently used crutch. Fortunately, whereas they were once the exclusive province of club statisticians, scorers and persons excessively fond of anoraks, the Internet has made them one of our planet's more widespread and interchangeable currencies. Numbers are the bedrock of sport – what better way to attempt to shed some light on the complexities of human existence than by doing something as natural as counting? Use those digits and decimals properly, not thoughtlessly, and you have the bedrock of any match report. Provided you research accordingly on the plane or at the hotel, it should be eminently possible to whizz off to Poland at half an hour's notice to cover an ice hockey game and produce a report that convinces all but the most knowledgeable reader you know what you are talking about. Journalism, in good part, is the art of instant expertise and bluff.

Be prepared, though, to dig below even the most self-contained statistics. Take the Division Two striker whose 43 goals in 28 games fail to persuade the Premiership manager to offer him the sort of contract that would allow him to quit his day job. Granted the assistance of statistics and video evidence, the boxes he fails to tick may be endless. How many of those shots or headers wound up where they were intended? How many were clean connections? How many fluky deflections did he profit from? How many mistimed tackles, useless keepers or slack markers aided his cause? Did the goals come against the division's weaker defences or in the latter stages of already-lost games? How many of those goals would have been flagged offside by an experienced referee's assistant?

Similarly, winning sequences can be deceptive. Manchester United may have won ten games on the trot, but while one should never underestimate the value of confidence and momentum, analysing the opposition over those ten games can promote greater accuracy. While two of the matches might have been played in a downpour, rendering the result something of a lottery, three of United's victims might have been utterly form-free, three riddled with injuries and the remaining two neither threatened by relegation nor in the running for prizes. There are, as the good book says with good reason, lies, damned lies and statistics. No number lacks context, and context, as ever, is all.

NOTE-TAKING

In one respect this is a hugely overrated practice. In my experience, the more copious are your notes, the less likely you are to go back through everything with the requisite rigour. There is no more point in noting down every foul, run or questionable decision than in ignoring everything and relying slavishly on memory. The clock is the constant, remorseless enemy, especially when you are writing at the same time. Less, in this case, is not infrequently more. By the same token, even an early item of seeming insignificance – a heavy tackle, a dropped pass – may, over the course of a contest, mushroom into one of huge import, whether to the final outcome or to the future of a team or individual.

The better you know your subject, the more able you are to discern the significant from the incidental. Instinct and experience will inform your decision as to what is worth noting, but certainty is impossible, which is why it helps to think visually. Devising a hierarchy or multi-tiered format is recommended. One time-honoured method is to divide each page of your notebook in half by means of a vertical line. Put the name of one team or combatant on the left, and the other on the right. Then, for each happening of potential consequence, note down the time (write 57 if it's the 57th minute, and circle it for emphasis) or the stage of the contest (the 57th over, the seventh game of the set). Try, too, to note facial and other physical reactions or tics – such observations add colour and depth. If a goal or try is scored, or somebody is booked or sent off, indicate its prominence by ringing or underlining it. If it lacks such obvious substance but you suspect that it may prove material to your report, do likewise, or add an asterisk. This way, when scanning your notes come writing-up time, your eye will be that much more easily drawn to the key moments.

WORD COUNTS

Until the advent of laptops and word counts, being asked for 650 words and delivering same was bedevilled by inexactitude. Counting was often a rushed process, leading to miscalculation. It was also blighted by the publication's own method of calculating story lengths. At the *Guardian*, for instance, prior to the advent of the Berliner format, the average number of words printed per line, five, was multiplied by the number of lines the production editor had allotted the story, giving an overall requirement. The governing principle was to ask for slightly more than necessary, the better to ensure the reporter did not come up short. Further complicating matters was the fact that one man's 650 words might be another's 680 – or 620. Anyone partial to multi-syllabled words would obviously be at somewhat greater risk of running over. Reporters who had worked on the sports desk found a way to ensure their work was published as written, knocking 10 per cent off the requested count. For all the time this saves, I have heard it said by more than one sports editor that he preferred his sub-editors to have something to cut: it made them feel more useful.

The most logical ploy I have ever come across was that practised by Brian Glanville, who would divide a large piece of notepaper into a grid: the number of boxes represented the number of words required. Come writing-up time, he would insert each word into a separate box: the number of crossings-out were astonishingly few. Sitting beside him as he simultaneously dispensed tales of meeting Lenny Bruce and talked Italian to his chums in Rome was a lesson as well as a privilege.

LANGUAGE

Whether creative, lyrical, apposite or merely sound, word selection is one of the major keys to effective journalism. In sports journalism, the task is rendered all the more vexing by the fact that the storylines, in essence, are so limited in range. As Tim Robbins' dense, slowly maturing pitcher Calvin 'Nuke' Laloush apprises a reporter in Ron Shelton's superlative celluloid homage to minor-league baseball and mateship, *Bull Durham*: 'Sometimes you win, sometimes you lose, sometimes it rains.' And nowhere is one's vocabulary tested so sorely as in the heat of a live match report. Hyperbole and repetition, excitability and injudiciousness: such are the inevitable consequences of writing against deadline while an event is unfolding. A colleague once told me he kept boredom at bay by aiming to insert a fresh word, one he had never used in print, into every match report. Another would choose a noun or adjective each time then repeat it as often as possible. Some started each paragraph with a specific letter so that it spelled out something rude and/or insulting. Groups of reporters would collectively nominate a word and agree, individually, to deploy it that day. Ah, the games we play.

Teaching someone how to write well is not unlike advising them how to compose a hit single. One woman's George Eliot is another woman's Danielle Steel. Nonetheless, a journalist's work is always subject to criticism and change, and not always for any explicable reason. Sometimes it is a dispute over fact or interpretation: the reporter takes one view, the reader/sub another. While preciousness is never recommended, some battles are worth fighting. I once had a tussle with a veteran sub over a cricket season preview: he disagreed with one of my prognostications and changed it to reflect his own view. I respected his experience, and his knowledge of the game, but as the reporter being paid for purportedly being in the know, I requested that the original be reinstated. Happily, he took it with good grace and we subsequently worked harmoniously for several years. On another occasion, a statistic I had included in a report was changed, not because the sub in question had ascertained that it was incorrect but because he could not believe it. Which brings to mind the night on one English national paper during the 1950 FIFA World Cup when the scoreline from Brazil – USA 1 England 0 – was construed as an error and rewritten: as 10–0 to England.

More often than not, disputes stem from the language or phrasing. All editors and sub-editors have their bêtes noires, words and phrases that have them reaching automatically for the delete button. Tabloids often have an aversion to adjectives; a heavy may take exception to colloquialisms and contractions. Subjectivity is all. One paper's cliché is another's trusty standby, used over and over again precisely because of its value as shorthand and its reassuring familiarity. Aside from those whose meaning has been warped by misuse – presently has no more in common with currently than disinterested has with uninterested – four words are guaranteed to send this particular subjective pedant into a minor frenzy: great, ever, fantastic and tragic/tragedy. I make no apology for re-emphasizing these bêtes noires.

The difficulty with the first three words underscores the contrast between the spoken and the written word: the most succinct distinction is that whereas explicit clarity is not always absolutely necessary when talking, readers demand it and deserve it. When wielded as a qualitative as opposed to quantitative tool, 'great' is possibly the most grievously abused word in the English language. Where once it was applied sparingly, and only to those of accepted and long-entrenched stature – most notably that illustrious Anglo-Russian clan headed by Alfred, Peter and Catherine – it is now trotted out unthinkingly whenever somebody does something for which the description 'good' is simply not effusive enough. Greatness can only be assessed over time, with hindsight; otherwise the word loses all substance and meaning. Much the same can be said of 'ever', as in 'Colin Partridge's first-ever Premiership goal': the Premiership has only been in existence since 1992. And don't get me started on such vile constructions as 'Neil Phinn's display last night was undoubtedly his greatest-ever performance in a City shirt'. As for 'fantastic', that stands one rung above 'great' in the ladder of contemporary overstatement. The question to ask yourself is this: was that shot so exceptional and/or phenomenal that it satisfied one's dreams? Depending on your dreams, of course, I would strongly suspect that this does not crop up terribly often. While commonly used nowadays to pour scorn on pitiable or obsessed human beings, 'tragic' retains much of its original power: witness horrors such as the Rwandan genocide, the Asian tsunami or the destruction of New Orleans. A true tragedy, in the Shakespearian sense, is one in which a character brings about their own fall, often by dint of the very asset/defect that accelerated their rise. If you are going to cite an own-goal, a muffed putt or a dropped catch as a 'tragedy', you might as well pop along to Westminster Abbey and expectorate all over The Bard's grave. It scarcely needs adding that to misuse this word is also to diminish the suffering of disaster victims and their families.

CONTENT

Your job is to bring the reader to the action, putting them in the seat next to you. Unless you are exceedingly adroit, and by contrast with a feature (see Chapter 8), there is no option over tense: it must be the past. Be careful, too, to work in harness with the information at the top of your report. If the strapline says 'League Cup semi-finals: Chelsea 75 Arsenal 1 – aggregate score 75–2 – Dan Steele reports from Highbury', followed by details of the scorers and times, don't begin the report with 'Chelsea walloped Arsenal 75–1 at Highbury last night, completing a 75–2 aggregate victory in the League Cup semi-finals as Frank Lampard scored a hat-trick spanning the 24th, 77th and 88th minutes.'

Blow-by-blow descriptions are particularly useful if you are reporting for a Sunday paper, where space is often at less of a premium, but try to avoid a 'and then this happened . . . then that' approach. Readers expect a more analytical approach. What was the significance of the result, to one or both sides? Why did Team X win? How did Team Y foul up? Did the addition of Player A have the anticipated impact on Team Y's fortunes? Did the loss of Player B to an ankle injury impair his side's form? The skill is to realise and accept that you cannot hope to squeeze in everything of apparent importance. If the emphasis of the story changes substantially between editions – a controversial comment is apt to do this – you may have to eliminate facts and elements that you believed were intrinsic to your first-edition piece. Sometimes, as is the risk with any story that purports to deliver news, one incident may dominate your report to the exclusion of all else. This may make you feel uneasy but that, I am afraid, is journalism.

The intro

Your first paragraph, henceforth to be referred to as the intro, is critical. No matter how fascinating or alluring the headline may be, unless the opening salvo adds to the impact, eyes and minds will wander. Intros must therefore serve two functions:

1 Distil the essence of a story, emphasising/alluding to its most interesting and hence newsworthy aspect(s).
2 Drag the reader in. Entice them to read on. Sell, sell, sell.

If you are your newspaper's lone representative, you have to cover all the bases. On major occasions, you may turn up to a press box mob-handed – *The Sunday Times* sent five reporters to one mid-1990s FA Cup final – though this can lead to duplication as well as greater breadth and depth. Your intro will distil and compress the most important information with all the care and precision of a sardine tin-packer while still finding space for some colour and an overview. As in: 'Quicker around the court, more forceful at the net, Andy Murray eased past Tim Henman and into the semi-finals of the French Open at the Stade Garros in Paris yesterday, forcing the former British No. 1 to accept that his best days are "behind me".' In 44 words (38 if the report is headed by a 'French Open' tagline and a 'Cyril Niceone reports from Paris' byline) you have the result, the winner's degree of superiority, the reason for it, and the most newsworthy line of the press conference. And while that particular intro would be better suited to a heavy or midmarket title, it would require only a small tinker to make it acceptable to a tabloid: 'Tim Henman admitted his best days are "behind me" after a crushing defeat by "Handy Andy" Murray left Wimbledon's favourite son facing the final curtain.' Nor is there any harm in a more visually creative approach: 'Head bowed, shoulders sagging, chin scraping the court, Tim Henman headed straight for his wife's arms after being thrashed by Andy Murray, then confessed his best days are "behind me".'

From theory to practice. Although the *Guardian* dispatched three other writers to Twickenham for the England–All Blacks match on 5 November, 2006, the opening paragraph of Rob Kitson's match report was an object lesson, written as if he were the only man on the spot. Everything is here: the opening of a rebuilt ground, a record attendance and a record hiding for England, and even – perhaps inevitably, since it is such a gift for keen metaphorists – Bonfire Night:

> *New-look stadium, same old story. This was supposed to be a day of celebration for English rugby but by the time the Bonfire Night fireworks were lit the record crowd of 82,076 had already witnessed an unprecedented roasting. The bald statistics – this was England's sixth successive loss and the biggest home defeat of all time – simply served to reinforce how far the world champions' star has fallen.*
>
> (Guardian, *6 November, 2006)*

Compare that with Alex Spink's first *three* paragraphs in the *Mirror*, which drew on quotes from England's beleaguered coach Andy Robinson and emphasise the reporter's view that the hosts were the architects of their own demise:

> *Martin Corry pointed the finger of blame at his own team after England made sure their sixth straight defeat was the biggest Twickenham had ever witnessed.*
>
> *Under-pressure boss Andy Robinson reached for the positives and hailed the All Blacks as a 'winning machine' after Dan Carter had helped himself to 26 points in a match which was over by half-time.*
>
> *But the plain truth of the matter was that the crisis-hit world champions were put to the sword only after shooting themselves in both feet.*
>
> (mirror.co.uk, *6 November, 2006)*

In the *Sun*, my erstwhile *Today* colleague Tony Roche led with a quote, underlining the tabloids' predilection for personality-based journalism: if a leading participant says something of interest, it should take precedence over the reporter's views:

> *Graham Henry summed up England's current plight in world rugby when he declared: 'We didn't put all the nails in the coffin.'*
>
> *New Zealand did not have to. England hammered home the rest for the visitors.*
>
> *The All Black coach virtually ignored the fact his team had inflicted what was the heaviest home defeat on England in their history.*
>
> (Sun Online, *6 November, 2006)*

In the *Daily Mail*, meanwhile, the correspondent was the similarly experienced Peter Jackson, the most persistent and respected of rugby's pack of newshounds. This is a comparatively new category of journalist: until the game went openly professional in 1995, rugby union news stories were almost as scarce as the hair on Zinedine Zidane's head. Jackson's failure to mention that the attendance was a ground record was uncharacteristic. As was the way – in contrast to his counterparts elsewhere – he focused on a disputed try that probably made not a jot of difference to the outcome:

> *England slumped to a record 40–21 defeat at Twickenham but the All Blacks admitted they were lucky to get away with a disputed video verdict.*
>
> *French referee Joel Jutge stunned the New Zealanders and a crowd of more than 82,000 by disallowing a try by England's Jamie Noon in the fifth minute.*

> *And All Blacks captain Richie McCaw admitted after the match: 'We were a bit lucky that it went our way. The call was in our favour and we managed to relieve the pressure. After that, the momentum swung our way.'*
>
> (dailymail.co.uk, *6 November, 2006)*

Note that, in all these cases, there is no reference to *when* the match was played.

In the same day's *Guardian*, Jeremy Alexander went to the other extreme. Drawing on a news item for inspiration when composing an intro to his report on Derby County's defeat of West Bromwich Albion, he merged art and football as possibly never before:

> *Football is determined to copy art in its daftest pretensions. On Friday the* Guardian *showed Jackson Pollock's Number 5, 1948, reportedly sold for $140m, and an obscure representation of Liverpool's passing patterns. They were practically indistinguishable. On Saturday Derby County reproduced My Bed, an embarrassing mess, all over the place. Like Tracy Emin they won but West Brom had all the subtle touches and rich colours, give or take their green and yellow stripes.*

On another page of that morning's *Guardian* was a report of another rugby union international, Paul Rees's on Wales's invigorating 29–29 draw with Australia, which had taken place on the Saturday. Not only does his intro look forward, as a good Sunday-for-Monday report should, it marches on as far as the World Cup, which was not due to begin until the late summer of the following *year*. Note, too, the dart at rugby league, symptomatic of a prejudice common to most rugby union reporters:

> *The Australia skills coach, Scott Johnson, predicted an afternoon for voyeurs, an orgy of attractive rugby, and, if the enthralling six-try draw offered a peek at what is in store at next year's World Cup, a tournament customarily decided by the team with the best defence, the sport stands to regain its core values, having resembled rugby league for far too long.*
>
> (Guardian, *6 November, 2006)*

Intriguingly, and not a little disturbingly, while the report continues at some length, up and down two legs of copy, not once is there any mention of the fact that the game had been played on the Saturday. Plenty of how and why but no when.

The body of the report

As touched on earlier, the lone representative of a publication is also responsible for covering any story or even stories that may emerge. It may be the timeless staples: criticism of the referee/umpire by the losing manager/coach, or criticism of the losing team by a former player/manager. It may be something meatier – a drug test, an incident involving flagrant cheating, a mass brawl. Never, in other words, imagine you are solely there to report a match, or that your duties end when the final whistle peeps.

Match reports – indeed, the greater mass of sportswriting – defy the diktats of the 'inverted pyramid', the structure touted for time immemorial as the only way to write a news story, a legacy of the pre-1980s when typesetters ruled the journalistic earth. It was called an 'inverted pyramid' on the basis that the most important elements should come early, and that the copy could be cut from the bottom without losing anything essential. Depending on space, however, the next paragraph or two after the intro to a match report may be reflective and more specific, an elaboration of events, the consequences thereof and the response of a key figure. Only after that will come a phase-by-phase breakdown and description of the contest in chronological order, ideally while teasing out the decisive areas of conflict – who dominated the midfield, the scrums, the close rallies, the fairways and greens, and why? That said, depending on space, this may well allow you to focus on a particular player.

If the word count permits, the more depth you can bring to a report, the better. Any insights are welcome provided they go beyond the prosaic ('And then he scored his 54th goal of the decade, and then it was ruled offside, and then he made amends . . . '). Depending on the publication, you should also cast forward to one or other of the protagonists' next important engagement by reporting and analysing injuries and possible suspensions, cup draws and so on. I reiterate: try to put your readers in the stadium. Make them hear the chants and sniff the hot dogs.

For the bigger occasions, where more than one reporter is on duty, there will be room for the so-called 'colour piece'. While this may be interpreted, wrongly, as implying that the report it complements is somehow devoid of light or shade, it does free the match reporter to stick to the script. A colour piece ought to do precisely what it says on the tin: splash the action with flavour, subtexts, tangential-but-relevant observations and, ideally, a vestige of wit and proportion. Challenging as it often is to find a suitable focus, a combination of preparatory and on-the-spot research should solve any dilemma. Because what you write is not so tightly bound by the confines of straight reportage and chronology, you have more time and freedom on your hands: use it wisely.

Seek out a coach or player before or even during the game, perhaps an administrator or club director. Home in on a particular player by all means – even an ex-player with memories of the same occasion a generation earlier – but don't forget those other participants, the crowd: the demographics, the mood, the chants, the roars, the boos, the slow handclaps. What else is going on in the neighbourhood that day? Is there an important running news story in another sphere that your match reflects in some way? You might well decide on your topic before the game starts – having discussed as much with your editor or sub so an appropriate photo can be found in good time – but never be inflexible: those of an athletic bent are nothing if not consistent in their capacity to defy probability and force a rapid rethink.

At the end comes what is variously called the tail, the payoff or the outro – the final sentence or paragraph. On no account should this be anticlimactic. Offer an overall verdict, quote a player or manager, or even crack a pertinent – and, ideally, funny – joke. But remember: it is your inalienable right to have the final word.

Rob Kitson's outro to his England–New Zealand match report reflected a well-practised tactic, that of completing the circle. Alighting on the presence of one significant spectator,

Sir Clive Woodward, who coached England to the 2003 World Cup, Kitson resumes the Bonfire Night thread and even throws in a literary reference:

> *It was all a far cry from the glory days under Sir Clive Woodward, back as a humble spectator for the first time since vacating the head coach's chair. Sir Clive tipped New Zealand to win beforehand and asked rhetorically why opposing teams come to London with all their players fit while England struggle to raise a quorum. It remains a burning issue but this is no time for excuses. Last night the bonfires of south-west London were ablaze with English vanities.*
>
> (Guardian, *6 November, 2006)*

PLAYERS READ THE PAPERS TOO

There is, of course, another audience to contend with. No matter what they may claim, or what they may learn to do with age and wisdom, players read the press. Mostly the *Sun* and the *Mirror* although the occasional *Daily Telegraph* and *Mail* has been spotted. Graham Thorpe, who played 100 Tests for England while enduring one of the country's less savoury celebrity break-ups of recent times, once availed me of his philosophy: 'If you want to read the good bits, you have to be prepared to take the bad. If you can't take the bad, don't read the good.'

I would never suggest that the players' feelings should always come first. There are many occasions when you have no option but to point out that X has had a stinker or Y's tackle was grossly over the top and warranted a lifetime suspension, even when X or Y are reliable sources with whom you have shared many an unsober evening. But sensitivity, in outlook and language, is warmly recommended. When you are about to let someone 'have it with both barrels' – as Graham Otway, a former colleague at *Today* and the *Sunday Times* would invariably announce when he had somebody in his sights during English cricket's woeful run at international level during the 1980s and early 1990s – pause before sending your story and consider whether you would like what you have just written to be written about you. Then decide whether you can justify the extent of your criticism. Let's face it: for all that the impact they have on the fans' emotions and weeks cannot be underestimated, missing an open goal, giving away a penalty, dropping a catch and going offside ad nauseam are not crimes and their perpetrators are not hardened sociopaths. There has to be a balance – sports journalists are nothing if they are not entertainers – but toning down the impassioned adjectives, using understatement or gentle wit, can reap dividends for the conscience.

When working for the less histrionic or effusive titles, turning down the volume is usually advisable; no matter how cool you play it, a tabloid sub-editor will almost certainly inject the requisite fire and brimstone. Maintaining principles and dignity is not easy, which is why the reporter I admire more than any other is David Foot, best known for his work with the *Guardian* but also a regular in the *Mail on Sunday*. Not only does he write as easily and fluently as most of us boil the kettle, splashing his canvas with colour and texture, his match reports, profiles, interviews, columns and biographies, even in his dotage, exude a warmth and compassion for his fellow humans utterly out of kilter with the times. I cannot recall him ever being harsh or derogatory. A proud exception.

Andy Afford has a better grasp than most of the contrast in responses and attitudes either side of the touchline. As a left-arm spinner for Nottinghamshire, he went close to national selection in the early 1990s, going on an England A tour of Sri Lanka, where we met and discovered we shared a mutual passion for Bruce Springsteen. Phil Tufnell barred his way to the Test XI but before he was 30 he realised that he had gone as far as he was going to go. One University degree later, he was editing *All Out Cricket*, a magazine that doubles as an in-house organ for the Professional Cricketers' Association and one of three monthly cricket titles currently on the WH Smith shelves. Now paid to observe cricketers himself (he also reported a few games for the *Guardian* in 2005), his recollections of how he used to regard journalists – more 'Aw!' than awe – are refreshingly frank and most illuminating.

> *As a player and a reasonably surly, opinionated and acerbic one at that, I had an attitude when dealing with the press of, at best, indifference. Being a cricketer wasn't the same in the 1980s and 1990s as it is now, in any number of ways. It was local papers looking for local stories when dealing with their county's pros. Very friendly (unless we were losing and being criticised for it!) and supportive.*
>
> *Things like deadlines, word count, etc., meant f*** all as a player. Not even a consideration. Back then my attitude was that if it was hard for the press to do their job, that was fine with me. It was amusing to think that a journalist would have to book a phone line at some ungodly hour in some god forsaken place, in order to do his job – served him right for not being able to play the game!*
>
> *If form was such that England recognition looked a possibility then the proper papers might venture north for an interview. These were big deals and set you apart from team mates so generally frowned upon by the management and players alike. You'd taken a few wickets and gone all Billy Big Time . . .*
>
> *There was no 24-hour media as today. Wisden Cricket Monthly and The Cricketer were very important in reflecting the views of players. The tabloids hardly covered [county] cricket and the broadsheets were where the sport lived. The Daily Telegraph was where cricket was best represented and if you managed a good write-up in it, you were doing well. Conversely, if Fred Trueman picked you out as one to watch in the Sunday redtops, then you might as well forget it!*
>
> *I feel that generally there is a herd mentality to reporting the sport and no one wants to miss a story or write about the 'wrong thing'. There is an outlook to the job that I don't like, the 'I'm never drinking again' culture in the evening, 'fancy him getting out at this time' when coping with deadlines, 'they should have bowled them out hours ago' so you could have avoided the traffic – a slightly hard-done-to take on life that is unappealing.*
>
> *Reporting standards are bloody brilliant at the top end. I love to see the Sunday papers filled with cricket. The profiles, the moments, all of the complementary coverage that makes it a great read with a cup of coffee. The blokes on Test match duty work like bastards during the Test. I'm less convinced on the [county] circuit.*
>
> *On reflection, my exposure to the media was very limited. But I handled it all at arm's length when I should have been, at the very least, more bloody friendly. Looking*

back it's a piece of piss to be interviewed compared to conducting and writing up a report that's entertaining, balanced and without so much ego that it detracts from the subject. I should have enjoyed the ride more!

I once felt the wrath of an aggrieved subject. Saturday at Lord's in the mid-1990s and the press box was united: Keith Brown, a rightful fixture in the Middlesex side as a gritty batsman, should not be keeping wicket. While undoubtedly agile and brave, he missed too many chances and lacked the requisite speed of hand or foot. In common with a few other reporters, I made this point and also reported that he fluffed a stumping. The next time I was at the ground, a few days later, he strolled over and requested a private word. We had never met before. I was a little wary – he was, after all, renowned as a useful boxer – but consented. He proceeded to tell me that, so far as he was concerned, he did not miss that stumping. I was entitled to write what I liked, he added, but inaccurate reporting was the thin end of the wedge, and if I did it again . . . The low growl and the measured menace did not seem to be worth testing. It is possible that he was right: the Lord's press box back then was next to the pavilion and hence at a terrible angle. He may also have been in denial. Correctly judging which is just one of the unconsidered items on a sportswriter's plate.

THE RUNNER

The most demanding form of match report is the runner, a report delivered in stages so as to ease the congestion on the sports desk and ensure that deadlines are more easily met. These were staples of those Green 'Uns and Pink 'Uns that once proliferated nationwide but are now, for logistical reasons, a dying breed. Not all Sunday papers demand runners, but all dailies require them to be done this way because of printing constraints. Most evening football matches end between 9.30 and 9.45, which only just about fits in with the deadline for second edition on the average national newspaper, which is around 10 p.m. As you might imagine, extra-time causes one or two tiny difficulties. The sub-editor has to write a holding, non-commital headline; the reporter must write an intro that hedges bets.

The normal format, for football and rugby matches, runs as follows: half the apportioned word-length at half-time, another quarter at three-quarter-time, and the final 25 per cent of copy split into a top and a tail – intro and outro – up to 10 minutes before the final whistle. So, say you have been asked for 600 words, you would file about 300 at half-time, 150 at three-quarter time and a 75-top, 75-tail to finish. Because the match has yet to finish, you will need to call the sub-editor handling your story and keep the line open until the whistle is blown, which enables you to dictate any necessary changes.

The worst nightmare, because of the length of a day's play, is cricket, and seldom more so than when you are reporting to England from the Caribbean, or to Australasia from England. Because of the respective time differences (five hours behind and up to 13 ahead), reporters covering Test matches in such instances have to file one piece for first edition (taking in play up to lunchtime in the Caribbean, say 18.00 GMT, or 21.30 Australian time), one for second edition after tea, and another, for third edition, as soon as possible after the close (though not in the case of Antipodean papers, whose readers have to wait until the following day for the final chapter). The story may twist and turn in all sorts of directions during that span, so taking care to hedge your bets, again, is paramount. Never will I forget the night at the *Independent* when I was awaiting Martin Johnson's report from Trinidad. England had been left to make 190-odd for a rare victory over the West Indies. The mood was expectant, even triumphalist. By the time stumps were drawn that night, just in time for third edition, England were tottering on 40 for 8. The rewrite was not unhurried.

Covering the World Series for a British newspaper is just as hazardous, and only partly because it follows a best-of-seven format. The combination of late starts (20.30 BST) and time difference (eight hours if the game is taking place on the West Coast) means that there is no prospect whatsoever of readers finding a report the next morning. Instead, it can be written at one's comparative leisure and will not be seen in print until after the *following* night's game. As with a Monday morning football report, delay any mention of the day the game was played as long as possible: writing 'Thursday night' in a report that will not be read until Saturday morning dates it terribly, so damage limitation is the aim. Again, no matter how decisive the result, resist any temptation to make predictions. Much the same set of caveats applies to major tennis and golf tournaments played in the States, although afternoon matches and early rounds can be accommodated.

Whereas Continental Europe (one hour's difference), Africa (two) and the Indian subcontinent (four-and-a-half) pose few if any headaches, Australasia is another major obstacle for a British sportswriter. Because Australia can be anything from eight to 11 hours ahead, and New Zealand 13, by the time your report on the first day's play of a Test match appears, the second is almost done and dusted. Which is why you will often find a report of the first day's play appearing alongside a pre-lunch report from the second, even if the story has taken a wholly different direction. Which may well make a nonsense of that first-day report, not to mention the accompanying headline. The 2006–07 Ashes series brought the Internet into sharper focus than ever as a newspaper's accomplice: in addition to podcasts, several national titles made their chief correspondent's report available on the Web almost as soon as play had finished, and hence virtually 24 hours before it could be read on paper. In the past, British reporters took advantage of that lengthy time difference, cogitating over dinner before writing up, but these fresh demands may well have put an end to that. That said, early figures for the *Daily Mail*[1] suggested these Web reports found few takers, underlining the enduring preference for print as the prime source of leisurely reading.

THE HOLDING STORY

Deadlines may also oblige you to write a piece before a match has begun. On a Saturday, for instance, some English nationals have early cut-off points for their European edition; more commonly, in midweek, football matches kick off too late for the first editions – which are usually only seen at the country's northern and southern extremities – to include full reports. In both cases, the space reserved will be filled instead, for that one edition, by a related story, ideally one that cannot be contradicted by the result. New Yorkers have it even worse, especially when a team from the city is playing on the West Coast, which is three hours behind: baseball games routinely start around 8.00 p.m. and regularly last anywhere between two and four hours, which means only the final edition, at best, will feature a report.

PRESS CONFERENCES

In most cases, if you are working for a national or regional paper with more than one daily edition, you will write a report, then rewrite it and file again about an hour later, possibly at a reduced or increased length depending on how eventful your match turned out to be by comparison with those elsewhere. This second bite at the cherry exists partly to facilitate a more considered report, but also to allow you to incorporate any significant comments arising from the subsequent press conference. Or, better yet, the thoughts of a player or manager you have managed to corner. In other words, be aware of what the pack, the competition, are doing, but don't be a sheep. The key here is to discern, quickly, what you simply *have* to quote – a key revelation that explains an incident; a controversial statement; a comment about the importance of the next match.

Sometimes, though, you do not need to reproduce, merely to report, in your own words, what was conveyed. Newspapers are obsessed with quotes, magazines too, but try not to use them as a substitute for thought or for more revelatory reporting. Besides, cutting quotes is a simple process: sportspeople seldom talk in complete sentences, nor do they always choose the right words, or the most succinct way of expressing a thought or feeling. Paraphrasing, provided it is accurate, is acceptable. '"I was very, very unhappy indeed with the way the lads played today," said Alex Shankly, the Lewes manager,' is easily trimmed to 'Alex Shankly, the Lewes manager, was not a happy bunny.'

A press conference can be more valuable, in fact, as a source of future material. The manager of the winning team might spend a few moments elaborating on why his star striker is having such a fruitful campaign, but only a fraction of those comments might warrant inclusion in a match report. Take them all down and save the bulk for a non-matchday feature or even a holding story. The opportunity may arrive the next day, or not for another six months, but it will almost invariably present itself at some stage. By the same token, the manager may say something that demands a separate story in its own right, in which case alert the desk and find out whether it can be accommodated that very night. The page designer may not thank you for saddling him with extra work but the story always comes first.

REPORTER AND CRITIC

A match reporter, in summation, is at once reporter, painter and critic. He or she is also a human being. The live report that grabbed my eye most forcefully in 2006 was not from the World Cup final, nor even that controversial game at The Oval that saw Pakistan become the first team to forfeit a Test (of which more anon), but the C&G Trophy final at Lord's. It supplemented the main report, by Richard Hobson, and was written by Christopher Martin-Jenkins, who had been commentating on the match for the BBC. It revolved around his difficulties in maintaining impartiality while his son, Robin, was batting or bowling for the eventual winners, Sussex. I cannot envisage a stiffer journalistic task. 'Towards the end,' CMJ began,

> *I received a charming email in the Test Match Special box from a proud sporting parent in Carlisle, commending me for the 'professionalism' with which I had communicated [sic] on my*

> *son's bowling role in Sussex's narrow success. It was as well, perhaps, that, earlier in the day, Robin had been [unjustly] given out just before I was due back on air . . . I would have found it hard to be diplomatic but I was as proud of his reaction [RMJ showed no dissent and walked straight off] as of his modest part in Sussex's success.*

He even quoted his boy: '"He's a very good umpire, it was a very good ball and I got very close to it," he said. Unquestionably his mother's son'.[2]

EXERCISE

Borrow or buy a DVD/video of an FA Cup final that you have not seen and write an 800-word running match report, for the newspaper of your choice, written as if contemporaneously. The more you research, the more realistic the report. Write 400 words during the first half then, within five minutes of the half-time whistle, email it to yourself; three-quarters of the way through the match, email another 200 covering ensuing developments. Finally, write and file the last chunk of 200 words – comprising an intro and a final paragraph or two to tack on to the end. Name full teams, substitutes and referee, just as you would expect to find at the end of a contemporary match report, plus attendance, half-time score and goalscorers with times. Adhere closely to the house style of your chosen publication.

Chapter 6

Breaking the news

The news story

> *This is an attempt at a true account of events at The Oval yesterday, but I cannot be entirely certain any of this really happened.*
>
> *(Matthew Engel,* Guardian, *27 August 1986)*

Not for the first time, nor the last, Matthew Engel wrote what I wish I had had the wherewithal to write. He even used the dreaded 'I' word without raising hackles. Columnists aside, newspapers actively discourage the 'I' word; on this occasion the exception was absolutely justified, but the rule makes sense: given that your byline generally lies above the copy, and that the reporter is almost never a relevant part of the story, to use the first-person singular is regarded as egotistical.

The above quotation was Engel's intro to a report on the opening day of the 1986 England v New Zealand Test at The Oval, my own Test debut as a reporter. Rather helpfully, Ian Botham had returned that day from a two-month suspension – he'd confessed, shock, horror, to having smoked cannabis in his time, and even inhaled – with a bang so resounding they might have heard it in Dunedin. With his first ball back, he took a wicket, equaling Dennis Lillee's Test aggregate record of 355; never being one for custom or tradition, much less superstition, Botham then proceeded to raise the bar with his 13th delivery. (Later in the same game, for good measure, he cracked the fastest 50 yet made for England in a Test. Please note the reluctance to use 'ever': by the time you read these words, it is far from unfeasible that Andrew Flintoff will have beaten it.) For the first-timer, it was a birthday cake from heaven complete with icing and cherry. Readers of the first edition of the *Manchester Evening News* might have recoiled at the excitable prose but at least it was in on time, dictated breathlessly from a public phonebox.

That was an occasion where what happened on the field was deemed worthy of being transplanted from back page to front. (When covering a major story, a sports journalist may be required to compose a different, usually briefer, version for the news pages, a more frequent occurrence as bats and balls cast their increasingly mesmeric spell over the public imagination. The recent emergence of the 'sports correspondent', a news reporter entrusted with covering financial, political and media-related issues pertaining to sport at the front end or main section of a newspaper, supplies further evidence of this spell.) Botham, after all, was to the mid-1980s what David Beckham was to the late-1990s. The main difference was Botham's distaste for the quiet life and his unwavering belief in his own invincibility, which saw him shoot himself in at least one toe on almost a daily basis, thus playing into the hands of those happy to provoke an exchange of fists or extract a handsome fee from a Sunday paper for an ugly slice of kiss-and-tell. Allied to his handlers' lack of expertise, this meant that, while he was frequently acclaimed as the most formidable Englishman since Alfred the Great – three parts Winston Churchill, four parts Richard the Lionheart, one part Alf Garnett – he was just as often a prime subject for the serious end of the *Nine O'Clock News* and grave editorials whose authors apparently bypassed childhood on the road to the pulpit. Nor, for Botham, was there an escape hatch to Madrid: unlike their footballing brethren, English cricketers can only earn a worthwhile living at domestic level if they stay in England. George Best had hinted at what was possible during the previous decade, but Botham spent the 1980s proving that, in terms of news, what went on inside the lines was no match for events beyond them. Any sports journalist operating in England knew the goalposts had moved as soon as hardened news reporters began, in the early 1980s, to be dispatched on cricket tours in order to 'dig the dirt', as it was dignified, on Botham.

IDENTIFYING A NEWS STORY

Nowadays there is no shortage of news stories for the sports journalist to tuck into. The more influence the moneyed classes exert, the cosier the nexus between sport, sponsor and media barons, the greater the responsibility of the journalist to expose the fissures and represent the exploited, i.e. the viewers and the large rump of sportspeople who are not paid a trillion pounds a minute. To catch the really big fish, it's simply a question of whether you have a) the nose of a bloodhound that has just had its adenoids seen to, and b) the stubborn persistence of a cat trying to persuade you that you really are most unlikely to be able to finish that *entire* pot of cream on your own.

The difficulty now is threefold:

1 If journalists were ever widely trusted by those in power, the paranoia we generate shows about as much sign of diminishing as Richard Branson's pension plan.
2 The Fifth Estate, as one might collectively term agents, press offices, public relations, promotion and marketing departments, has emerged. These held little sway in Britain until the early 1970s, when the tabloids, stirred into action by the *Sun*, started peeking into too many closets and exposing one too many skeletons. During Edward Heath's brief reign at No.10 (1970–74), a *News of the World* sting saw one of his ministers, Lord Lambton, caught cavorting with marijuana and prostitutes thanks to a camera and microphone concealed in a teddy bear. Even as late as the mid-1990s, it was possible to grab a quick chat on the phone to the Tottenham manager, gently mediated by a press officer whose time was largely devoted to editing the match programme. Those days have gone, for good I am utterly certain. The Fifth Estate is a shield, yet another wall distancing public from performers, a media for the media to contend with; another layer with a vested interest in controlling the availability and flow of information. Not that it is above leaking the odd titbit of extremely tasty and/or inflammatory information if it

serves a wider purpose. Say a club wants to get shot of its mutinous centre-forward, accidentally-on-purpose letting slip that he was once tried for bigamy in Turkey, an incident previously hushed up by all concerned, would do nicely.

3 The seemingly insatiable demand for, and supply of, instant information leaves less room for the properly researched story. Yet some stories take years to gestate. Just as cricket's match-fixing crisis of the mid-1990s was gathering steam, I was told in strictest confidence by an Australian friend, Mark Ray, then cricket correspondent of the *Melbourne Age*, that he had it on utterly reliable authority (a trusted contact on the Australian Cricket Board) that Shane Warne and Mark Waugh had been secretly fined for furnishing a bookmaker with pertinent information that could be used in fixing odds. Even though the information – state of the pitch, weather prospects, injuries – could have easily been gleaned from elsewhere, this was a serious matter, the act of keeping the fines secret a further nail in the coffin of open and transparent governance. The one problem was that Mark's contact was not prepared to go on the record. We had to sit and wait. I can recall one Saturday morning when we were about to go into print – me in the *Sunday Times* – only for Mark to call me urgently to insist that the contact had changed his mind and that we would have to wait a bit longer. Four years after our original conversation, Phil Wilkins, another Australian journalist, broke the story.

Journalists prepared to risk reputation, pocket and neck by rooting around in the grubby undergrowth of government and corporate corruption are a tiny minority and seldom encouraged. The editorial logic is cold and plain: why lavish fees and expenses on lengthy investigations without any guarantee of a printable story? Better, by far, to invest in a honey trap that yields an off-the-record quote from a vengeful employee alleging that his horrendously cruel boss, who just happens to be a famous movie director/Chancellor of the Exchequer/chat show host, might once, perhaps, have misappropriated a fiver from the Christmas dinner box to pay a chemist's prescription on behalf of his ailing 96-year-old mother. The flaws of celebrities are considered of greater interest than genuine wrongdoing.

Sport is not so terribly different. David Conn, an award-winning journalist and author who preceded all this frippery by qualifying as a lawyer, writes an admirable and thought-provoking weekly column for the *Guardian* investigating football economics – the fragility of the professional game beneath those billion-pound TV deals and eight-figure contracts, the growing threat to century-old institutions, the illusions, the corruption and incompetence. During a rousing Annual Sport Journalism lecture at the University of Brighton in 2006, he made the pertinent point that what he was doing, rather than being exceptional, should be de rigeur for all journalists. 'All' he ever did was check out a company at Companies House, which anybody can do, ascertain any revealing figures or changes of personnel or responsibilities, and pick up the phone. What amazed him, when he began focusing on stories of this ilk at the *Independent* a few years previously, was how sparse the competition was.

Since the 1980s heyday of the *Inside Track* team at the *Sunday Times*, investigative sports reporting – a comparatively new area but one made inevitable by the financial growth of professional sport in the 1960s – had withered, as it had elsewhere. That said, jobs such as 'sports news correspondent' or 'chief sports reporter' have surfaced in recent years, posts usually filled by those with a background and steeling in general news, such as Denis Campbell at the *Observer* and Paul Kelso at the *Guardian*, their function to report and analyse the latest development from a political/financial/media angle. When I started out, this was usually the lot of the athletics correspondent, the likes of John Rodda (*Guardian*) and Cliff Temple (*Sunday Times*): they were considered more able, because of their familiarity with the International Olympic Committee, bidding procedures and steroid abuse, to obtain or follow up such a story. Alan Hubbard (initially at the *Observer*, latterly for the *Independent on Sunday*) and John Goodbody (*The Times*) have long concentrated on sports politics, primarily those concerning the shadowy world of Olympic bids and drug policy. Steven Downes (*Sunday Times*) and Duncan Mackay (*Guardian*, *Observer*) have also distinguished themselves in this area, and justly won awards. Academics such as my University of Brighton colleagues John Sugden and Alan Tomlinson have done their fair share of prodding and prying into the affairs of FIFA, as, more famously, has Andrew Jennings.

It was Jennings's exposure of the Olympic movement's darker side that made him Public Enemy No. 1. Walking out on the BBC after the Corporation refused to screen an hour-long documentary about the connection between Scotland Yard and cocaine, he wrote a book about the subject and then embarked on a series of uncompromising investigations into the hypocrisy and corruption of the Olympic movement, whether solo or in cahoots with Vyv Simson and Clare Sambrook. The first of these, *The Lords of the Rings*, was retitled rather more bluntly in the States as *Dishonest Games*. Jennings's reports and documentaries have won awards from the Royal Television Society and at the New York TV Festival; he has even received an 'Integrity in Journalism' award at the United Nations. 'Of course,' he assured me, 'I am not a sports journalist – not since my stint on the *Burnley Evening Star* in the mid-1960s. But I have strong views on how sports journalists cover sports investigations – or rather don't.'[1]

Yet for all that the tide may be showing signs of turning, the vast majority of sports editors in my experience still deem such stories as sexy as a corduroy jacket, dictated to as they are by daily deadlines and budgetary constraints, not to mention fear of legal action by, and alienation from, powerful forces with whom they prefer to pursue a course of mutually productive co-existence. The aim, it follows, must be to persuade them otherwise, and the only way to accomplish that is to dig. 'Kids today,' believes Jennings:

> *are interested in interesting things. There's no more room for papers to proclaim that their reporter is the 'Voice of Football' because they're not. There's too much they don't know. What is interesting? Fans might think 'I thought that Blatter was a bad 'un' so you go and try and prove he is. I had 80,000 hits on my website within a few days of my* Panorama *documentary about FIFA [taking bribes]. More recently, I did a documentary on Jack Warner and their ticket racket for the* Mail *– I was able to post 70 pages of evidence on the web: you can't do that with newspapers. I didn't think, when I was first sniffing around the Fascist boots of [former IOC kingpin] Juan Antonio Samaranch, that I'd still be digging into Olympic corruption.*
>
> *I can remember when the populars did investigations – they saw it was good for business. [Paul] Kelso in the* Guardian *doesn't really get any stories because he has to produce material every day, under deadline pressures. TV has much bigger budgets than newspapers and magazines.*[2]

Did he ever feel he was banging his head against a wall?

> *No, never. I knew I didn't have the full story – you never do – so you let it run. Maybe you divert for a few months and then return. You don't see any initiative in the UK press to report [the FIFA bribes story]. They're smug and lazy, waiting for the wires to deliver. Blatter's people planted a story in the* Guardian *via David Owen, saying that someone on the FIFA committee, from Paraguay, had taken bribes but that 'it would seem' that Blatter himself was not involved. When do you ever see 'it would seem' in an official document? I can't believe this kind of spin-doctor, damage limitation, planted story would get in the front end of the* Guardian. *It would have been smelled by the real reporters and editors in the grown-up sections.*
>
> *The trouble is that FIFA don't put out press releases, and nor do the IOC for that matter – so you see nothing in the papers. The story was only seen in the* Mail, *my book, and on* Panorama. *I had 2.9 million viewers for that, which is more people than buy the* Mail *every day, and not all of them read the sports pages. Which is why the bright young journalists are going into TV. The editors of papers aren't watching TV – they're busy putting the papers to bed and maybe having the big game on.*
>
> *The IOC have been better since Samaranch left. But who's asking questions about them? In Mainland Europe yes, not England. The level of thievery in volleyball is huge. People think that if a sport isn't on Sky it isn't important. Editors have determined arbitrarily what the market is. During Colin Gibson's reign at the* Mail *he pushed investigations with panache but nobody followed them up. Where are the sports editors to push them? I've got documents, half of which haven't been published yet.*[3]

DEVELOPING A NEWS STORY

Speaking from a strictly professional perspective, one handy by-product of the media's obsession with sport is that a story emanating from one branch of the Fourth Estate can find extended life in others: even the mildest on-air utterance or comment in a ghosted column can generate headlines and fill space. The more controversial the better. Take the former England batsman-turned-pundit Geoff Boycott, who recently espoused the view that Duncan Fletcher, the England coach, had outlived his usefulness, even though the national team had risen from bottom to second in the world Test rankings and regained the Ashes after a near-two-decade famine.[4] The cause of Boycott's discontent was the side's performances in the one-day arena: the 2007 World Cup was but a few months away, and England's recent displays in the competition had been somewhat embarrassing for the nation that plays more limited-overs cricket than any of its rivals. Printed on what is widely referred to as a 'slow' day – Monday papers are primarily reflective of the weekend's events – it also helped that fixture lists for a Monday are thin, obliging editors to be creative rather than using live events as a crutch.

The *Daily Telegraph*'s rivals were grateful for Boycott's candour. *The Times* devoted an entire page to his broadside. Christopher Martin-Jenkins tapped out a firm and lengthy rebuttal ('With every respect to Geoffrey Boycott's profound knowledge of, and deep passion for, cricket, his opinion . . . is patent rubbish'). Geoffrey Dean elicited pro-Fletcher noises from Micky Stewart, one of Fletcher's predecessors, Keith Medlycott, the highly regarded former coach of Surrey, and two county stalwarts, Dougie Brown of Warwickshire and Paul Nixon of Leicestershire, both of whom had toured under Fletcher. Between those pieces loomed a large, cleverly-chosen photo of Fletcher, a dead ringer for a sad clown with his face caked in sun cream and his mouth seemingly moulded into a pout; below lurked a box containing a few lines on each of the four contenders the paper's correspondents believed were in line to succeed him. And yes, mentions of the *Daily Telegraph* as the primary source of all this juicy material were utterly conspicuous by their absence. The *Telegraph* would have expected nothing else. Giving other papers ideas is an inevitable consequence of being in a business where industrial espionage is seldom required, so easy is it to steal. Long before they had a presence on the Internet, local and regional papers were a constant source of stories for the nationals. Although a national reporter or sub-editor living in the area may simply filch their handiwork, the original reporter is normally the mainspring, whether seeking career advancement, a tip fee (you can earn up to £50 for supplying a diary story, and perhaps even more merely for supplying the necessary information and leads) or a freelance payment for a rewrite.

To evade detection, the last of these may necessitate using a 'cod' byline or pseudonym: by and large, it is frowned upon, and it can even be a breach of contract for full-time employees on one paper to write articles under their own name for another, even if it is not a direct rival. Even when there is no contract involved, having your name in two competing publications can lead to loss of work from one or even both. A realistic and reasonable editor will accept that being a freelance makes such conflicts of interest inevitable, but not all editors conform to such an ideal. I fell out with the *Daily Telegraph* during the winter of 1989 after I was informed they would only offer me work for the following cricket season if my byline stopped appearing in the *Sunday Correspondent*, for whom I was covering football and rugby. As a regular but non-contracted freelance, I felt this was a grossly unfair imposition, and politely declined. The *Sunday Correspondent* went out of business shortly afterwards. By then, fortunately, I had realised the paper was living on borrowed time and moved on, somewhat guiltily, to the *Independent on Sunday*, one of the prime reasons for whose imminent launch had been to see off the *Correspondent*. In mitigation, I can only point out the frequency with which the words 'freelance' and 'insecure' occupy the same sentence.

BALANCED REPORTING

The main imperative in any news story, given that it will invariably offer two or even more competing and contradictory viewpoints, is to represent those of all factions, facilitating balance. Only then is it possible to legitimately claim accuracy.

News stories are where your contacts book earns its corn. Phone numbers, snail-mail and electronic addresses, regularly updated, can be stored in your computer, or on your mobile phone, but a backup copy is a must. Over time, you will ascertain those contacts who can be depended on for an authoritative comment, whether revealing or insightful. When the former England defender Gareth Southgate was appointed manager of Middlesbrough shortly after retiring, the fact that I had not covered football in earnest for several seasons did nothing to dull a pleasing sense of inevitability. I was working on the *Sunday Times* during his formative years at Crystal Palace and remember vividly how quickly and enthusiastically colleagues latched on to him as one of the English game's more thoughtful and eloquent practitioners, seeking him out for quotes with remarkable frequency for one so inexperienced.

Key information may well be culled from indirect or unquotable sources – a quote from another publication; an off-the-record chat, even a rumour. As touched on already, rather than claim this as unimpeachable fact or alienating a valued contact, words and phrases such as 'apparently' and 'it is understood that' are reliable standbys, shorthand for 'I can't swear on my mother's life that this is the truth, but it is what I was told by a trustworthy source, and to the best of my knowledge it is correct'. In the case of one club or organisation disputing the word of another, obtain a statement from somebody in authority – a chief executive, a chairman, a director. This will often be forthcoming anyway, in the form of a press release, though this should be treated with circumspection and followed up (of which more anon). If lifting a purported fact from another newspaper or media outlet that you cannot verify, insert the rider 'reportedly' – as in 'Tiger Woods reportedly announced his retirement yesterday'. It may not turn out to be true, but the fact that it was reported by a reputable publication is generally regarded as sufficient justification.

Obviously, deadline pressures mean that eliciting all integral viewpoints is not always possible. At the very least, therefore, endeavour to contact the relevant parties. Insertion of the time-honoured get-out clause – 'Lou Seefa was unavailable for comment' – signifies that the requisite effort has been made. By the same token, subsequent events may well prove that one or other of the parties has been economical with the truth: on a daily newspaper especially, you are powerless to prevent this. Content yourself in the knowledge that you reported the story, as it stood the day your publication went to press, as fairly and accurately as you could.

HAIRGATE

Stories that stem directly from events on the field are the most obvious starting point. Perhaps the most resonant recent example of how a sporting contest can ignite an international furore emerged on Sunday 20 August, 2006, when, for the first time in 129 years of Test cricket, a match was forfeited. The long and the short of it was that Darrell Hair, an experienced if resolutely controversial umpire, decreed, midway through the fourth day, that Pakistan had been guilty of tampering with the ball, and duly fined the tourists five penalty runs – another first. Inzamam-ul-Haq, the captain, was so aggrieved, he protested by waiting 40 minutes before leading his team out after tea; by then, Hair and fellow umpire Billy Doctrove, while keeping strict counsel and refusing to make contact with the players, had adhered to the laws, lifted the bails and declared England the winners. With no allegation made against a specific player, nor so much as a frame of Sky Sports' live coverage available to the prosecution, the International Cricket Council announced that it was standing by its man and that, as captain, Inzamam would have to appear before a disciplinary hearing scheduled for the following Friday.

The timing was less than impeccable. Relations between West and East had recently been splintered anew by Israel's invasion of Lebanon. British Hindus, moreover, were trying to distance themselves from the arrest of eight alleged would-be terrorists in east London. For Shariyar Khan, chairman of the Pakistan Cricket Board and career politician (a common mix in Pakistan), a contest between England and Pakistan thus carried a heightened importance. Here, he argued – in hindsight, admittedly – was something to cherish, a proud symbol of sport's capacity to teach politicians and religion a thing or two about humanity. Unfortunately, for all that the Pakistani newspaper *The News* led its front page with a punny headline – 'Hold your nerves – Hair comes trouble' – the fact that the victims (albeit not necessarily the villains) were the sons of Karachi and Lahore could scarcely have been more certain to unpick scars further afield.

Mike Marqusee was quick to reinforce this.

> *In 1992, the Pakistani team were slandered as ball-tampering cheats by much of the British media; the coverage included derogatory comments not only about the players, but about their country, culture, and religion. This time English commentators and fans have for the most part backed Inzamam and criticised Hair. That's a sign of progress. However, on the same day the Pakistanis were being called cheats at The Oval, two men of Asian appearance were ejected from an airplane in response to the racist paranoia of fellow passengers. With a one-day international series yet to play, no one can be sure what the repercussions of this affair will be.*[5]

The same morning, a *Guardian* leader contended that the row could 'only fuel the alienation felt by some British Muslims at a time of great strain'.[6]

Cricket lovers can be relied upon to cheer whenever their fix knocks football off the back pages, not least on the opening weekend of a Premiership campaign. This, though, was an extremely guilty pleasure. That the story led front pages in Britain, Pakistan and India, and even prompted in-depth coverage in the United States and Israel, confirmed two time-honoured verities:

1. Cricket, more than any other high-profile sport, reflects the major issues of the day – because of its Commonwealth origins, no other major professional pastime so frequently pits black against white, new world against old, haves against have nots.
2. Cricket is still widely seen as a barometer of England's soul. Consider the following headline and standfirst-cum-subhead atop Chuck Culpepper's report in the *LA Times*:[7]

> *When a Match Becomes a Scandal, That's Not Cricket*
>
> Pakistan's historic forfeiture against England jostles the sport's genteel image

The space devoted to what the *New York Times* characterised as an 'imbroglio' was staggering. On the Monday morning came proof that, even though the BBC's *10 O'Clock News* was still covering the unfolding saga live from The Oval on Sunday night, newspapers still know how to adapt with alacrity to sudden developments. The *Guardian* sports section boasted no fewer than nine articles on the Test, only one of which referred to the state of the match; the story was also given top billing on the front page of the main paper and was the subject of a leading article. *The Times* carried six pieces on its sports pages, accompanied by sundry timelines and stats, plus a front-page story and leader. The *Daily Mail* had six stories on the sports pages but had long since resolved to use its front page to promote its serialisation of newsreader George Alagiah's new book and its exclusive warnings about the perils of multiculturalism ('My Fears For Apartheid UK' raged the headline), pushing the cricket to page five. This, mind, was no mean feat either, since the story squeezed into comparative insignificance below revealed that the French authorities were to reopen investigations into the death of Princess Diana.

Come day two, the *Sun* claimed to have discovered 'exclusively' that, on the Saturday of the match, the England coach Duncan Fletcher had urged the match referee, Mike Procter, once a teammate in Rhodesia, to keep a keen eye on the Pakistan bowlers. Even though this was by no means an exclusive observation, not to mention highly speculative – Fletcher and Procter had been spotted talking – it was repeated by competitors. The *Sun* also ran four stories across its back three pages, some pointed comments from former Test umpire Harold 'Dickie' Bird (who would have kept the match going) and a lead for its 'The *Sun* Says' editorial column, which called for 'cool heads' and decried Shariyar's linkage between sport and religion. Plus a neatly lifted, vigorously reheated interview with Imran Khan, originally published the previous day in *The Nation*, a Pakistan newspaper, wherein the one-time Test captain, accomplished playboy and would-be Prime Minister of Pakistan denounced Hair, who had upset Asian teams consistently over the years, as a 'mini-Hitler'.

While less histrionic, the *Daily Telegraph* sports section that Tuesday contained eight stories on the forfeiture; *The Times* had nine plus another leader and a raft of letters. It also boasted the most measured response. Referring to the absence of televisual evidence for umpire Hair's claim, Giles Smith summed up why, since there were no visual exhibits to support Hair, this story was such a boon for print journalism: 'Here, awkwardly for television, lay a story with, at its centre, the absence of television pictures.' In almost all these instances, as with any running story, the reader was reminded of the story so far.

Kept bubbling by journalists in Pakistan, England and Australia, the 'Hairgate' saga entered a fresh phase the following Friday, though this had nothing to do with journalistic endeavour and everything to do with how media-savvy organisations have learned to play the game. The ICC chief executive, the Australian Malcolm Speed, a qualified lawyer, authorised the release to the media of a series of emails wherein Hair said he would retire on condition he was paid $500,000, i.e. the remainder of his contract, give or take. Of course, it suited the by-now highly embarrassed ICC for the intransigent, troublesome Hair to be portrayed as a blackmailing blackguard. Back to the front pages he went. Many columnists and leader writers, and by no means exclusively those of an Australian persuasion, drew the inevitable conclusion: he had been hung out to dry. Speed was similarly adamant: his learned friends had informed him he had no option: he *had* to leak the emails, to cover the ICC's back.

Finally, on 28 September, nearly six weeks after 'Hairgate' began, the verdict came in. After a two-day ICC hearing at the scene of the crime, the umpire's decision, almost unprecedentedly, was reversed: following examination of the ball by expert witnesses, it was held that there was no evidence to justify Hair's imposition of a five-run penalty. However, having caused the match to be abandoned, costing the England and Wales Cricket Board £800,000 and the game much shame, Inzamam's decision to keep his players off the field saw him suspended from his country's next four one-day internationals for 'bringing the game into disrepute'. The governing body, moreover, announced that Hair would not stand in the Champions Trophy tournament to be held in India later that month. The stated reason – security concerns – was denied by the Board of Control for Cricket in India. In Pakistan, the result and reasoning of the hearing was accepted without much demur. Honour had, to a greater or lesser extent, been restored. Almost without exception, given a day to mull the matter over, English and Australian correspondents pitched into the ICC with venom.

The next chapter ensued in early November, at the annual ICC board meeting in Bombay. Revealingly, it was precipitated by a leak from an ICC official to an Indian TV station,[8] stating that a motion had been tabled by the Asian bloc – India, Pakistan, Sri Lanka and Bangladesh – calling for Hair's eviction from the umpires' panel, and carried by a 7–3 vote. To no great astonishment, the only dissenters cited were Australia, England and New Zealand. Naturally, the ICC initially refused to confirm the TV report, whereupon the following day brought a somewhat po-faced statement from its new president, Percy Sonn. 'The board has discussed this matter with great sincerity, lots of attention and come to the conclusion that they've lost confidence in Mr Hair.'[9] By leaving it to the Fourth Estate to break the news – on the understanding, of course, that the leaker's identity was not divulged – the ICC had bought itself some breathing-space. Once again, an inept governing body had found the media a handy accomplice.

Later that month, uncoincidentally, Hair was voted 'Umpire of the Season' by the predominately Caucasian readers of *The Wisden Cricketer*, reaping fully two-thirds of the nominations. That he had been passed over the previous week for a place on the list of umpires for British first-class matches in 2007 – he had been seeking to qualify by residence – must have struck him as more than a little ironic. Soon afterwards, he revealed he was consulting his learned friends. A few days later, he was awarded a place on the umpires' reserve list. This one could run and run.

THE PRESS CONFERENCE

Another reliable source of stories is the press conference – or 'the presser' as Australians, I believe, first referred to this hardy institution. Habitually called by email, it is vital to bear in mind that they exist at the behest of a governing body, venue, club, agent, broadcaster or sponsor. More often than not, there is a contractual obligation, to promote an event or team or individual: Wimbledon is about to start; Liverpool have just signed a new goalkeeper; the Royal & Ancient has changed a golfing rule; Don King has found a cross-dressing karate champion to take the ring with Mike Tyson.

Press conferences, though, are a double-edged sword. On the one hand, in these cosseted, image-obsessed times, the opportunity to ask questions of a player or coach for longer than a microsecond is not to be missed. Being en masse can also embolden the individual: it is psychologically easier, I would argue, to ask a probing question in a 50-to-one or even five-to-one environment. On the other hand, it also suits the promoter to get all those nasty questions answered in one fell swoop, with a lawyer, manager, agent or PR at hand for advice and direction. If a prickly question is asked, the aide can always step in. Better that than take the chance that a series of one-on-ones might lead to damaging deviation from the party line.

Moreover, in the interests of exclusivity, many journalists in such a situation suppress their most pressing questions for fear of giving the game away, of giving rivals a story that might otherwise not have registered, hoping instead to address those questions in private. That, though, has always seemed too risky to me, even in less fettered times. I have always been quite prepared to share the fruits of an answer so long as the question does not go unanswered. Mind you, there is never any guarantee that answers will be forthcoming, or at least not quotable ones. Huw Richards, who was at The Oval reporting for the *Herald Tribune*, assured me after the Inzamam hearing that Ranjan Madugalle, who chaired it, gave what could only be construed as a masterclass in stonewalling, responding to one question at extraordinary length without ever coming close to answering it. Politicians have a lot to answer for.

'Press Days', a looser extension of the press conference, are exceedingly helpful. Staged by clubs at the start of a season, photographers snap away while journalists talk to players, managers and coaches. You may only use one or two of the quotes or stories that day, but store the rest up. They can keep you going for a season or more.

There is, however, an element of bluff, even industrial secrecy, about all this. Readers familiar with televised press conferences may strongly suspect that you have derived your quotes from that source, but many will not be so attuned to the journalistic process. Either way, there is no need to write, '"That Rooney – he'll be the death of me," Sir Alex Ferguson told a press conference yesterday.' The 'told a press conference' may be accurate, but it is a needless detail: 'said' is sufficient. Besides, that's three precious words saved.

You can never tell where or how a story might take root, nor how it might flower and branch out. Take the rapid rise to prominence in English cricket of Kevin Pietersen, the South African-born batsman rebranded as 'KP' following his resoundingly successful entrée to the Test arena in the Ashes-winning summer of 2005. Reporters being each other's most avid and attentive readers, of course, I'd initially been alerted to Pietersen early in 2001 when Vic Marks wrote a column in the *Observer* about a South African spinner who had just joined Nottinghamshire. He suggested Pietersen might be the solution, once he had qualified by residence four years hence, to England's shortcomings in that department. Pietersen made headlines all right, but with the bat rather than the ball. So much so, *Wisden Cricket Monthly* asked me to interview him. We spoke on the phone. He sounded confident, almost brash, but then that was precisely how I had come to expect white South African sportsmen to sound. As someone interested in making the England team as good as possible – hell, 'we' hadn't won the Ashes since Live Aid 1 – and simultaneously aware that most sportspeople downplay their confidence for appearances' sake, it was an encouraging sound.

That said, I was not overly disposed to like him. Apartheid had given me permanent blinkers: to paraphrase the *Spitting Image* song of a decade or so earlier, I'd met exceedingly few white South Africans I could stomach. All the same, as he explained his predicament, I warmed to him. He had left his homeland, he insisted, because his future as a cricketer there had been undermined by the quota system: a minimum number of players in South African provincial teams had to be 'of colour', a controversial but – in my view anyway – wholly justifiable attempt to compensate for the soul-destroying iniquities of sport under Apartheid. All the same, this personalising of the issue, as opposed to debating it in the abstract, made me think anew, just as it should. Unless your heart is made of reinforced stone, anytime you meet or talk to someone, rather than simply write about them from the safe distance of an office, your perspective is bound to alter to some extent.

The result was an empathetic piece. Strangely, the fact that a cricketer can earn a great deal more in England than South Africa slipped my mind: in mitigation, with hindsight, Pietersen was spearheading the latest wave of economic migrants from Johannesburg and Cape Town, spurred by the post-Apartheid political changes that left white South Africans feeling vulnerable. Shortly after the interview was published, I received an email from John Young, a South African cricket writer and teacher. Nice piece: shame I'd let Pietersen 'off the hook', as he delicately put it. If he was *that* sure of himself, or *that* good, why didn't he stay and battle his way through? Young was right: here was a priceless instance of allowing a soft centre to compromise a reporter's disinterested perspective.

Five summers and approximately six different exotic hairstyles later, Pietersen's autobiography was published, with extracts serialised in the *Daily Mail*. One such reiterated the essence of our discussion: he'd been forced, he said, to flee South Africa by the quota system. This quote was duly treated as news. Indeed, when helping me compile a selection of the week's quotations for the Sports Journalists Association website, Steven Downes, the editor of said site, emailed that particular quote. The fact that it was about as newsy to me as the death of Queen Victoria was ultimately irrelevant. In 2001, Kevin Pietersen was a promising nobody and *Wisden Cricket Monthly* had around 20,000 readers; in 2006, Kevin Pietersen was public property and the *Daily Mail* had nearly 100 times as many page-turners.

More recently, a story of sorts sprang from a suspicion, a quick scan of my bookshelves and a seemingly telling statistic. In moving home, I made the possibly irrevocable decision to give away some of my old editions of *The Cricketer's Who's Who*, an invaluably chunky annual published for the past quarter-century containing salient details about every county cricketer who played a first-class game or 'List A' one-day match during the previous season – mugshot, birthday, career statistics, career highlights, name of parents and schools, nickname, favourite musician, pet peeve. I had kept them in the knowledge that, every blue moon or so, an idea might strike that might require me to check what X said about Y ten years earlier, or how his form had waxed and waned over the course of his career. In the spring of 2004 came vindication.

Over the preceding few years, as the number of British Asians in county ranks had swollen, so those of Anglo-Caribbean origin appeared to have withered. I mentioned this to John Stern, editor of the newborn *The Wisden Cricketer*, the product of a merger between *Wisden Cricket Monthly* and *The Cricketer*: it caught his imagination. Upon closer inspection, aided in good part by those aforementioned mugshots, I tallied the number of Anglo-Caribbean players in the 2004 *Who's Who* and compared the result with the figures for 10 and 20 years previously. The 1984 edition, published three years after Roland Butcher became the first Anglo-Caribbean player to represent England, featured no fewer than nine such players who had, or would, play for England. The 1994 edition featured 33, only four of whom had international careers ahead of them. The 2004 edition featured 18 eligibles, only two of whom have been called upon to defend St George. In 1990, the front cover of *Wisden Cricket Monthly* had featured four Anglo-Caribbean fast bowlers who were about to fly back to the islands in England blazers.

Suspicions borne out, I spoke to dozens of interested parties that spring and early summer: players and academics, chief executives and coaches, mothers, fathers and brothers. Why had this decline occurred? The replies ranged wide, from the decay of West Indies cricket and the counter-lure of football to waning immigration and, yes, racism. I left the final word with Mark Alleyne, the foremost success story: graduating from North London's Haringey Cricket College for wayward and unemployed black youths, he had become the most successful county captain of the twenty-first century to date, and now coaches Gloucestershire. 'I say to the guys, "I don't have to prove I'm black – I *am* black." I'm very proud of it. Now let's get on with what we came here to do.'

Thanks both to Stern's refreshing willingness to publish a proper investigation and to the concurrent tour by the West Indies, which made it topical, the resulting piece, headlined 'Whatever Happened to the Black Cricketer?', ran for 4,200-odd words – possibly the longest sporting article yet printed in a British consumer magazine. Two differing abridged versions appeared in the London *Evening Standard* and the *Observer* – one of 1,300 words, one of 2,500; one adapted and edited by me, the other by my trusted friend Neil Robinson. Albeit only because Jim Hall, my University College Falmouth course leader, stuck up a poster and I filled out the appropriate form, it won the UK section of the inaugural EU Journalism Award 'For Diversity, Against Discrimination'. A freelance must always be their own best publicist.

Another productive source of stories is memory. In the summer of 1987, during the brief life of the *London Daily News*, I went to The Oval to interview the former Surrey and England left-arm spinner, Tony Lock. As much as my own desire to meet one of the most indomitable characters of 1950s sport, what prompted it was a spectacularly flamboyant diving catch by Phil Edmonds, his 1987 successor and a *Daily News* columnist, in a recently completed match against Pakistan. Lock himself had been an agile, showmanlike fielder, and his views on Edmonds's catch, as well as contemporary spin bowling, were eminently worth having. I also wanted to ask him about the one major blight on his career: the accusations that he bowled illegally, throwing his faster ball without apparently realising it – or so he claimed – until he saw film of himself. I had seen footage of the Test in the Caribbean in 1954 when he was called for chucking, and more evidence besides; I could not believe he was not called more often. He reiterated the explanation then waved his hand down at the field of play, indicating the bowler, Phil DeFreitas. I cannot recall the exact words, but the message was unmistakeable: DeFreitas was 'a chucker'. It was too ludicrous for words, a knee-jerk of a dart from a man painfully if fairly maligned.

Although I was not due to file the ensuing article for a day or so, I informed the news editor, Ian Cole, of Lock's claim. That evening, he rang me at home, said he needed a back-page lead for the first edition, and asked if I could write up Lock's allegation. Reluctantly, I agreed. Amid talk of writs, the fallout after the paper hit the newsstands led to a swift retraction. I was remiss on two counts: a) in overestimating my audience and assuming they would be just as conversant as I was with the fact that Lock the pot was calling the kettle black; and b) in mentioning it at all. The desire for a byline should never drown out the voice of reason.

RESCHEDULING THE NEWS

As mentioned in the context of the Saturday-for-Monday post-match press briefing, the capacity to keep one's powder dry is a key tool in a reporter's repertoire. A post-match press conference, for instance, may throw up something that is too peripheral or tangential to the game under discussion, something that might serve as the basis of another story for the next day, or even later in the week. In such circumstances, reporters will consult each other and decide on a mutually convenient plan of action. 'We're a bit light on space today,' one might confide, 'but there's acres to fill tomorrow and I'll have a better chance of getting that story in then. What about you?' And so the word spreads. An agreement to hold the story will be made. A story a day keeps the guillotine at bay.

The proliferation of tours and World Cups has led to another side of what might be called news rescheduling. Take the Germany 2006 World Cup. With the England team scheduled to be gainfully occupied on the field every four days or so, and with hotels and flights adding up to tens of thousands of pounds, reporters accompanying the squad had to find non-match stories to write on the intervening days. Previews and postscripts, yes; columns and historically based features, yes, but also less formal press conferences wherein reporters would be informed of a time and place at which, say, Rio Ferdinand or the manager of England's next opponents would be available for questioning: the better to keep the press sweet, fulfil obligations to sponsors, give the impression of open governance, and keep the team in the public eye for the best reasons. Though this mini-conference might have taken place as little as an hour after a match, the ensuing articles – cleverly packaged and published to give the impression that Ferdinand had granted an interview specifically to the paper concerned – might not appear for another 48 hours, or more. Again, the reporters concerned would have agreed among themselves what day would best suit.

PRESS RELEASES

Welcome to the lazy journalist's route to a story. Plopping into editors' and reporters' inboxes at an unholy rate, these must be treated with a moderate amount of scepticism. Some, even most, are little more than advertorials: adverts or promotional material masquerading as vital information. They seek to ensure that everybody gets the same message and prints it without demur. They have certainly advanced in content and cunning: a release regarding a transfer might include a paragraph or two outlining the barest bones – how delighted Club A are to announce that Player X has left Club B and joined them on a whoppingly generous three-year contract – followed by a stream of quotes from the delighted manager, the delighted chief executive and the delighted player, perhaps even his delighted agent. All, in other words, that a poor editor and an indolent reporter might reasonably ask for. But while the deal may have been signposted some time previously, confirmation should trigger a number of responses. Is the new deal better than the one he was on? And if not, why not? Did his previous manager consider him expendable or too much trouble? Was he fleeing town because of a clandestine affair? Did he disagree with the manager's tactics? Was it all symptomatic, conversely, of his former club's economic plight? Is there an ex-teammate or boss who can shed some light? And so forth. Again, think like a fan.

To answer these questions, go down to the training ground or pick up the phone, armed to the teeth with your deep knowledge of the background. Contact the player/manager/ex-manager/chief executive/chairman, if needs be via a press officer. It won't always be possible – and local and regional reporters usually have the advantage here – but it is incumbent on you to at least attempt to squeeze more from this particular lemon and hence back up your own assertions. You won't be alone, but if the initial response is 'Bloody hell, you're the fifteenth reporter to ring me this morning' don't be meek about it, or too apologetic. In fact, it is advisable to pre-empt any such outbursts by beginning the conversation thus: 'Hi, Sir Alex, baby, I know I'm the fifteenth reporter to ring you this morning, but . . . ', though you might just as easily omit the 'baby' bit.

THE SELL

Intros, as we have said, sell a story every bit as well as a good headline, and this is especially true of news. In this context, given that there are no scorelines or match details to lean on, there is even more reason for the intro to encompass four of the key elements – who, what, where and when. The rest of the story examines and relates the how and the why while elaborating on the what, although the why may be briefly summed up in the second par. This is easier on a heavy, where opening paragraphs may be 70+ words long, less so on a tabloid, where 20 is the norm and opportunities to use two sentences – enabling a short, punchy start – are scarce, leading to the likes of:

> *Liverpool's brilliant 3–0 defeat of Anderlecht was marred by a race row. The Belgians' sub Nenad Jestrovic was sent off after racially abusing Kop ace Momo Sissoko.*[10]

This *Sun* intro is another example of how a match can produce a news story as well as a report. Note how the intro has been split in two – 'don't overburden the reader while he's on the loo' is the message. Note, too, that the score is mentioned – this is not a match report – and that there is no mention at all of *when* the incident occurred. This is not industry practice, but the *Sun* makes its own rules. And immediacy, especially in this dangerous age of instant partial knowledge, is all.

Now, let's examine how the *Guardian*, more or less the *Sun*'s spiritual and polar opposite, handled this story:

> *Anderlecht's striker Nenad Jestrovic faces severe sanction from Uefa after the referee Kim Milton Nielsen dismissed the Serbian substitute – who had been on the pitch for only five minutes – for allegedly racially abusing Mohamed Sissoko as Liverpool moved to within a point of the knockout phase last night.*[11]

Note that this *was* a match report: for space and design reasons, the news story and the run-of-play occupied the same slot. Some might argue that there is too much information loaded into one paragraph, let alone one sentence – both teams are mentioned, as is the racial incident and Liverpool's standing in Europe – but I doubt many *Guardian* readers would do so. The gory details are saved for the second par:

> *Jestrovic had clashed with the Mali international and, in front of the official, is claimed to have muttered 'Fuck off, black' at Sissoko in the 75th minute. The Liverpool player*

claimed not to have understood what was said but the outburst was heard by Nielsen, who had no hesitation in dismissing the substitute before confirming to the Uefa delegate present, Knud Stadsgaard, that the abuse had been racial. The officials refused to comment publicly last night, but Jestrovic offered his version of events. 'He [Sissoko] called me a son of a bitch,' he said. 'I told him to fuck off, and the referee sent me off. I do not understand why.'

Note the liberal use of the F-word. For the most part, newspapers and magazines still replace the full offending word with asterisks – f*** – in order to spare readers' sensitivities, though this is increasingly less the norm. In this case, the printing of the full word seems justified, amplifying as it does the magnitude of Jestrovic's crime.

The news element might also be a statement or threat, as in the following intro to another *Sun* yarn:

Jose Mourinho laid into his Chelsea Euro flops last night – and then threatened to lay out Arsène Wenger.[12]

Note the lack of quotes, replaced by an interpretation (not necessarily either just or valid) that distils the essence of the story. The intriguing thing here is that the Chelsea manager, who called his Arsenal counterpart a 'voyeur' and was angered by Wenger's allegation that he is 'stupid', actually said: 'Now it's time to stop. But if he doesn't, it's time to fight.' Which could be construed merely as a threat to involve lawyers. In addition, astonishingly, in a story that stretched on for a dozen paragraphs, there was not a single mention of Chelsea's opponents, still less the score.

Again, let's go to the opposite extreme. This is the *Guardian* intro:

Arsène Wenger and Jose Mourinho stepped up their increasingly poisonous war of words when the Arsenal manager called his opposite number 'stupid' and Mourinho revealed that Chelsea have compiled a 120-page file of comments that Wenger has made about them over the past 12 months and seemed to suggest that they would forward it to the football authorities if the Frenchman continued in the same fashion.[13]

Note three things. First, Wenger is 'the Arsenal manager' but Mourinho, apparently, needs no introduction. Second, there is no mention of the latter threatening any violence. In fact, Mourinho is quoted as saying: 'I accept [this] answer being strong but it's time to stop. But if he doesn't stop we are there for a fight.' Which is, I think you will agree, not quite the same as threatening to lay someone out. Third, there is no mention of *when* the incident occurred.

Now, the two-sentence intro:

After two fine last-ditch wins to square the series in India, England are not about to inflict major surgery on the team that served so well when the going got tough. But a brace of excellent practice matches in Hamilton, on a top-notch surface against competitive opposition, have revealed that there is work to be done before Wednesday's opening one-day match against the Black Caps in Christchurch.[14]

This works, even though it's a slim story. In actual fact, it is a preview masking as a news story. The 'have revealed' bit is a giveaway – nothing remotely earth-shattering has been revealed: the fact that the subs (most likely) or that fine correspondent Mike Selvey used such a classic tabloid dramatisation demonstrates that 1) even the *Guardian* jazzes things up these days, and 2) the broadsheets have learned much more from the tabloids than vice versa.

But back to hard news. Last year I handed out to my first-year students a selection of opening paragraphs published in the national press, all of which related to comments made by Roy Keane that were censored by Manchester United's own TV channel. I asked them to suggest ways in which they differ and duplicate each other, which would, I hoped, help identify which intro belonged to which newspaper – or, at least the correct market sector.

1 Manchester United last night sensationally pulled the plug on Roy Keane after their skipper slaughtered his team-mates following their 4–1 humiliation at Middlesbrough.
2 Roy Keane's no-nonsense verdict on Manchester United's humiliating defeat at Middlesbrough forced club officials and MUTV into an embarrassing climbdown last night.
3 Chaos reigned at Manchester United last night as the stricken club vetoed an official Roy Keane interview that laid bare the shocking inadequacies of Sir Alex Ferguson's team.
4 Manchester United's season went from bad to worse last night when Roy Keane castigated his team-mates in an interview so explosive that Sir Alex Ferguson and his chief executive David Gill immediately banned it from being shown on the club's in-house television station.
5 Roy Keane has slammed FIVE Manchester United team-mates on MUTV as not good enough.
6 Manchester United were last night forced to pull the plug on an explosive interview in which Roy Keane identified the culprits for the club's malaise. Keane's frank assessments of the team are nothing new, but this time, pointing the finger at underachieving team-mates, he was so outspoken that the club's in-house television station was forced into a desperate cover-up.

Note the following:

1 Almost without exception, the journalists use the phrase 'last night'. This was, in all probability, a bit of a fib; the incident, if memory serves, happened during the afternoon. In bygone times, 'yesterday' would have sufficed. But the desire for immediacy now means that anything that happens after about 4.00 p.m. is classified as 'last night'.
2 Intro 2 does not use the 'last night' until the end: this is because the only other place to insert it would have been after 'Middlesbrough', which would imply, wrongly, that the defeat against Boro had happened the previous night.
3 Intro 6 comprises two sentences.
4 Intros 2 and 5 refer to MUTV, the United TV channel, presuming a knowledge the others do not.
5 Only intro 4 stated that Sir Alex Ferguson himself had vetoed the Keane item, and only two of the other stories subsequently mentioned Ferguson's involvement. Indeed, one

report said that it was 'understood' that he played no part, which may be true. Equally, it could be shorthand for 'sorry, but I don't actually know for sure, but my mate who sweeps the reception area is pretty sure he had nothing to do with it'.

6 Intro 1, in using 'slaughtered', should never have reached a breakfast table.

For the record, the correct answers were:

Intro 1: *Daily Mirror*
Intro 2: *Daily Telegraph*
Intro 3: *Daily Mail*
Intro 4: *Guardian*
Intro 5: *Sun*
Intro 6: *The Times*

LIBEL

On the basis that even a single syllable of misinformation could be damaging, I do not propose to elaborate on this, other than to heartily recommend, to those seeking to practise journalism in England, the reporter's bible, *McNae's Essential Law for Journalists* (Oxford University Press). Other countries have their own tomes dedicated to legal correctness. The latest *McNae* was published in 2005, but beware: the ever-changing nature of the law of the land means it is updated every two years, so ensure you always consult the most contemporary volume.

Whatever else you do to ensure your copy does not fall foul of our learned if expensive friends, there is one inflexible rule: remember, after conducting an interview, to keep all your notes, even if it means doing so for decades – as was so vivdly demonstrated in court 56 of London's High Court in November 2006, when Matthew Fisher rather belatedly sued former bandmates Gary Brooker and fellow songwriter Keith Reid for backdated royalties accruing from Procul Harum's 1967 hit *A Whiter Shade of Pale*. Lawsuits have scant respect for the passing of time.

EXERCISE

Examine a sports news story across a broad variety of publications, paper and virtual. Divide a piece of paper in two with a vertical line and list either side of it which publications give the story a positive slant and which a negative. Take another piece of paper and list the facts that are most and least common. Note those that deploy the 'exclusive' tagline and ask yourself whether they are justified. Now write a 400-word version of the story that you believe reflects the facts – as you understand them – of the story. As always, specify the target publication at the top of your copy. A journalist who does not write with an audience in mind deludes himself that he knows how to communicate.

Chapter 7

'Hi,' said Muhammad, amiably

The interview

He's starting to feel resentment. The hour he has promised for the interview has overrun by 30 minutes and I'm still grasping his hand and pleading with him to stay. 'Just one more, pleeease,' I beg. 'It's something I've always wanted to ask you.'

'Go on,' he says.

'Why did your cheek always puff out when you kicked the ball?'

'Just a habit,' he smiles. 'They called me "Puffer" at West Ham. Do you remember Gordon Pirie, the famous middle-distance runner?'

'No,' I reply.

'Whaat!' he shrieks aghast, 'I thought you knew something about sport.'

'No,' I smile, 'I know nothing about sport, but keep talking, I'm learning.'

(Paul Kimmage meets Sir Geoff Hurst, Sunday Times, *28 May, 2006)*

While facts may be sacred in journalism, prising information out of people in the form of quotes has gradually become the holy grail. Think of the most banal statement you can imagine – 'Yes, I did quite enjoy that time I won a million on the lottery'; 'Yes, I was disappointed that we lost 16–0 after they'd had five players sent off in the first 10 minutes'; 'No, I don't like it when people jam red-hot pokers into my bottom on a Friday afternoon, or a Tuesday morning for that matter.' Chances are, it has been in print at some time over the past quotes-obsessed decade. That players now receive media training has done little to unmuddy the waters.

Time was, as recently as the 1970s and 1980s, when, in the newspaper world, quotes were kept to a bare minimum in broadsheets such as the *Daily Telegraph* and *The Times*. Expanding broadcasting schedules and the medium's emphasis on personality, however, kindled a greater clamour for celebrity, nationally and locally, and with that a greater emphasis on the utterings of both perpetrators and witnesses, no matter how banal or unrevealing. It would be wrong to suggest that the heavies print quotes as slavishly as do tabloids, but the difference is shrinking fast. Which seems curious, given that saying nothing, and at great length at that, has evolved into a fine if slimy art.

Obtaining quotes, whether for the purposes of a news story or a magazine interview, can be a fraught and tiresome business. Gone are the days when people were almost invariably honoured to be interviewed. In a world where the laws governing invasion of privacy are forever being challenged, where a five-minute chat on the phone can turn into a global front-page splash, where seemingly innocent statements can be juxtaposed with misleading headlines and photos, scepticism and fear are now the watchword. Journalism, let us not forget, is supposed to rank alongside estate agency, and just above genocidal dictator, as the public's idea of a trustworthy profession. On the other hand, I read a poll recently that ranked journalists fourth on the list of jobs women would like their partner to have. Make of that what you will.

As already mentioned, gaining access to sportspeople means circumventing various intimidating obstacles, principally the boards, associations, clubs, agents, managers and PR consultants who strive so assiduously to protect and control their employees and clients as well as their own self-image. If there is one thing managers, coaches and teammates can generally be relied upon to do, moreover, it is that they will protect their charges and colleagues. Nevertheless, even if they have something to hide, the majority of people still consent when approached for an interview. There are several reasons why:

1. They have something to sell, and a mention in your publication will bring attention to it and hence promote it. What they are selling may also be the version of themselves they want you, and the general public, to see.
2. They have a message, a theory or a discovery to communicate. Again, the intention is to impress or persuade.
3. They want to see their name in lights.
4. They are contractually obliged. If Tiger Woods signs a new deal with Nike, he will do interviews, for all branches of the media, that enable the brand to be promoted – a big photo in a magazine with him wearing a Nike cap, supplemented by the occasional plug for how fabulous the people at Nike are, will do the trick nicely. Similarly, if David Beckham's people tie up a deal for a newspaper column, Beckham is obliged to spend at least five minutes of his precious time actually talking to the journalist who will be responsible for putting 'his' column together.

It is advisable to give the general impression, when approaching a would-be interviewee, that he or she is doing you and your publication the biggest favour anyone has done for mankind since God decided Adam needed one fewer rib. Nevertheless, always keep in mind that they will only assent to your request if there is something, anything, in it for them. I apologise for sounding cynical, but to state otherwise would be to encourage naivety.

Only once have I ever secured an interview as a favour, and I can't say I ever want to repeat the experience. The subject was Jack Dunnett, then president of the Football League, and also my cousin's husband. It was at the dawn of live TV coverage of League football, just over 20 years ago, and I was reporting for *City Limits*, a left-wing alternative to *Time Out*, the London listings magazine, that had no more than 20,000 readers a week. I'm sure Jack, who never gave interviews to the press, thought it was a bit of a ramshackle operation. Come the day of the interview, he was surprised to see me accompanied by a photographer, and refused to let him in. The favour came, it seemed, with a condition. Which did not go down too well back at the office. In fact, the magazine got their own back. When the interview was printed, they used a photo of Kevin Keegan, then the most instantly recognisable English footballer to a general audience such as the one that read *City Limits*. Under it was a caption which read something along the lines of: 'We know it's a photo of KK but what else could we do when Jack Dunnett refuses to have his photo taken?'

MODES OF INTERVIEW

Ideally, every interview you conduct should be face-to-face. That way you can notice *how* your questions are answered: any signs of nervousness or uncertainty, anything that adds flesh to the words, the better to present a multi-dimensional portrait of your subject. Also, if you are with someone as they answer, the way they react may prompt further questions, questions you may not have planned to ask. Whatever the circumstances, ensure that, in addition to tape-recording the interview (and first, always, ask the subject if they mind), you take back-up notes. The ability to write in shorthand will make this infinitely easier.

Remember, however, that tape recordings are inadmissible as evidence in court, whereas a notebook containing a contemporaneous shorthand note, according to my esteemed colleague Jackie Errigo, who lectures in media law at the University of Brighton, 'is generally regarded as sound and credible by courts'. The Reynolds defence to defamation requires evidence of 'responsible journalism': this means producing notes pertaining to what was asked, what was answered and when, and so on. 'The reasoning,' explains Jackie, 'has been that shorthand notes cannot be easily manipulated after the event, whereas, rightly or wrongly, it has been felt that tapes could be edited and altered. I know this does not keep up with technology – it is possible nowadays to spot edits in tapes in a way that never existed before – but the "notes good, tapes bad" view prevails. No-one has ever, either, suggested that one could tear a page from a shorthand book and rewrite it to make it appear contemporaneous.'

In reality, especially in sports journalism, face-to-face interviews are not always practical. You may want a response to a news story from either an interested party or an expert, but you don't have the time to get to wherever they are. Especially if they live overseas. Or their schedules may make it impossible for them to find the time for something that may take an hour or more. After all, if someone has travelled a fair way to interview you, you are less likely to be able to get rid of them in five minutes. You certainly can't put the phone down on them.

Until the advent of the Internet, telephone interviews were the favoured alternative, the next-best option to being in the same room. These can be unsatisfactory on a number of levels. Recording a conversation is now possible, of course, but relying on machinery is not advisable. I have learned to distrust tape recorders; I take down the quotes as I'm talking and listening and cradling the phone, which can be a bit of a strain, and not necessarily the best means either of getting the most out of the conversation or even of getting all the words down – which is, of course, where shorthand comes in.

Relying on sound alone also deprives you of the aforementioned extra dimensions – the body language, the state of their kitchen, the books on their shelves, how they talk to their spouses and children and colleagues. On the other hand, you should always make the best of what you've got, so keep an ear out for tone and hesitation, whether their voices modulate and whether the speed at which they speak varies.

The Internet is both a step down and a step up. It is a step up because you can email a list of questions and have them answered with greater deliberation, thus ensuring accuracy – or at least improving your chances of doing so. This way, however, the interviewee controls the interview: there is no opportunity to react to a particular answer and take the conversation down another, possibly more revealing, road. You can fire back a list of supplementary questions, based on those initial responses, but in my experience it is unusual for a subject to devote any more of their time to you than they already have. However, this does not mean, nor should ever mean, that you don't try to clarify.

The email interview is also a step down because all you have to go on are the words. There is seldom a tone, at least no detectable tone, in interviews of this nature. And answers are more likely to be shorter and less instructive if you are not there to push the subject.

ARRANGEMENTS

All too often, as mentioned, arrangements for the interview must be made through a third party, especially when it comes to interviewing sportspeople at the top and even in the middle of their fields. For agents, managers and media relations departments, though, the agenda is often in direct conflict with yours: much as they value the oxygen of publicity, there is such a thing as noxious oxygen, and good reporting, one can seldom tire of reiterating, is all about exposing what others wish to suppress. Much as they are regarded with derision and suspicion, these people are merely trying, like you, to do their job. Respecting that, and treating them accordingly, improves your prospects of getting what you ultimately want, so stifle any sense of superiority and resist curtness. Without them, you may be sunk. With them, you have access.

Then again, for all that these PR operatives have succeeded in wrapping most leading sportspeople in cotton wool of a calibre normally seen exclusively at Harrods, distancing clients from their audience in a manner their counterparts in cinema mastered long ago, there are other means of obtaining interviews and reducing that gap, primarily:

1. Doorstepping – literally finding out the subject's address, home or office, and going there. A practice much favoured by tabloids.
2. Finding out a direct phone number, address or email address, either through a contact or fellow journalist. The Internet has made this easier, too. Sending a formal letter, whether by mail or as an attachment, is a good way of clarifying your purpose, not to mention avoiding the nerves that go with making a cold call. It may take rather longer, though, to receive a response.

Bear in mind that there are good times and bad times to make a phone call. Obviously, after 10.00 p.m. or before 7.00 a.m. is a tad risky, and if you know your subject has young children, say, and rarely spends much time with them, try and avoid the times when you are most likely to intrude. A good reporter will know these circumstances and act accordingly. Also, the first time you ring, if you haven't arranged a time with a third party, ask the subject, if now is not a convenient time to talk, when would be. It is probably best to assume that the first time, being a surprise, is never convenient. The more prominent the person, the more likely they are to need to shift the balance of power so they control matters. Telling you to ring back later is a trusty way of achieving this.

Also, be conscious of time differences. Don't ring an American at 7.00 a.m. GMT, or an Australian at 4.00 p.m. GMT. Unless, of course, the story is too big to wait, in which case protocol goes out the window.

THE INTERROGATION

Before conducting the interview, find out as much about your subject as possible. Depending on their fame or noteworthiness, the available sources are forever multiplying. We now have newspaper libraries and cuttings services, books and magazines, TV documentaries, DVDs and videos. Collections of quotes are invaluable, notably regularly updated nuggets such as Phil Shaw's *The Book of Football Quotations* (Mainstream) and David Hopps's *Great Cricket Quotes* (Robson Books). These allow you to quote back to the subject something he or she may have said, or that somebody has said about them. This will impress them and perhaps prompt a greater sense of trust.

There is no excuse for not being au fait with every important aspect of the subject's life or career. And the more informed you seem to be, the more the subject – whose ego will be duly massaged – will respect you and relax. Making your subject feel comfortable, and perhaps lowering their defences, is the key to a good interview. The more they relax and enjoy it – and most people get a kick out of talking about themselves – the more likely they are to give you more of their time. I once arranged to interview Ian Botham for the *Independent*, while he was in the middle of playing in a match for Worcestershire: initially he agreed to 45 minutes, but it was a rainy day, the tent was comfortable, we hit it off and talked, ultimately, for an hour and a half. That I was so palpably in thrall to his every utterance no doubt helped.

Before conducting the interview, deadline permitting – magazines and weekend papers are more likely to afford this sort of luxury – talk to the subject's colleagues and opponents, manager and/or coach, friends and family. This will almost certainly enable you to glean invaluable insights. Thus armed, make a list of questions and keep it close by during the interview. Perhaps ask a friend or relative what they, as a fan of either the interviewee or his/her sport, might like to know. It is definitely worthwhile trawling through the cuttings to discover any questions that have troubled or inspired your subject in the past, though care should be taken to check whether any published responses have been subject to formal denial or subsequent contradiction. Do not, moreover, list so many questions that you have no chance of asking them all. If you have a sensitive one to ask, one that you suspect may anger the interviewee, it is essential to prepare the way by preceding this with some less taxing ones. So start off light, easing the interviewee in, and save the awkward posers for once you've established a rapport. A compliment to kick things off never hurts. Without wishing to advocate deception, if they think you are a fan, they are more likely to open up.

Remember to keep the questions concise and straightforward, and your choice of wording simple. Sportspeople, by and large, are not intellectuals – why should they be? Not only does their scholastic education tend to be short, they rely on their bodies and powers of concentration; coaches and managers worth their salt know full well to communicate instructions as plainly as possible. Confuse them with long statements and unfamiliar words and a mist is likely to descend. It is wiser, therefore, not to take the risk. A student recently asked me, before interviewing the former Olympic swimmer Karen Pickering, to approve his list of questions. The first used the word 'prevailing', which I suggested he changed to 'current'. Better to play safe.

Unless you have no option ('Did you cheat/take that bung?'), don't ask questions that encourage or permit a 'yes' or 'no' answer. Open-ended questions such as 'why' or 'how' encourage an expansive answer. If they respond with a reply that jars with you, don't be afraid to argue. And if that awkward question attracts a blank response, or a refusal to answer, go back to it at a later stage, when you have built a better rapport.

Talking about the subject's childhood, or parents, is a good way to kick things off. It will almost certainly reveal something interesting. It will also put the subject at ease. So will a reminder of their finest hour, or a low moment they might have learned from. Given the healthy dose of mistrust and disrespect your presence may generate, given your choice of profession, demonstrate your knowledge of them and their discipline at every opportunity, stressing the fact that you can and do speak the same language.

Listen to the answers carefully: they may prompt a secondary question, or even take you down a path you weren't anticipating. In other words, don't be rigid. Be flexible, too, in how you structure the interview. That said, you must always control its course. Your subject, if they are experienced in these matters, may use their own form of flattery to distract you, or attempt to take you down a path of their own choosing. Be strong. Don't be deflected from your purpose. And remember that people very rarely just 'say' things: they assert, they speak haltingly, they hesitate, they deny, they agree, they laugh – and so on. Convey this to your reader.

Remember, too, to look the subject in the eye at all times – or, at least, when you're not looking down at your notebook, and only do that when you absolutely have to. And always take heed, as mentioned earlier, of body language. Your subject may be the Queen, or the PM, or a movie star, but they're still human beings.

Be wary, therefore, of wayward memories. They may state with seemingly cast-iron conviction that a certain incident took place during the 1999 FA Cup third round, or that they have won seven winner's medals, but never rely on this. Double- and even triple-check.

COPY APPROVAL

For journalists if not their grateful subjects, one of the more disturbing developments of recent years has been the demand for copy approval. Fuelled by the desire for image control (not *all* publicity is good publicity) and a fear of litigation, this might seem an eminently reasonable request, not least since it will almost certainly persuade the author to be more scrupulous, more circumspect and more sensitive towards their subject's feelings. On the other hand, imagine interviewing somebody who has been found guilty of match-fixing and being contractually obliged to write something with which he could not possibly take exception. Under such censorious circumstances, fair comment, not to mention truth, is all too often the casualty. Letting the facts – and the words – speak for themselves may be the aim of the game but the art of journalism lies in the way you structure an article, and what you choose to emphasise. Compromised journalism is insipid, anodyne journalism. And anodyne journalism is not the same as disinterested journalism. It is far closer to, if not indistinguishable from, a press release.

Bar ghosted columns, my earliest memory of giving a subject copy approval dates back to the early 1990s, when, while working for the *Independent*, I interviewed Micky Stewart, then manager/coach of the England cricket team. It was a thoroughly pleasant afternoon in his back garden, an enlightening discussion with a born optimist who evidently loved the game to distraction and was plainly doing his utmost to suppress the contempt in which he held the media. His team were gradually improving – albeit still no match for Australia, West Indies or Pakistan – but the fact remained that English cricket was still in the doldrums and he was perceived as being as big a part of the problem as he was of the solution.

He asked to see the article before it was published; his employers, the Test and County Cricket Board, demanded this as part of his contract of employment. To have refused – or taken the shrewder option, namely assenting without actually delivering – would have been to risk alienating a contact. This is always a delicate matter, and strikes at the very heart of a journalist's lot, and I will return to this shortly. The short answer to the dilemma is that there are no easy answers, much less definitive ones, other, that is, than to reiterate my conviction that compromise is a journalist's most grievous enemy.

While hurriedly writing up, I turned to Peter Ball and David Hopps's original *The Book of Cricket Quotations*, and found an illuminating soundbite from Stewart, culled from an interview conducted while he was captaining Surrey to the 1971 County Championship, an interview I had, by chance, seen in a newspaper library the previous year, in the *Daily Express* if memory serves. It made painful reading: 'I find I am playing every ball, bowling every ball and fielding every ball. The captaincy has cost me over six hundred runs a season. I am snapping at my wife and children and sleeping no more than four hours a night.' This struck me as a priceless insight and I duly reproduced the first and third sentences in my intro. As much as an author can ever assess a piece of writing without a barrowload of self-justification and a pair of ultra-thick blinkers, the article, I felt, was fair, accurate and yes, a wee bit compromised. Not that Stewart had done anything to justify anyone's wrath; the accent he placed on fitness and preparation had assuredly benefited his charges and improved results, although this inflexibly Roundheaded approach would soon lead to the axing of my favourite Cavalier, David Gower, which would in turn prompt an MCC petition and even irate questions in the House of Commons. At length, I faxed the final edit to the TCCB and then filed it to the *Independent*: I awaited a phonecall, or a return fax, from Lord's or Stewart, but none ensued. Taking this to indicate that all was well, I relaxed. The sports editor and sub-editor were happy, which is all a freelance needs to know.

Then, barely five minutes before the page was due to go to press, Stewart rang me. He wasn't terribly happy about the intro, claiming it was a misquote, and asked me to make the necessary alterations. I flapped. Futile as it was, I argued briefly, citing my sources and asking him why he hadn't pointed this out when Ball and Hopps's book had been published more than five years earlier, not to mention why he hadn't called me an hour or two earlier. What mystified me was why he should want to disown a 20-year-old comment, not least since it was neither controversial nor self-damning. I can now see that he might not have wanted to be projected as a whinger – or worse, an obsessive – but hindsight is a cruel teacher. Facts, though, had to be faced: if I declined to delete the quotation, legal proceedings might result; nor was there any sense in a cricket reporter alienating the national coach without good cause, especially a freelance whose antics might prejudice the newspaper in question's prospects of future interviews. While I am willing to give him the benefit of the doubt, I rather suspect he knew exactly what he was doing in leaving it so late to make the correction. Changing an intro with the page about to go 'live', can be as nightmarish as it gets for a journalist. As previously stressed, it is the means by which we invite the reader in, the paragraph we agonise over most. I was professional enough to substitute another paragraph but I learned a valuable lesson.

Although there is rarely a contractual obligation to supply copy approval, it may be imposed as a precondition of the interview. Even if the request is informal it is probably best to accede. However, unless you are obliged to submit the entire article, there is no need to do anything more than send the quotes you intend to use. Unless they are to be presented on the page in a Q&A format (questions followed by answers with no editorial content), where you use them in the narrative, and the context in which you couch them, should always be your prerogative.

As to your response if asked to pay a fee for the interviewee's time and trouble (highly unusual, admittedly, in my experience of sportsfolk), resist any urge to fulminate about how it should, if anything, be the other way around. Instead, state clearly and simply that it is not the policy of your publication to do so. Such tactics are far more common in television, of course, where editorial budgets – if not always audiences – are bigger and take such costs into account.

If the subject insists they will not co-operate without a fee, and claims that your publication will attract extra sales through their presence within its pages (possible, depending on whether the article is billed on the front page), the wisest way to counter this is a) stress that your publication is offering them both a soapbox and the oxygen of free publicity, then b) emphasise that if the readers were even to suspect that money had changed hands (and word has a strange habit of getting out), they would feel short-changed and be less likely to trust what ultimately appeared on the page. You might even dare suggest that you, the journalist, would be far more likely to feel entitled to adopt a critical or disparaging tone if money entered the equation. If pressed, by all means ask the sports editor whether £100, say, can be spared: the answer may well be yes. Depending on the status of the interviewee – and the more exalted that is, the likelier they are to have an inflated opinion of their own worth – the chances are that such an offer, while made in (fairly) good faith, will be considered derisory: either way, the decision will be made for you.

WRITING IT UP

As with a match report, transport the reader into your shoes: put them where you were for that half-hour or even five minutes, in the room, inside the subject's memories. Make them smell the coffee; show them the furniture; introduce them to the family. Anything germane is game provided it broadens the reader's view or challenges their preconceptions and cannot lead to charges of voyeurism or of unreasonably invading privacy.

Early on, too, establish a reason for interviewing your subject at this particular time. That they may simply have been available is never sufficient, and should never, on any account, be revealed to your readers: the mechanics are never as interesting as journalists might like to imagine. However obvious it may seem – and the standfirst may even do the job for you – do not neglect this pertinent detail. Your subject may be about to make his debut for the national team, make his record-breaking 123rd appearance or face his former club, or be the subject of an upcoming TV documentary. On the day the England rugby union side were scheduled to face Argentina at Twickenham in 2006 trailing a run of six successive defeats, the *Daily Telegraph* printed an interview with David Duckham, a member of the last England XV to suffer such a fallow sequence 34 years earlier.[1] The next day, after England had lost again, the *Sunday Telegraph* published another interview with one of Duckham's colleagues, Andy Ripley.[2] It was a calculated risk: even if England had prevailed against Argentina, the lesser stature of their opponents would have done little to ward off the doom and gloom shrouding the world champions' form in the build-up to defending their crown in France the following September. In addition, the fact that Ripley had participated in the match that ended his team's run of seven consecutive losses – an unexpected triumph in South Africa – lent the interview a positive hue.

Paul Kimmage hit the spot with customary accuracy with the opening paragraphs of his Geoff Hurst interview:

> *It is a Thursday evening in London and Sir Geoff Hurst is sitting in a lounge of the Grosvenor House hotel telling me things about the future of David Beckham, Wayne Rooney, Michael Owen and Steven Gerrard that are raising the hairs on my head.*
>
> *Apology: During this time it completely slipped my mind to ask his views on Rooney's metatarsal. Another apology: There was no discussion either of Owen's fitness, Theo Walcott's age, or who should partner Peter Crouch up front in Germany.*
>
> *And if you've tuned in expecting an expert opinion on England's chances next month, well, apologies again but I couldn't stop asking him about the bang.*
>
> *The bang is what awaits Beckham, Rooney, Owen and Gerrard and the other England stars a few years from now when they return to the real world after a life on planet football. The bang is the 40 years of Hurst since 1966.*
>
> *The bang is sitting on a deserted train travelling from Ipswich to Chelmsford after covering a Sunday game for Anglia TV in 1982. He has put the 60 quid for the shift in his pocket and could murder a cup of tea but the buffet car is closed and there is no roving trolley.*
>
> *A guard arrives and checks his ticket: 'No buffet car this evening?' Hurst inquires. 'Not on Sunday,' the guard replies. But five minutes later the guard offers him a cup of tea that he has poured from his flask. 'I'm sorry Geoff,' he sighs, 'but this is the train that hit your brother on the day he killed himself. I was working that day.'*[3]

It may be noticed that nowhere within those 270 words is there any direct explanation for the timing of the interview. The isolated reference to '1966' is the lone clue, albeit a sizeable one, given that mere mention of that year triggers an instant response among the vast majority of Englishmen: 1966 means England's footballers winning the World Cup and Hurst scoring what remains the only hat-trick in the tournament's decider. Overseas readers and others were catered for by the so-called 'furniture' (see Glossary). Across the top half of the first page of the double-spread towered a vast photograph of Hurst celebrating – as the caption confirms – England's third goal in the 1966 World Cup final. Underneath that was the headline '40 years of Hurst', with the final word set in much larger type and spanning virtually the width of the page: a deft play on a line from the 1996 hit 'Three Lions On The Shirt' ('Thirty years of hurt . . . '). Beneath that lay the section title – 'The Big Interview: Sir Geoff Hurst', denoting it as a regular item – and below that a standfirst: 'You would think life as a bona fide national hero was a breeze. But life after 1966 has had many twists and turns, finds Paul Kimmage'. The accompanying mugshot of the author testifies to his standing within the paper, as the sports section's interviewer-in-chief. There were also four more photos on the spread – two contemporary, two old – and a pullout quote: 'I've had a good life and played at a good time and I don't want to knock the present game, but the circus around it is madness'. The package was completed by a factbox encompassing Hurst's birthdate, career details and current occupation. The inclusion and even the wording of the last fact – 'Hurst is now director of football for McDonald's, which is an official partner of the World Cup. In April it celebrated the creation of 10,000 new grassroots coaches in the UK' – was almost certainly a precondition for the interview.

When it comes to committing your subject's responses to print, much the trickiest technical aspect is deciding what to include and what to omit. As is the case with a match report, only immeasurably more so, the overmatter should be considerable. Some statements will fall naturally by the wayside – the repetitive, the bland, the blindingly obvious or the unrevealing deviation – but you still ought to have more than you require. I know I always spend more time cutting and editing than I do writing. One extremely useful aid in this regard is the (strictly unofficial) licence you have to compress quotes. Few of us speak in structured, complete sentences. If your subject uses the wrong word to describe something, or expresses themselves inaccurately or inelegantly, or gets a fact wrong, you are there to spare their blushes. Unless you have a justifiable reason for doing so – and *schadenfreude*, finding pleasure in the pain of others, is seldom if ever that – why make someone you don't know look foolish? By the same token, feel free to cut a quote down, so long as you don't distort the meaning.

For instance, let's say the subject says: 'No, I wouldn't consider retiring until I've fulfilled all my goals, and there are still a few left, so I'll carry on until I've run out of ambitions.' This can easily be cut back to 'I still have goals, and I intend to fulfil them.' There is a fine balance to maintain, between representing the subject accurately, capturing their voice and tone, and turning their utterings into something intelligible, that doesn't waste space. Your own ability to express yourself economically will help you sculpt the words of others.

Also, there is no harm in reported speech – 'I used to be scared of hard balls as a boy but my dad helped me get over it by bowling rocks at me,' is a quote you would probably want to keep intact, but if space was tight, and this was not the most revealing quote, you can simply report it: 'Davis's father overcame his fear of hard balls by bowling rocks at him.'

This would save you ten words, which in the context of an 800-word space, may be extremely helpful.

There are times, moreover, when a change may necessitate the use of square brackets as a means of clarification. You are effectively saying to the reader 'He didn't actually use this word, but this is what he meant'. Take a sentence such as: 'That so-and-so raked his studs down my thigh.' If the so-and-so in question has yet to be identified within the piece, insert [David Ronson] after 'That so-and-so'. Similarly, if a piece of germane information is missing, use square brackets to make amends, as in 'Fortunately for that so-and-so, by the time we played Tranmere again, Ronson had moved on [to Preston North End].' Or 'I never liked [former world heavyweight champion] Mike Tyson until he bit [Evander Holyfield's] ear' rather than 'I never liked that Tyson bloke until he bit that other bloke's ear'. It is not absolutely necessary to use square brackets – you can insert the fact as if the interviewee had mentioned it – but it is more transparent and honest. As mentioned previously, if they swear, it is normally best to spare sensitivities with asterisks, as in 'That so-and-so really is a bit of a s***.' Ascertain the house rules in this regard.

The quotes you choose should be designed to reveal as much about the subject as possible, but don't use them to convey information you can easily, and more succinctly, supply in your own words – such as age, number of children, career achievements and so on. What we want are explanations and insights, glimpses of the mind and life behind those muscles and hand-eye coordination, and, above all, what motivates them. If interviewing an up-and-coming player about their aspirations can be interesting, what fascinates is to find out how the leading sportspeople do what they do, and maintain the edge they need to stay ahead.

In all but the most exceptional cases, resist any temptation to bring out your subject's accent or dialect. 'By the toime I'm finishin' my career, oi'll be the best jockey ever to ride a 'orse' may be an accurate quotation but it serves only to make the subject seem quaint at best. It may also be construed as mockery. Over the course of 1,200 words, moreover, it can be wearing for the reader, not to say confusing.

Take care, too, to distinguish between full and partial quotes, and to punctuate them accordingly. If it is a complete sentence, the punctuation comes inside the quote; if not, it comes outside. Partial quotes may be as thin as a single adjective – 'brilliant', 'terrible', 'corrupt' – but be careful not to emulate those naughty film-poster people. You know the score: '"Unmissable" – *The Mirror*' may be extracted from a review wherein the sentence in question actually read: 'This is about as unmissable as an earthquake.'

One other point, a pedantic one: if you are running a quote over a number of paragraphs, you must use opening speechmarks at the start of every paragraph but only at the very end of the quote do you insert the closing quotemarks. Also, when it comes to attribution, try to mention this as early as possible in the quote. As in this entirely fictitious example: 'I hate football,' said the Fareham Rovers centre-forward, Lionel Lycro. 'It's the worst time I've ever had. In fact, I'm not sure why I wanted to become a footballer. I guess it was because I didn't want to be a fisherman like my mum.' Introducing a quote as 'He said' followed by a comma or a colon, is acceptable but I almost invariably introduce the first sentence or clause of the quote then insert the attribution: it is good to let the audience know as early as possible who is talking. Try not to reproduce five pars of quotes and only drop in a 'he said' at the very end.

Make sure, too, to use the most pertinent attributes. Some subjects have a number of hats, but when introducing them only use those that are strictly relevant. Mr Lycro, in this instance, is a Fareham centre-forward before he is a man, a boyfriend, an owner of a string of chip shops or even a fervent admirer of Avril Lavigne. Unless they also happen to be a Lord, an Earl or a Russian spy, save such details for later, provided you feel they shed some worthwhile light on the subject's character. In the unlikely event of your being confronted with the choice of whether or not to reveal that subject is homosexual, there is no reason to betray their right to privacy unless they are a hypocrite about their sexuality (cf. innumerable politicians) or you are specifically investigating homosexuality in sport.

Now comes the dilemma. To quote or not to quote, that is the question. In one respect the answer is straightforward: if you are told that what the interviewee is about to say – or has just said – is 'off the record', respect it. The only exception would be if Saddam Hussein, say, had informed you that he had commanded his army to round up and execute a group of militant Sunnis, in contrast to the official line, namely that they had killed each other.

Fortunately, sport seldom poses such ethical or moral predicaments, though it is always wise to be on your guard. If you are determined, nevertheless, to include the fact or comment concerned without attributing it, you can remove the quotes and use one of those reliable escape clauses: 'It is understood that . . . ' or 'Sources say . . . '. While it may well be the interviewee's intention to get the fact or comment into the public domain, you are unlikely to know this: by airing it, therefore, you are risking incurring their displeasure and/or wrath. One way round it, of course, is to send a copy of the final article to the subject concerned, but this is not always practicable or desirable. As with the risk of alienating a potential future contact by refusing copy approval, it is one you alone can weigh up. Are you likely to need to talk to this person again? Will they henceforth refuse to speak to your publication? There is one former England cricket captain about whose behaviour I once wrote some decidedly uncomplimentary things in a book, all of which he richly deserved. I have been asked to interview him on a number of occasions since but have always declined. All I can urge is that you judge each situation on its merits.

The difficulty in deciding what quotes to use does not, however, stop there. A number of conflicting issues are worth considering. First, what are the most interesting and/or revealing answers to your questions? Keep the audience uppermost in mind: are you addressing teenage males or middle-aged women, fans or experts, families or expats? Second, what, if seen in print, might upset the interviewee or their employer? Third, whose interests are paramount: the publication's, the reader's or your own (and the last two should be one and the same)? Given that your relationship with the editor is intrinsic to your prospects of continued employment by that publication, it is obviously in your best interests to prioritise whoever commissions you. On the other hand, in terms both of compassion and pragmatism, boxing clever is the only way.

Back, then, to agendas. There are times when sportspeople, coaches and managers especially, make statements in press conferences or interviews designed solely to needle or unsettle a future opponent. In some instances they might even say something they know full well to be untrue, such as 'That Davy Lee-Jones is a brilliant full-back – can't think why they aren't picking him' or 'You know Davis has been having trouble with his missus.' Broadly speaking, it is just about possible to term this a 'plant': using a third party, i.e. the media, to spread word of something that may or may not be factually correct. While there are far more sinister examples one could cite, the intention behind such a knowing falsehood may merely be to undermine an opponent or persuade those entrusted with selecting an opposing team to choose someone whose abilities do not warrant it, neither of which are criminal actions. Indeed, they contribute to the mind games that make sport so fascinating. Detecting such an agenda is inordinately difficult; even suspecting it usually takes a sizeable leap of the imagination. Seek a second opinion, of course, but checking out whether Davis's marriage really is in trouble is seldom practical.

For the most part, there are very few occasions in which there is any firm agenda, bar self-justification that is. The key here is to let the words do the talking. If your subject says something offensive, controversial or contradictory and you sincerely believe it is in the public interest that they be seen in their true colours – even if you profoundly disagree with their stance – forget those protective impulses and quote away. Tempting as it may be, there is no need to intercede, to editorialise: as the adage goes, 'let them hang themselves'.

Sometimes, mind, honesty, however well-intentioned, carries a price. Derek Pringle, then a Test cricketer, now cricket correspondent for the *Daily Telegraph*, reminded me recently of a minor kerfuffle in the early 1990s, when something I quoted him as saying – about ball-tampering, if memory serves – resulted in his club, Essex, slapping him with a far from immodest fine. While he may have meant every word, not a single one of which was anything less than reasonable or astute, neither of us guessed the extent of feather-ruffling they would incite. An innocent miscalculation, in other words. In recalling the episode, he also reminded me that I had offered to take him out for dinner at a restaurant of his choice. He had, in fact, proposed the most expensive London eaterie he could think of, but since the paper refused to compensate me for any such outgoing, I took him to a gig instead. He still insists I owe him some grub.

All of which brings us back to the possibility of alienating a contact or, more importantly, causing offence. While you may be absolutely sure of their intent, the words you deploy and the way you construct a report or article – or the way a headline is written – may still leave them open to more than one level of interpretation, even when you have no gripe whatsoever with your interviewee and the tone is positive, even complimentary. Keeping your subjects sweet while reporting what they do and say fairly and honestly is a balancing act capable of reducing even the ablest juggler to a cack-handed wreck, affecting as it may do your long-term prospects as well as the short. My then wife and I once spent six anxious months fearing the worst after one interviewee instituted legal proceedings. I crossed paths with the man concerned (conveniently, perhaps, my memory has erased his name) while researching a lengthy article about Jewish football that was ultimately published in a magazine aimed at London Jews. A chunk of it was devoted to what I saw as his harsh and unappreciative treatment by Tottenham Hotspur, the club he had supported all his life, during the course of which I gently suggested that his devotion was such that he had married his daughter off to the club's centre-half, Paul Miller, though the pair had subsequently broken up. The tone of that section was uniformly favourable, wholly sympathetic, and not swayed in the slightest by the knowledge that I had ventured into a world for which I would have no further professional need. Unfortunately, as is often the case, one sentence cancelled out everything around it: he interpreted the line about his daughter as a slight, and instructed his lawyer to seek damages. I consulted the National Union of Journalists: there was nothing they could do to help. Perhaps recognising that proving his case might have been a good deal more complex than frightening a tiny publication with meagre resources, the plaintiff settled out of court, albeit not before the magazine had stumped up £2,000 in costs; I contributed half. I have no regrets about what I wrote, nor any doubts that there is an even greater need for care when writing for niche publications aimed at a specific community.

In these ludicrously litigious times, perhaps the one rule to bear in mind above all others is to ensure that you record every word of an interview. The following tragic story will, I trust, illustrate why.

In 1992, British athletics, to all intents and purposes, was run by Andy Norman, a former policeman with fingers in quite a few pies. As promotions officer for UK Athletics, he organised all the televised meetings that brought a modicum of wealth to a sport still gingerly dipping its toes into the confusing waters of professionalism. He also acted as an agent for leading track and field exponents. As was made clear by an edition of the BBC sports magazine programme, *On the Line* – whose brief, in essence, was to dig behind the scores and expose wrongdoing – he was no kindly benefactor and assuredly not a man to be trusted. That he had left his wife to set up home with Fatima Whitbread, the Olympic javelin medallist, did nothing to dissuade those inclined to believe he was abusing his position by bribery, manipulation and naked profiteering. The allegations mounted, among the most persistent that he had been guilty of perverting samples in a doping inquiry involving one of his clients. Yet his status as a one-time law enforcer meant that, so far as officialdom was concerned, he should always be taken at his word. Which is why, as the sportswriter Steven Downes puts it, 'he thought he was invulnerable'.[4]

One summery week in 1993, shortly before the World Athletics Championships in Stuttgart, Chris Nawrat, an unreconstructed maverick and fearlessly creative sports editor of the *Sunday Times*, had a dilemma. Being the organised type, and averse to the easy option of allowing a match report to spearhead his section, he liked to plan his lead story well in advance. Aided by his trusty calendar of major sporting events, this meant he could commission stories linked to a specific event and would therefore not have to panic come the weekend. On this occasion, however, he was bereft of inspiration. Cue a bright idea: why not ask Cliff Temple, the paper's longstanding athletics correspondent, to investigate Norman's many conflicts of interest. Temple duly obliged. Because he also coached athletes and arranged meetings without taking a penny for himself, athletes and journalists alike respected Temple: not only did he know what he was writing about; he was trustworthy. Unfortunately, he was also trying, with scant success, to overcome the pain of a broken marriage.

Temple's article was emblazoned across two pages of the *Sunday Times*. Norman, whose past and present clients, Sally Gunnell and Linford Christie, would beat the world in Stuttgart, was livid. 'Even though *On the Line* had already done most of the story, his bullying nature wouldn't let it go,' attests Downes, who had been subjected to Norman's intimidatory tactics himself and subsequently wrote (with Duncan Mackay) a splendidly searching book about the Norman era, *Running Scared*. Norman rang Temple and threatened him. If he didn't cease his investigations, he warned, he would put it around that Temple was sexually harassing the female athletes he coached, among them the Olympic medallist Shireen Bailey. Unbeknown to Norman, Temple recorded the entire half-hour conversation, then lodged a copy of the tape with Nawrat for safekeeping.

The following February, Temple threw himself under a train. The coroner expressed the view that Norman's threats would have been enough to push him over the edge. Downes, who also worked for the *Sunday Times* and had heard the Norman–Temple tape, reported the sorry saga for *Channel 4 News* and *News at 10*; Norman was sacked from his job the next day. The Channel 4 News investigation won Downes a Royal Television Society award.

The last Downes heard, Norman had been thrown out of the family home by Fatima Whitbread and was living in a council flat. Even so, Downes understands, his influence within UK Athletics remains quiet but deadly.

EXERCISE

Interview a member of your family, write it up and show the final version to them. Note how they react. What do they take exception to? What makes them turn a redder shade of pale? Ask them to imagine the article being published: what alterations would they have liked you to make? What do they demand there and then? What do they consent to after further debate? Now reverse the process: monitor how many alterations you request and how great a struggle you put up.

Chapter 8

Beneath the mud

The feature

'How does a feature differ from an essay?' Thus runs one of the first questions that springs to the lips of the average first-year journalism student. The answer is unvarying; make that the short, Paul Daniels of an answer: 'Not a lot.'

The Jack Daniels answer usually meanders like this. An essay is an examination of a specified subject. An academic essay is that and more – longer, more structured, more research-based, and littered with references to the theories of purported experts in the field. Both of these *must* be read, if only by a humble teacher. There is, however, no obligation to read a feature. Luring the reader in is therefore even more important than it is in a news story or match report, both of which are more about information than interpretation.

The most conspicuous way an academic essay differs from a journalistic feature lies in its use of references. In the former you use endnotes or footnotes; in a journalistic feature, there should always be a full acknowledgement of the source of the quote or information within the body copy. Such as: 'As Louis De Ville, the former French international No.10 and rugby union correspondent of *L'Equipe*, pointed out in his seminal 1935 study of left-footed fly-halves, *Vive les gauches*, dropping goals is more difficult for right-footers.' This is not to say that every journalist always owns up to his sources – few do – merely that it is less than honest not to do so. Saving precious words is a legitimate excuse; passing off the thoughts of others as your own, as opposed to crediting where credit is due, is not.

In academic essays, what is valued most is the opinion. In journalism, the idea is also to impress upon the reader the *qualifications* of the author, his or her *right* to opine as they do, hence the full and proper accreditation *within* the copy. A player or coach commenting on a tactic, a manager commenting on a player, a manager assessing another manager, a chief executive explaining the difficulties of running a club: these are authorities worthy of note, even a modicum of trust.

All that notwithstanding, when teaching I always ask students both to credit their sources within copy ('said Thomas Petty, the ex-New Zealand Davis Cup player . . . ') and to disclose the full source at the end of a feature, by way of endnotes. Such is the temptation to plagiarise, and so manifold the available sources, the penalty may be expulsion: safety-first is preferable to lasting regret.

A newspaper or magazine feature also differs in a number of subtle ways:

1 Depending, of course, on the subject matter, there is seldom any excuse to thrust yourself into the narrative of an essay; this is doubly true of a feature. So no 'in my opinions', however humble: your byline makes that clear enough.
2 You have more scope with the intro – use a drop intro to set it all up, or a pertinent quote, whether insightful or revealingly ludicrous.
3 There is more room for humour and colour: inform first and foremost but don't forget, provided the subject matter warrants it, to entertain.

The salient point is that anything that does not constitute news (either a breaking story, the latest chapter in a developing story or a match report) or opinion is, by definition, a feature. Broadly speaking, there are three types, all based around interviews:

1 an interview focusing on the subject's career and views, buttressed by the reflections of colleagues;
2 the news feature, adding depth and background to a breaking or running news story;
3 the issue-based feature, taking a current topic and examining it from a particular perspective with the help of one or more experts. In such cases, the article is not *about* the expert but what he/she has to say, leaving you to deliver the final verdict – or perhaps perch, Solomon-like, on the fence. This may also be a celebratory-cum-analytical look back at an event 50 years on with the help of one of the participants, or an extended preview of an event. In effect, previews occupy the middle ground between news and features and can therefore be written in either style.

As sports pages continue to multiply, the additional space is more likely to be given over to features than to extended coverage of the previous day's matches, which involve travel and hence are more expensive than those that can be constructed from the basis of a telephone call or two from home or office. No less helpfully to editors panicking about how to fill their pages, features, which place a greater emphasis on accompanying photos, graphics and visuals, also occupy more space. They are, furthermore, less time-sensitive than news stories, which means, in turn, that they can be planned further in advance without excessive fear of being overtaken by events. Subsequent developments on the day of publication, or after the piece has been dispatched for editing, may necessitate a tweak or even a rewrite, but that is easily resolved without major surgical alterations. The shelf-life of a feature, moreover, is less restricted. That said, they are almost invariably tied in to some development, event or anniversary, so they still have a sell-by date. And don't imagine that a longer shelf-life necessarily means longer deadlines: one of the key skills a journalist must master is the fine art, when a news story demands more in-depth coverage, of turning round a lengthy feature at extremely short notice.

You may be granted anything from 400 words to 1,500 – or, in the case of magazines and supplements, up to 10,000. In newspaper terms, the average length is around 800–1,200; magazines tend to have more pages and hence more room.

Features have more scope for individualism, idiosyncrasy and specialised vocabulary. They also allow for longer paragraphs and more complex or adventurous modes of expression. None of this excuses poor grammar or structure. When it comes to the intro, virtually anything goes, depending on how much space is at your disposal. The livelier and more intriguing the better. Seduce, seduce, seduce.

> *Today Lisbon is almost, but not quite, back in Portuguese hands at the end of the most hysterically exuberant occupation any city has ever known.*[1]

Hugh McIlvanney's uncharacteristically short intro to his piece for the *Observer* on Celtic's historic 1967 European Cup triumph, written for publication four days after the fact, covers neither the who, the when nor even the what. But that does not make it any the less enticing. There is exaggeration, sure, but of a harmless, warmly humorous nature. It reflects the sense of occasion without revealing much else. He was depending on his readers' knowledge: anyone reading a British Sunday paper that May weekend would have known what he was on about. Having set the scene, he was free to ruminate over the prolonged Glaswegian celebrations.

George Plimpton, a Harvard graduate who founded and edited the widely respected *Paris Review*, is best known as the first sports journalist to mix it on the field with the professionals and turn the experience into memorable reportage: *Sports Illustrated* sent him on what one observer characterised as the 'imaginary nightmare' assignment – pitching to leading Major Leaguers such as Frank Robinson and Ernie Banks; he also trained with the Detroit Lions gridiron team and turned the experience into a book, *Paper Lion*, which was subsequently filmed as a movie. In 1973 and 1974 he followed Hank Aaron around North America's ballparks as the latter pursued Babe Ruth's career record of 714 home runs. Published in *Sports Illustrated*, the ensuing feature, 'Final Twist of the Drama', certainly benefited from the space the magazine was able to give Plimpton: there was certainly no British publication in 1974, sporting or otherwise, prepared to hand a journalist 7,500 words in which to write about a piece of athletic history; indeed, there is only one now – *OSM*. Here, in all but one respect, was an object lesson in capturing a moment in time: Plimpton allows us to glimpse the record-breaking 715th home run from the perspective of Aaron himself, the pitcher who conceded it, the TV commentators, even the fan who caught the ball in the stands in Atlanta. Yet nowhere, remarkably, is there any mention of the agonies Aaron endured en route, chiefly the poison-pen letters and death threats from racists who believed a black man had no right to usurp the mighty Babe. Nonetheless, the following intro demonstrates that simplicity and clarity are the hallmarks of the most eloquent writers:

> *It was a simple act by an unassuming man which touched an enormous circle of people, indeed an entire country. It provided an instant that people would remember for decades – exactly what they were doing at the time of the home run that beat Babe Ruth's great record, whether they were watching it on a television set, or heard it over the car radio while driving along a turnpike at night, or even whether a neighbour leaned over a fence and told them about it the next morning.*[2]

A feature should not – at least not obviously – be a thinkpiece. For the most part, you should be the conduit, the cipher, for the views of acknowledged experts. That said, your views will be clear, in the way you structure the argument, in the quotes you choose, in the way you use them, and in the conclusion you draw. Again, unless your presence in the story is essential (which is about as often as a golfer sinks a hole-in-one), none of this should tempt you to use the dreaded first-person singular.

As with news stories, only more so, research is the be-all and end-all. You must know your subject inside out. And, as ever, you should have far more material than you can use – the key to successful feature writing is your ability to meld all this knowledge into a succinct whole. I reiterate: time permitting, the cutting and editing ought to take longer than the writing.

Such is the prevailing wind in journalism, the more voices you employ to discuss an issue, the more weight it will have. Be careful, though, to make sure each has something different to say. Don't delude yourself into thinking that six people saying 'Drugs are a bad thing' is sufficient. At the very least, each quotee should make their point in a way that differs from the others. Quoting a player claiming that his club's directors are corrupt carries weight; for a member of that selfsame board to do so patently carries more: both are worth using. If one interviewee offers a witheringly sarcastic response and another proffers much the same answer in graver tones, both may be worth using. Vantage point, tone and strength of conviction are all integral factors.

As for structure, while there are no hard and fast rules, I tend to think in terms of classical musical composition: the intro – which may span more than one paragraph – is the overture; then comes the exposition and development, the meat of the story; and finally the recapitulation and perhaps a coda – i.e. a summary and conclusion.

In terms of language, features – primarily because space is less of a constraint – offer more freedom, but don't get carried away. By all means use rhetorical questions, be provocative, quote songs or movies, crack jokes – whatever helps you to get your point across more effectively. But never forget that, as with all journalistic writing, *any* form of writing, clarity is all. Making readers titter is all very well, but what you really want is for them to either nod their head approvingly or fling the paper across the room in disgust. Neutral reactions are the avowed enemy.

And remember to be on your guard for legals. The world of features may seem somewhat gentle by comparison with the harder-nosed sphere of news, but this may lull you into a false sense of security. In a news feature you must guard against contempt of court, and the risk of libel is always there.

EXERCISE

Check out the most prominent sporting news story in your local newspaper. It may relate to a proposed ground development, a takeover bid by a millionaire publican, a row over financial discrepancies, even a tiff between manager and centre-forward. Seek out the reporter who wrote it and tell them you are doing a college assignment. Ask if you can visit them at the newspaper's offices, where you can trace the source of the story and check for any other relevant cuttings. Find out the phone numbers of the main protagonists and interview them, obtaining their differing points of view. Then write it all up as a feature for a specified national or even overseas publication, giving it an overriding theme rather than trying to present it as news.

Chapter 9

Me, the jury

Expressing yourself (responsibly)

Being a columnist is not hugely unlike playing God. In exchange for hitting your deadline and filling the space, you get to play judge, jury and bailiff. You may decide that wit, whimsy and cynicism are your strongest suits and sharpest weapons. You may prefer confrontation and provocation: standing on your soapbox, eschewing all pretence at balance and aiming directly for the jugular, a stance expertly adopted by the likes of John Sadler of the *Sun* and Peter Wilson of the *Daily Mirror* (and perhaps best described – in reluctant homage to contemporary British journalism's Rottweiler-in-chief – as Littlejohnesque). You might even opt, unfashionably, for the wise-as-a-monastery-owl approach, as practised so admirably by Hugh McIlvanney, Paul Hayward and Richard Williams, for whom substance is all. The danger lies in the fact that you are also being granted – as the Beastie Boys so eloquently put it – 'licence to ill'.

At the height of cricket's ball-tampering fiasco in August 2006 came a pertinent reminder of how easy it is for writers, and columnists in particular, to give offence. Writing about Darrell Hair, Simon Barnes went directly for the jugular:

> *So now we know it. Officials are more important than players, laws are more important than people, one man's vanity is more important than the pleasure of millions, principles are more important than common sense, intransigence is better than decency, vindictiveness is better than compromise, trouble is much more fun than peaceful co-operation and a fat man's dignity is more important than mutual understanding between nations.*[1]

To me this was plainly ironic, but one journalist I know was unable to see this and considered the word 'fat' to have crossed the line between fair comment and gratuitous abuse. 'I thought hard about whether to use that word,' explains Barnes, 'but the point I was making was "consider how it looks to Pakistanis".'[2] The 'umpire-is-God brigade' may have taken offence, he reasoned, but he did not have the slightest problem with that.

Being a TV pundit involves even more risk. Shortly before this, Dean Jones, the former Australian Test batsman-turned-freelance commentator, had been fired from one of his gigs for observing, after a Sri Lankan batsman had been dismissed, that it was another wicket 'for the terrorist' – the bowler in question being Hashim Amla, a heavily bearded South African Muslim of Indian descent. 'Peter Roebuck, writing in the *Hindu*, tacitly supported Dean Jones,' complained my friend, the Indian sportswriter Gulu Ezekiel. 'He claimed worse things happen in the world, like wars and ethnic cleansing.'[3] Duly prodded, I found an article in the *Hindustan Times* by Mukul Kesavan, who also condemned Roebuck, as well as Harsha Bhogle of the *Indian Express*. That this was a journalist writing about other journalists undermines the column's validity not one whit. Besides, here was an example, not so much of dog eat dog, as dog takes dog back to school and gives him a lesson in manners, the perils of casual thought, and linguistics:

> *Jones's critics, [Roebuck] wrote, '. . . hiss and snarl like cornered canines'. They were slavering dogs because they were using up stores of indignation that might be better used denouncing ethnic cleansing, grinding poverty and the bombing of the innocent. Right. Just as Roebuck might be better employed digging up landmines in Lebanon or tending lepers in India instead of turning out copy for the sports pages.*
>
> *But we get the point. Border and Roebuck are saying that Jones is basically a good guy and that given the scale of evil in the world, his offence was trivial. He was stupid, idiotic, foolish and insensitive in saying what he did but not bigoted.*
>
> *Roebuck nudged us towards the reasonable conclusion. 'Does anyone suppose, though, that his comment betrayed the secrets of his soul? Has any rancour been detected therein?' If you're not used to Roebuck's rhetoric, this meant Jones didn't mean it, couldn't have meant it because everyone knew that Jones wasn't a bigot or a racist.*
>
> *This was the same defence that [Australian cricketer] Darren Lehmann mounted when he called the Sri Lankans 'black cunts'. It was also the defence used by Jewish friends of Mel Gibson (another man who has spent some growing-up time in Australia) after his anti-Semitic outburst. Mel, they said, 'wasn't like that'. Wasn't like what? What does a man's track record have to be before a bigoted comment made by him qualifies as bigotry?*[4]

Incidentally, just in case you might be labouring under the illusion that the media have suddenly discovered principles, it is worth mentioning Ron Atkinson, the football manager-turned-pundit who in April 2004 casually let slip a racist insult aimed at Chelsea's Marcel Desailly. As with Jones, the fact that the comment was made when Atkinson thought he was off-air was no defence whatsoever. He duly lost his job, not to mention a weekly ghosted column fee from the *Guardian*. By autumn 2006, he was back on British screens in a documentary series, *Big Ron Manager*.

Wit is perhaps the columnist's most prized asset, enabling serious points to be made in an entertaining manner. Making proclamations as if from on high is to risk alienating the reader; cloaking them in humour sweetens the pill.

Take Martin Johnson, who made his name as cricket correspondent at the *Independent* before moving to the *Daily Telegraph* as a columnist and feature writer. As the only journalist who can fairly be said to have inspired an Ashes victory – the England team's only shortcomings in Australia in 1986, he quipped, lay in batting, bowling and fielding – he occupies a hallowed throne. Aided by the fact that his tenure at the *Independent* coincided with a period in which the national team were both soap opera and standing joke, he merged run-of-play with running gags drawing on everyday objects and speech, every crack constructed and set up as if he were Leicestershire's answer to Woody Allen. If anything, if only because the plot was so unvarying, the details of the match were comparatively incidental. Twenty years later he was still mining the same chucklesome seam: 'If you were to look into the reasons for England's opening-day performance,' he reported from Brisbane during the opening Test of the 2006–07 Ashes series, 'then the finger could properly be pointed at a build-up itinerary equivalent to practising for Everest by mounting the stairs in a pair of carpet slippers. In modern parlance they were "undercooked", although "half-baked" is another way of putting it.'[5]

If humour seldom travels well, the common language that is sport makes this one arena in which it does. Writing in *Sports Illustrated* shortly after the Ryder Cup lineups were announced in late August of 2006, Rick Reilly, 10-time winner of the US National Sportswriter of the Year award, went even further than Thomas Boswell in attempting to bury the legend of the myopic American. 'Have you seen the US team?' he harrumphed in characteristically sly fashion. 'It has all the intimidation power of the Liechtenstein navy . . . We've lost seven of the last ten. Can't they at least give us Canada?' The tone of the article – reprinted, unusually, in *The Times* – was plain from the opening sentences:

> *I like warm beer and hairy-legged women. I drive a car so small, you could park it in the glove compartment of a Hummer. I enjoy funny brown cigarettes in the loo. That's because, as of now, I am officially a European. I have turned European because I'm bloody sick of the US getting the haggis stomped out of it . . .*

By the end, however, one detected a certain relenting: 'Wait. Excuse me? You say all true Euros love Monty [Colin Montgomerie]? (Pause.) OK, forget the whole thing.' Reilly was even bold enough to take the greatest risk a sports journalist can make by way of previewing an event, dubbing the US team 'the single worst squad we've ever taken to a Ryder Cup', a carefree verdict thoroughly vindicated by the outcome.[6]

Reilly's sardonic barfly approach, resolutely conversational, typifies one of those traditionally quintessential differences between English and American sportswriters. Mind you, this disparity is less marked than it once was, due in good part to the influence of *Sports Illustrated* and *Rolling Stone*, two lively American publications that treated their subjects with a blend of fond appreciation and irreverent detachment and found their way to British newsagents during the 'swinging sixties', encouraging aspiring and even wizened journalists to spread their wings.

Portrayed by Nicholas Dawidoff as 'one of the great populist newsmen of his time', Jimmy Breslin, a fast-talking, cigar-crunching, no-holds-barring New Yorker, personified this bond as well as any, even when scolding his readers. 'The Mets lose an awful lot? Listen, mister. Think a little bit. When was the last time you won anything out of life?' He dedicated his 1962 account of the Mets' abysmal maiden season – *Can't Anybody Here Play This Game?* – to 'the 922,530 brave souls who paid their way into the Polo Grounds in 1962. Never has so much misery loved so much company.'[7]

As with what makes good writing, tone and wit are subjective perceptions, immeasurable and unproveable. Explaining why one joke makes you titter and another containing 99 per cent of the same words induces severe groaning can be a bit like trying to elucidate why hot chocolate tastes better than cold chicken. Timing – which in journalistic terms means punctuation, sentence construction and overall structure – is all. Still, without wishing to seem in any way patriotic (my sides are considerably more at risk when exposed to *Frasier* or *Seinfeld* than *Little Britain* or *My Family*), the contemporary sportswriter who makes me giggle most consistently is Giles Smith of *The Times*, although Harry Pearson in the *Guardian* is not all that far behind. And not simply because the former commissioned me to interview my favourite songwriters during his stint as music editor at the *Independent*, even if it does help that he wrote *Lost in Music,* the funniest book I have ever read about the pitfalls of youthful obsession.

Standing back from the events of a curious week in the Premiership, Smith alighted on the 'extraordinary' revelation by Chelsea FC (his lifelong sporting passion) that their French full-back, William Gallas, had threatened to score an own-goal if he was not released from his contract.

> *[This] raises numerous urgent questions, not least among them, what kind of own goal did Gallas have in mind? A scruffy and seemingly accidental deflection from a corner at some random moment in the second half, or a first-minute, 45-yard solo run through a baffled defence, rounding the goalkeeper and tucking the ball into the bottom corner, before wheeling away in the direction of the Chelsea bench with his finger over his lips? I'm thinking the latter. Gallas was, after all, and by all accounts, very keen to move. Either way, this affair clearly has repercussions way beyond the small cast of people involved. Straight away it casts into suspicion, both in the future and retrospectively, all own goals.*

The distinction 'between basic incompetence and a desire for regular first-team football under Arsène Wenger', he concluded, 'is suddenly a very hard one to draw'.[8] This might not tickle your fancy, but the natural comic writer's sense of rhythm is plain, as evinced by a lengthy description of a clearly preposterous own-goal followed by a crisp, seemingly throwaway, four-word sentence: 'I'm thinking the latter.' What made me laugh aloud, and what I most appreciate as a fellow manipulator of words, was the selection and deployment of language: the wryly delicious subversion of cliché ('and by all accounts'); the skilful use of both understatement ('very keen to move') and exaggeration ('numerous urgent questions'); best of all, the mock grandiosity ('both in the future and retrospectively') that so expertly captures and punctures the tendency of administrators, press officers, journalists and fans in general, and TV and radio commentators in particular, to invest sport with a little too much gravitas.

'If nothing springs to mind for a column, I take the dog for a walk or ride a horse.' Thus does Simon Barnes describe his modus operandi. 'I've also been lucky in my editors, for different reasons. When Keith Blackmore was head of sport at *The Times* he would come up with a half-baked idea on the train and throw it at me. Tim Hallisey, the current sports editor, is also a terrific supporter. He's less intrusive, which makes me more self-motivated.'[9]

Nor is it necessary to be a full-time sportswriter to be a sports columnist worthy of repeated inspection. The Radio 5 Live and former Radio 1 DJ Nicky Campbell delivers terrific copy for the *Guardian*, astute as well as funny, albeit with an overt Scottish slant; neither Simon Hattenstone, Marina Hyde (both *Guardian*) nor Giles Smith has ever, to my knowledge, reported a football match, yet all write about footballers convincingly and winningly. Nor is it absolutely necessary to agree with a column to derive something from it or even enjoy it. And as with any form of opinion-based reporting, if not more so, the reward in writing one lies with persuading just one leopard to exchange spots for stripes – or at least make them reconsider their choice of fur pattern.

There is, of course, a line between giggling and sniggering. Nobody in my experience has trampled over it quite so entertainingly, or carelessly, as Frances Edmonds, another outsider. Her day job was with the EC in Brussels: as with the mirth-makers mentioned in the previous paragraph, the fact that she had no need to deal with her subjects on a regular basis was assuredly no hindrance. Aided by the fact that her husband happened to be the maverick England spinner Phil Edmonds, she wrote two uproarious cricket tour diaries in 1986 and 1987, their insightful if sometimes cruel and scurrilous contents exemplified by this verdict on Ian Botham's intellect: 'I'd always been brought up to mistrust anyone whose bodyweight in kilos was numerically superior to his HQ.'[10]

The best columns are those that compel the reader to reconsider. Take Matthew Syed's attempt to tackle the conundrum that is Michael Schumacher. The German driver's cv may contain a list of achievements unparalleled in his sport, but few non-Germans or non-Ferrari employees ever warmed to him: this was not so much the result of any anti-Germanic, post-World War hangover, nor even because his dominance robbed petrolheads for so long of any vestige of drama or even worthwhile competition, but because of his willingness to embrace questionable tactics that might easily have cost rivals their lives. The day after his final grand prix, wherein a fourth-placed finish confirmed him in the decidedly unusual position of runner-up in the Formula One standings, Syed examined Schumacher through the filter of the once-successful sportsman.

> *As anyone who endured his hawkish glance and witnessed his visceral competitiveness will testify, Schumacher was driven by a passion for Formula One that bordered on obsession. And a jolly good thing, too. Where would sport be without vehemence? Where would be the grandeur and the heroism, the joy and the heartbreak? Give me a warrior who craves victory for its own sake any day rather than the tepid careerism exemplified by so many British sportsmen, whose puny ambition is slaked by a few measly drops from the National Lottery Sports Fund. Of course, the critics have been lining up to condemn the German for the moral dubiousness of some of his actions without seeming to realise that most human beings are prone to behaving dubiously when they care deeply about something. John McEnroe berated line judges, Rocky Marciano punched below the belt, but we forgave them both. Even as we debate the probity of Schumacher's actions, can we not acknowledge that they sprang from the hallowed place that cradled sport's soul?*[11]

As easy and tempting as it is to bluff under such circumstances – after all, a column spanning 800–1,200 words, the customary range, is not a vast amount of space to fill – good research is the passport to a persuasive column, especially when it comprises, as many now do, one longish rant and a clutch of shorter ones. Know your mind, yes, but know your subject better.

THE GHOSTLY ART

Conceived as a drawcard for readers before television entered the scene, the idea of contracting a well-known figure to sound off in a newspaper column via an interpreter – i.e. a reporter or ghostwriter – had its roots firmly in sport. Even though those roots have spread extensively, full-backs, fast bowlers and front-rowers remain much the most in-demand. This is largely attributable, of course, to the widespread perception of athletic types as being under-educated, semi-literate and either unable or unwilling to put pen to paper or forefinger to keyboard, though there are countless exceptions to this not entirely unjustified slight. For practical reasons, however, ghosting makes sense. To rely on a professional sportsman to churn out an interesting weekly column on time and to length is largely unrealistic.

Originally the sole province of local papers and national tabloids but now a staple for all, the thoughts of leading personalities command and consume more space than ever before. The process goes something like this: sports editor decides a weekly column from ace badminton player Josafeen Barrington, who has just become the first Briton to win the Jakarta Open, will liven his pages up. He offers her a retainer then assigns a reporter with – at the very least – a broad knowledge of badminton to talk to her once a week on a topical subject. This may constitute a chat in a pub or a changing-room but is far more likely to be conducted over the phone. There is a great deal of skill involved, notably an ability to turn rambling, disjointed sentences and hesitant, perhaps contradictory statements into a coherent whole, not to mention stretching a five-minute chinwag into 800 printable words. I once did just that for the *Independent*, grabbing that precise length of time with Alan Hansen while checking in for a flight to New York. Nobody complained. I can also recall a rather more hands-on experience, interviewing the former West Indies fast bowler Michael Holding for his *Today* column while perambulating round The Oval during a Test match in 1988. What with all the arms stretching out to shake his hand and the constant friendly interruptions ('Hi Mikey, can you sign this for my aunt in Jamaica? She knows your cousin.' 'Hey, Mikey, why you not bowl anymore?' 'Mikey, you lookin' *good* my man!'), it took us the best part of an hour to get back to the press box. As an insight into life as an idol, it was a nugget I shall always treasure.

Before beginning the interview, ensure you have a theme in mind: how *does* it feel to be nursing a broken leg while your teammates are jetting off to Madrid for the Champions League final? Ensure you have at least one back-up idea in case you are unable to squeeze out enough meaty material. Direct operations; dictate the course of the conversation, just as you would any interview. Ask the questions the subject's fans would most like answered: you will soon be made aware of what is off limits. In many respects your priority is to be a sub-editor – the subject may not say exactly what they mean, or use the appropriate words – and also a fact-checker. You should no more take an assertion ('Telford United have lost

17 of their last 18 games') at face value than duplicate a sentence such as 'If memory serves, Cardiff have never won the FA Cup'. Check everything. As the ancient adage goes, if in doubt, leave it out.

Creativity is permitted, even encouraged: your ghostee will never complain if you make him or her sound cleverer or more historically aware than they actually are. Only once can I recall a ghostee – Holding – ring me back to make a correction after reading the results of a conversation, though he was unusual, in those pre-agent days, in bothering to read it in the first place. The chief imperative, however, is to capture the subject's voice. Make it believable. Don't use too many sub-clauses or polysyllabled words. Try to make the tone of the piece reflect the character. A po-faced column under Gavin Henson's name insisting the Welsh Rugby Union are lovely fellows to a man would be no more credible than a jokey one purporting to be the handiwork of Alex Ferguson.

The best example of how *not* to do it? Try this: 'Sehwag in repose at the crease has resembled a cat ready to pounce on anything which comes his way. A cobra in coil, a panther on haunches, a falcon in that strategic patrolling of the sky.'[12] Thus ran part of a recent column in an Indian newspaper credited to Graham Gooch, the former England cricket captain. Granted, many England cricket captains have been Oxbridge graduates, but it is a widely known fact that Gooch, an earthy character, is not one of them. As his admirers well know and accept, metaphors of that ilk do not come readily to him, much less a word such as 'repose' or a phrase such as 'strategic patrolling of the sky'. Elegantly as it may read, to present his musings in such a way is as daft and as insulting to the reader as it is unprofessional.

Ghosting can be a profitable skill. For one thing, developing and nurturing a relationship with a local or national hero can lead to advance warning of a news development or a quotable source when a story breaks. He or she might also, one day, be seeking a ghost for their autobiography. The following cautionary tale concerns Ian Ridley, then a highly respected *Observer* football writer and now *Mail on Sunday* correspondent as well as one of the co-creators of Sky TV's *Dream Team*, with whom I share a literary agent, the estimable John Pawsey. Approached to write an autobiography on behalf of the Arsenal and England footballer, Tony Adams, the choice was straightforward: a decent advance payment and a small share of any royalties, or a smaller advance and a more substantial slice of the profits. Ridley opted for the former, anticipating that the sales would not be enormous and that the royalties would therefore be meagre; predicting book sales, after all, is about as precise a science as counting raindrops. As it transpired, the book, *Addicted*, sold by the truckload, in part because of Arsenal's success on the field under Adams's captaincy but primarily because of Adams's refreshingly naked honesty about his alcoholism. I can only say that, under the circumstances, I would have been no less cautious.

Ghosting is a much-maligned facet of journalism. Consistently turning out interesting and readable columns of this nature should not be sniffed at, not least because to do so requires a mastery of so many journalistic skills. Which is why, whenever I do not see a 'Steve Gerrard was talking to Nora Tatty' or 'Interview by Rod Tueart' at the bottom of a column that has plainly been assembled by someone other than the person whose name and mugshot is at the top, my usually well-suppressed homicidal tendencies have a habit of resurfacing. While I recognise that the essence of this particular game lies in a newspaper's ability to persuade readers that this particular assemblage of vowels and consonants is the work of the advertised celebrity-author, the fact that several sports editors now credit the ghost is surely an acknowledgement that the masquerade is over, that the public is fully conversant with the way these things work. Insist, if you can, on honesty, and on credit where it's due.

Again, though, it can be easy to cause offence. Spoof columns and diaries have been growing in popularity since *Private Eye* began publishing its hilarious 'Dear Bill' letters during the early 1980s, which appeared to have been written by Denis Thatcher, boozy husband of the reigning Prime Minister, to the *Daily Telegraph* columnist Bill Deedes. However, not everybody gets the joke. The *Guardian* recently published a series of articles entitled 'Chris Bryant's Manchester Diary', purporting to be written by the Labour MP.[13] The lighthearted tone alerted most, though the closing line – 'Chris Bryant was speaking to Ros Taylor' – was deceptive. The same form of disclaimer had also punctuated Chris Douglas and Andrew Nickolds' uproarious cricket creation Dave Podmore, a *Guardian* regular for several years, but since it is also used for genuine ghosted articles, it is perhaps not all that surprising that Bryant subsequently informed the paper that some people believed he had been responsible. An apology was duly published. A century and a half on, Abraham Lincoln's theory remains the watchword: you can fool some of the people all of the time, and all of the people some of the time, but you can't fool all of the people all of the time.

EXERCISE

Research and compose an 800-word column on the perils of drugs in sport, using at least one quote from a known and respected authority on the subject, whether first-hand or second. Write another on the same subject, observing the same strictures, but this time from the opposing vantage point. Now blend the two into a coherent, balanced entity that fits the same space.

Chapter 10

The advantage of distance

Periodical journalism

Parkinson's Law, I would argue, is more applicable to journalism than any other activity. Having time on one's hands, to the average reporter, is a heavier burden than a six-digit mortgage and a five-figure overdraft. Ask an experienced campaigner to dash off 800 words in 20 minutes and he'll be downing a pint after 19. Tell him he has a week to produce a considered 1,500-word analysis of the function of the wing-back and he'll research for an hour or two, fret about it for six days, start writing deep into the seventh then request a minor extension on the grounds that he's just about to unearth an absolutely invaluable nugget of information.

To others, however, the looser the deadline and fatter the wordage, the better. For such contrary creatures (and yes, I count myself among them), more words + more time = heaven. Which is where magazines, documentaries and books come in, their function, in most cases, to promote deeper insight and broader coverage. The downsides, nonetheless, are plain. Specialist monthly publications are only slightly less susceptible to the tyrannies of breaking news; printing schedules mean it can be a fortnight or more between press day and publication; a daily or even weekly paper has the decided advantage of being able to make amends reasonably quickly.

Although that emphasis on catering for as many tastes as possible remains, the publications under consideration should also encompass weekend papers: not only do they boast more pages than the dailies, but earlier deadlines for the sundry sections dictate a features-based agenda. As you may already have surmised, discerning between newspapers and magazines these days is the devil's own job.

'Hollywood doesn't make many movies about life at magazines because magazines are a conduit to celebrity,' reasoned Ed Needham on the 2006 release of *The Devil Wears Prada*, a movie about life at the fashion magazine *Vogue*. Newspapers, on the other hand, have been the subject of many a film, from *The Front Page* to *The Paper,* each more raucous than the last. By contrast, the *Rolling Stone* office – as featured in that ultimate guilty pleasure of a movie *Almost Famous*, written and directed by former *Stone* staffer Cameron Crowe – is eerily reminiscent of a 'university library'. Or so attests Needham, once editor of that unusually liberal and highly influential American organ himself. The *New Yorker*, moreover, was 'so quiet you can hear the photocopier on standby'. Admittedly, staff at one of the 'beerier' titles

Needham has worked on, *FHM*, dreamed up a game to pass all those prolonged hours called 'Balls Across The Nose': this apparently involved a work experience underling sitting sideways on a chair with an unlit cigarette in his mouth, whereupon 'the bigger boys would then attempt to dislodge the cigarette, without hitting him in the face, by throwing an American football at it'.[1] Such exceptions, though, do little to undermine the rule. Ranging from brisk trade and business (*Restaurant Business*, *Motor Trader*, *Marketing Week*) to passionate consumer titles (*Shoot*, *Wisden Cricket Monthly*, *Mojo*), my experiences have been consistent: as the number of pages rises and the tension of deadlines is diffused, so staffs shrink and volume sinks.

Whereas the immediacy of daily newspapers, and their greater responsiveness, will always give them a singular edge over magazines, distinguishing between the two is, as mentioned above, growing increasingly difficult. Facilitated by advances in printing technology, which made it possible to produce more pages at a faster rate, the huge expansion in newspaper pagination over the past decade has compelled publishers to look to magazines for inspiration. Because magazines generally have more pages, visuals, varied design and presentation exert more influence; this was duly mirrored when newspapers began introducing specialist sections on travel, gardening, motoring and personal finance, as well as business and sport: mini-magazines all. The process quickened with the spread of websites, which not only beat the papers to the news but also adopted magazine design values.

Yet distinctions between newspapers and periodicals remain. When considering journalism that is not for live or daily consumption, the key is to remind yourself that:

1. What you lose in immediacy you gain, ideally, in distance and hence perspective and proportion; the heat of the moment and the hot breath of a tight deadline cannot be relied upon to add up to a definitively trustworthy assessment.
2. Remembering to buy something once a month or once a year, or shelling out for a subscription, is much more taxing/expensive than instilling a daily habit easily delegated to a local dealer-cum-supplier. It can safely be assumed, therefore, that your audience is more committed, which in turn means that you can often assume more knowledge of the subject on their part, and hence a greater thirst for the teeniest titbits.
3. 'News' is an elastic, strictly relative concept. Information, even about something that happened long ago, can be news.
4. Magazines feed newspapers. It is now customary for publishers to email press releases to newspaper editors and reporters just before the latest edition arrives on the newsstands. The copy will plug an exclusive interview and offer it, via the syndication department, for publication, in part or in its entirety, in exchange for a mention of the magazine in the copy and/or a credit at the bottom of the piece. With other publications free to quote any particularly succulent items, this can be free advertising on a highly lucrative scale.

One impressive example of the greater depth a magazine can still offer could be found in *Observer Sports Monthly* the month after the 2006 FIFA World Cup: a lengthy account by Jason Burke of the Italian match-fixing saga that had seen some of Serie A's loudest and proudest clubs punished by relegation and points deductions. Reams of news and web pages had already been eaten up by the subject but the space that editor Jason Cowley was able to grant Burke, a foreign correspondent familiar with the world's hottest spots, enabled him to add shade, nuance and balance to an issue that had mostly been portrayed in black and white.

Much the same could be said of *The Wisden Cricketer*'s coverage later that summer of 'Hairgate'. Though appearing nearly a month after umpire Darrell Hair had declared England the winners of the fourth Test against Pakistan by a forfeiture, printing deadlines meant a somewhat different reality: editor John Stern had had barely a week to tear up his flatplan, commission seven pages' worth of fresh material and shift and/or omit features that were now of lesser import. Those seven pages were nothing if not comprehensive, spanning as they did:

1 an introduction bringing any tourists from Mars up to date with the story so far, accompanied by Philip Brown's already iconic photo of Hair lifting the bails to end the match and a headline and standfirst pulling together the essential strands – '5 penalty runs, 2 proud men, 1 huge row' (*Four Weddings And A Funeral* and *The Cook, The Thief, His Wife And Her Lover* the diverse celluloid references there) followed by a string of hunting metaphors playing on the official's surname: 'Darrell Hair started a hare at The Oval that ran the press pack a merry, moral dance for a week. TWC picks up the scent';
2 a day-by-day diary of events as they unfolded, running in vertical strips across the end-columns of five pages and culminating in extracts from the emails between the ICC and Hair;
3 a view from Julian Guyer, who covered the story for Agence France Presse, on whether the laws of the game might have allowed Hair to stop short of abandoning the match, and whether the match referee, Mike Procter, might have intervened;
4 an enlightening if occasionally apologetic explanation by Kamran Abassi, a Yorkshire-born journalist of Pakistani stock, as to why the Pakistanis reacted so furiously to the allegations of ball-tampering;
5 opposing responses to the question 'Has Darrell Hair been made a scapegoat by the ICC?' from, respectively, John Townsend of the *West Australian* and Stephen Brenkley of the *Independent*;
6 a stirring defence of ball-tampering from Mike Selvey of the *Guardian*, once an England seamer;
7 a cool-headed overview of the impending ICC hearing from Christopher Martin-Jenkins, making abundantly clear his belief that Pakistan's decision not to retake the field until it was too late was 'beyond the pale'.

In addition, there was a report of the match in its entirety, a privilege monthlies enjoy and dailies don't. Such is the depth of coverage to which newspapers aspire but rarely, for obvious reasons, attain. Yet all this time and space comes at a price. For a sportswriter, moreover, that price is heftier than most.

A monthly specialist title such as *Four-Four-Two*, *Rugby World* or *The Wisden Cricketer* may have a far larger palette, but deadlines (staggered to enable a tolerable copy flow) and printing schedules, allied to choc-a-bloc fixture lists and the permanent threat of injury, mean that *not* looking foolish with extreme regularity is a considerable feat. The last-named title might go to press at the end of a Test match and trumpet a glorious, record-smithereening victory for England on the cover, complete with a large photo of a grinning captain and a headline reading 'Captain Courageous', only for a defeat of historically shameful proportions to follow by the time the magazine hits the shelves, followed in turn by said captain's confession to a Sunday tabloid that he had cheated a young fan by selling him a bat signed by his gardener's niece. Yet the readers, because they have bought a specialist product, are more demanding, less forgiving. The name of the game is knowledge, anticipation, lateral thinking – and, of course, balls. You have my permission to translate that last word in any way you wish.

EXERCISE

Select a prominent sporting news story local to where you live. Then, over the course of a month, collect relevant newspaper, magazine and web cuttings in a folder. At the end of that month, write a 1,500-word feature targeting a specified publication and incorporating at least two fresh interviews with key protagonists. Supply a headline (25 characters maximum), a standfirst/summary (25–30 words) and two pullout quotes (70 characters each) together with suggested photographs/illustrations/graphics, bearing in mind at all times the style and editorial approach of your target publication.

Chapter 11

Live and exclusive

Broadcasting

EARLY DAYS

Competition for print journalists came as radio took wing between the world wars. Until the second half of the century, telephones were, for most, a luxury; not until then did delivering copy to newspapers by pigeon or messenger boy become prehistoric. The immediacy of the broadcasts hit newspaper sales – why wait to read about a match that evening, or indeed the following day, when you could hear it unfold as it happens? In time, the two would prove complementary: the desire to relive the action, and obtain greater detail and measured judgements, would keep print reporters in business. Indeed, it was a measure of the symbiotic relationship between print and broadcasting that, in the autumn of 2006, my old *London Daily News* and *Sunday Times* colleague Mihir Bose left the *Daily Telegraph* to become the BBC's first sports editor.

Broadcasting House first aired its perennial Saturday afternoon *Sports Report* in 1948, furnishing Caribbean listeners with ball-by-ball commentaries on the West Indies' three Test matches in England in 1939, even though Britons – eight million of whose homes were equipped with a wireless set of some description – were scheduled to receive but a fraction of the coverage. Such was the gratitude of the sporting authorities at such free promotion that, unlike their more commercially minded American counterparts, it would be many decades before they realised their wares had a market value, a value the next stage of the broadcasting revolution would ultimately hike to the skies.

Sports broadcasting blossomed initially in the aftermath of World War I. In the United States, boxing was first out of the traps: April 1921 brought what is claimed to be the first live radio broadcast of a sports event – a fight between Johnny Dundee and Johnny Ray, courtesy of KDKA in Pittsburgh. Three months later, a reported 300,000 tuned in for the Jack Dempsey–Georges Carpentier heavyweight title duel. Later that year, at the Sydney Cricket Ground in Australia, Len Watt, a former grade player, was handed a microphone at the start of a testimonial match for Charles Bannerman, scorer of the very first Test century in 1877, and instructed to 'go on talking'; come the next tour by MCC/England, in 1924–25, a Sydney station was broadcasting regular commentaries on the city's two Tests from inside the scorebox.[1] January 1927 saw the first British outside broadcast of a sporting encounter, the England v Wales rugby union match from Twickenham. A plan of the field divided into numbered squares was published in the *Radio Times* so that reference could be made to the position of play. Later that same month, the BBC aired the first live soccer commentary, Arsenal against Sheffield United; the Sport and Outside Broadcasts department's inaugural cricket broadcasts – Essex v New Zealand – followed that summer.

Reading extracts from those early commentaries and reports, resurrected and lovingly preserved by David Rayvern-Allen, reminds you of what a novelty it all was.

> *'I am speaking to you from a little box right alongside the scorers,' announced Howard Marshall during The Oval Test against the West Indies in August 1933. 'It is a lovely summer afternoon with the sun shining and the players casting long shadows on the turf, and a big and enthusiastic crowd sitting round the ground. As a matter of fact, when I came over Vauxhall Bridge on my way here this morning and saw grey clouds stretching away in the distance I was a little uneasy about the weather. Still, the wind came from the north-east and the clouds were high, and the omens generally were propitious. I always like The Oval – it is a friendly, informal sort of place. Incidentally, it is burnt pretty brown just now except for the patch of emerald green out there in the middle. As soon as I got here the news was going about. I will break off now to say that Martindale has just sent Marriott's off-stump cartwheeling out of the ground, and the English innings has closed for 312.'*[2]

Note the obsession with the weather and the short shrift given to events on the field. With none of those nosy cameras to keep them honest – or at least none that would make any difference; Pathe's cameras were there but they produced their newsreels for distribution to cinemas up to a week later – those boys could get away with pretty much anything.

And so, inexorably, came the jackboot-march of television, fuelled primarily by another postwar thirst for leisure and pleasure. That said, it took time to exert the grip it enjoys today, due in good measure to the antipathy of the BBC's Lord Reith, a staunch conservative by trade and sometime pal of Benito Mussolini, towards 'seeing by wireless'.[3] In 2006, James Murdoch, son of Rupert and BSkyB's chief executive, would claim that Reith took 'a pretty firm view of the need to keep the lower classes in their place'.[4] The knock-back drove that remarkable inventor and unfettered socialist John Logie Baird, who envisaged television as entertainment and enlightenment for the masses, to do business with the Americans instead. Despite initial resistance, the medium was soon being embraced with gusto.

A Japanese website claims that the first televised sports event was an elementary school baseball game in that country, in September 1931.[5] NBC would beg to differ, having screened its first baseball game in May 1930: the second half of a college doubleheader between the Princeton Tigers and the Columbia Lions in New York. A single camera was positioned on a platform behind home plate, the armchair audience estimated at 400.[6] Three months later, NBC broadcast its first professional game, between Brooklyn's Dodgers and Cincinnati's Reds. Commentary duties fell, aptly, to the folksy Red Barber, the most distinctive and fondly remembered of all baseball voices. When boxing joined in the next year, with a bout between Mickey Walker and Benny Leonard, what viewers saw, according to B.R. Bearden, was 'a reddish-orange picture about half the size of a standard business card'.[7] The first nationally broadcast professional gridiron game came along in 1934; in the same year, the Ford Motor Company paid $100,000 to sponsor live commentary on the World Series.

Eventually, grudgingly, Reith had allowed the test transmissions of Baird's television system over the BBC network in 1936 (at the opening of the BBC's first TV studio at Alexandra Palace, typically, his Lordship was on holiday in Scotland, snubbing Baird to the last).[8] As Steven Barnett relates, the first live BBC transmission from Wimbledon came in June the next year, though there were only 2,000 sets in circulation.[9] October 1937 brought the world's first televised motor race (the Imperial Trophy Road Race from Crystal Palace), the next year a gush of new frontiers: the first televised soccer international (England v Scotland), FA Cup final (Huddersfield v Preston North End), Test match (England v Australia) and Boat Race. By the early 1950s, only 10 per cent of British householders owned a television, and 9 per cent of their US counterparts; come the end of the 1960s, penetration in both nations had reached 90 per cent.[10]

The ramifications would be more profound than anyone could have imagined, not least for print journalists. As Richard Holt and Tony Mason related:

> *From Pierce Egan in the early 19th century to Neville Cardus between the wars, sports reporting involved a process of selection, dramatising, interpretation and reflection. The same has been true of the last 50 years with one critical difference: technology has provided fans with visual access to live sport within the privacy of their own homes, removed from the communal atmosphere, the stadium compressed onto a small screen with a spectacle 'mediated' by a sports producer selecting shots and by a commentator. No longer the sole providers of match reports, the popular press took to the 'human interest' angles not covered on television. The back page was turned into a kind of sports magazine. This had begun in a modest way between the wars but assumed enormous importance from the 1960s onwards. The contemporary media, led by the popular press but with commercial radio and satellite television in hot pursuit, have turned sport into 'male soap opera'.*[11]

The 1950s, as Holt and Mason see it, were 'the last decade when spectator sport [in Britain] was still produced for live consumption'.[12] Postwar attendances, reflecting that era's sense of relief at returning to something approaching normality (rationing notwithstanding), were immense. County Championship cricket fixtures drew ten times the crowds they do today. The 1948 three-day Lancashire–Yorkshire match drew 67,000. The record gates for the top three Football League divisions were all recorded between 1947 and 1950; the biggest single day's total attendance, 1.27m, was recorded at Christmas 1949. There was, of course, little competition for the working man's hard-earned shillings. Between 1968 and 1975, thanks in good part to the deterrent of hooliganism as well as the rise of Saturday trading, total League attendances declined by 15 per cent.[13]

Television encroached comparatively slowly. While eager to promote annual events that could be relied upon to attract big crowds regardless – such as The Derby and Wimbledon – sporting bodies took time to permit regular live coverage of the bread-and-butter. US sports, more willing to embrace sponsorship, were quicker off the mark: the first live baseball telecast arrived in 1939, the first club to sell TV rights were the Boston Braves in 1948, the first pay-TV baseball broadcast as early as 1964. Not until the 1980s did the Football League grant its assent. In the previous decade, the FA Cup final was still the only domestic football screened live – on *both* major channels. In those early postwar days, the concern, according to Barnett, was less that television would deplete attendances than that cinemas would 're-diffuse' the pictures and charge for admission.[14] The aggrieved parties formed the Association for the Protection of Copyright in Sports and asked for reassurances from the BBC that it would not be party to such piracy. Stewards of the British Boxing Board of Control, stated the chairman of the governing body in late 1947, 'remain unconvinced that Television . . . cannot be but detrimental to Professional Boxing'. Ernest Marples MP would counter this, claiming sporting events were 'the most effective spectacle on television'.[15]

Keenly aware of the impending competition from commercial television – ITV was launched in September 1955 – the BBC drew up a list of events 'from which the BBC would not wish to be excluded': Wimbledon, the Wightman and Davis Cups, major horse races, world boxing title fights, rugby union's International Championship, the FA Cup final, football internationals, Test matches and, lastly and leastly, by way of affirming the Oxbridge blood coursing through Broadcasting House, the Boat Race. This would in time form the basis of the so-called Listed Events, the sporting 'Crown Jewels' decreed by the House of Commons to be part of the national fabric; inclusion on that list would for decades prevent the respective sports from selling their product to the highest bidder.

Yet even at a time when viewers were limited to around 12 hours' transmission per day, the broadcasters' reliance on sport as cheap programming was palpable (even by the late 1980s, transmissions cost £16,500 per hour, cheaper than everything bar films and cartoons).[16] In the week of Laker's only slightly imperfect Manchester masterpiece in 1956, televised live on the BBC, there was extensive coverage of two county cricket matches, athletics, showjumping and archery.[17] Even more instructively, such was the rivalry between the Football League and the FA, and so profound the impact on League attendances in previous years, the former blocked live transmission of the 1952 Cup final after a request that it be put back a week was rejected. Sales of sets boomed for Coronation Year yet it was only in the face of stern opposition that the classic 'Matthews Final' of 1953 was witnessed by the nation. The few such squabbles in the US, by contrast, were between the three main networks, thrusters all. In 1956, CBS began televising NFL games to selected markets; four years later ABC became the first network to sign a contract with the American Football League. As early as 1962, moreover, the NFL signed an agreement permitting CBS to screen all regular season NFL games, while *Monday Night Football* debuted in 1970.

Live commentary, though, was neither the be-all nor the end-all. Cue the gradual birth, to spice things up and afford purportedly enhanced insight, of pre- and post-match interviews and punditry, as well as conventional reporting of sports news, such as transfers, appointments and selections. First aired in 1954, *Sportsview* would find a niche as a midweek magazine programme as keen to debate issues as show games. Indeed, that industrious historian Asa Briggs, author of the magisterial five-volume *History of Broadcasting in the United Kingdom*, would write enthusiastically about its impact: 'It was with *Sportsview* as a main weapon in its armoury that the BBC faced competition in sport from commercial television.'[18] Taking its cue from across the Atlantic – ABC's busy anthology *Wide World of Sports*, inventively produced by Roone Arledge, had debuted in 1961 – *World of Sport*, ITV's challenger to *Grandstand*, entered the arena in 1964. This was also the year those cheerily brassy strains of the *Match of the Day* theme were first heard on the newborn BBC2.

Many viewed the gradual adoption of TV as the primary source of information with displeasure and scepticism, casting it as a detriment to sportswriting, encouraging as it did the soundbite, the superficial, straight-after-the-final-whistle comment from a tired, sweaty participant-celebrity, at the expense of thoughtful analysis and uncompromised reporting. As Holt saw it, television 'more than anything else has transformed the image of the professional sportsman or woman from the skilled artisan to the dubious cinematic status of "star".'[19]

The resistance of broadcasters to live sport, though, could also be traced to its sheer inconvenience. Unlike soap operas, sitcoms or documentaries, sport is disobedient. Yes, kick-off times can be manipulated to suit television schedules; yes, television has done its level best to repackage and remould sport through highlights and action replays; yet without the need to please its principal sponsor, professional cricket would never have adopted coloured kit or 20-over games. But *Eastenders* doesn't go to extra time or sudden-death overtime; *The Office* is never rained off. A football or rugby match, moreover, is virtually the only time a commercial channel goes more than 25 minutes between ad breaks. With elections, royal marriages and funerals few and far between, news broadcasts forming a tiny proportion of the average day's fare and concerts easily shoehorned into schedules, live sport constitutes the broadcasters' biggest headache. That they are nevertheless prepared to offer sums equivalent to most nations' GNP for transmission rights underlines the mutually beneficial nature of a sometimes fraught relationship.

WHAT MAKES A GOOD BROADCAST JOURNALIST?

So much for the backdrop. In broadcasting, it is what is out front that counts. Time is the enemy, even more so than for print journalists. According to Ralph Dellor, a veteran of *Grandstand* and *Match of the Day* and one of the BBC's leading all-round sports broadcasters since making his debut on Radio London in the autumn of 1970, a 30-second match report for radio, at the customary rate of three words per second, amounts to just 90 words. Try to cram more in and the result will be unintelligible. Overdo the excitement, and humiliation may beckon, as I discovered one Saturday in the mid-1980s when, in the infancy of commercial radio, I reported a match at Highbury for a Midlands station. Introduced by a presenter who made Chris Moyles sound restrained, I made the fatal error of trying to match his freneticism: what emerged from my mouth might have been comprehensible to Superman, but listeners in Solihull and Droitwich would have learned more had a drunk monkey been chattering down the line.

The contrast with print is sobering. Even a two-paragraph snippet about a Serie A match in an English paper can command 100 words. The *Sunday Times* regularly runs 1,200-word match reports. I wrote dozens of that length for the paper on games as comparatively insignificant as a Fourth Division local derby. For the most part, television, and radio to an only slightly lesser extent, have no time – or inclination for that matter – to dig to the depths a print journalist would regard as their duty. Dellor, who also has decades of sportswriting experience gained with the likes of the *Daily Telegraph, Wisden Cricket Monthly* and *Cricinfo*, amplifies the divide:

> *On radio or TV, it's difficult to do anything more than a score log. It's difficult to adequately paint the picture. In print you can edit and cut words – and you have subs to help if you overrun your word length. The process is more important in broadcasting: trying to get the flavour and facts across is more time-consuming. You are trying to put the information over in a fluent, conversational way. And in trying to get that fluency, you are bound to speak quicker. I'm probably old-fashioned: I don't like to hear people reading from a script for radio – and you can almost always tell because of the deliberation with which the report is spoken. One example is 'however' – we don't say 'however' in conversation. When I did football reports for* Grandstand *I was out of vision. I worked very hard at making it seem as if I was not reading from a script. The key to good TV or radio reporting is the appearance of spontaneity. People said they liked my* Grandstand *football reports because I sounded enthusiastic.*
>
> *If you're reporting to pictures but out of vision, you are governed by the available footage. The producer will put the footage on screen then you write around that. I think it's the opposite with news programmes, where they use a lot of generic library footage, which is not felt to be appropriate for sport because you are expected to have that immediacy. News reports to camera are not scripted, or at least mine aren't. You order your thoughts, much like after-dinner speaking. I write a running order. I think about the intro, the core elements and the conclusion.*[20]

Logistics, though, meant that for much of his career Dellor seldom saw a football match to its conclusion.

> *When reporting for* Grandstand, *you often had to leave a ground well before the end of a game and go back to the studio. I left 20 minutes before the end of my first game, at Loftus Road, QPR's home ground, and dashed to the Lime Grove studios nearby, where I discovered the result. Of course, as luck would have it, I missed a few goals. At the next match I covered, at West Ham, another TV reporter, Peter Lorenzo, came up to me in the press box and told me he felt sorry for me, missing all those goals. 'Do you mind if I offer you a piece of advice?' he said, standing with his back to the pitch. 'Don't take any notice of what happens out there,' he went on, waving in the direction of the pitch. He said he spent 15 seconds covering the intro, 15 seconds on the story and 15 on the conclusion, which seemed eminently sensible. Some write their thoughts down, some don't.*[21]

Flying by the seat of one's pants is an occupational hazard. Dellor once left a Leicester–Aston Villa game at half-time.

> *A car was waiting for me outside the ground and I was driven to the BBC's Nottingham studios. Along the way we listened to the game on the radio and when we got there*

I phoned the Press Association reporter at the game and he filled me in with the details. Once I was doing a hockey report for the BBC when I was supposed to be doing a Sunday League cricket match at Southampton. By the time I finally arrived it was raining: I didn't see a ball bowled.

When reporting on screen, he is 'entirely conversational'. If not perfect, practice certainly makes for fewer imperfections.

You should have as many rehearsals as possible, and not necessarily with the cameraman. You know from experience how much you can get in. You are often asked for 30 seconds when they want 40, but then you get into the double-bluff and do 50. It's the opposite of print journalism, where they ask for more than they need. When you have a producer talking in your ear you have to split your brain in two. I used to do Today's Sport *after* Grandstand. *There was no script, no autocue. Towards the end the producer would be counting down from 10 – if you could say 'goodnight' when he got to one you knew you were doing OK.*

If I was starting now I'd prefer to do radio cricket commentary. That's what has given me the most satisfaction. On television you are always being told to keep quiet, not to talk too much.

It's more obvious in broadcasting whether you can or cannot do the job, because there are no sub-editors to save you. TV has restrictions: it's a bit clinical. There's no opportunity to express yourself unless you are a maverick like David Lloyd [Sky Sports cricket commentator], though there's more room for mavericks now. I prefer the disciplined approach. So many radio commentators say 'He's hammered it away for four' without describing the ball or the shot. On TV you can see what's happened so you should add to the pictures rather than describe them.

I found football commentary easier – you're just relating what's going on out there. It's only *about the discipline. In cricket you need to have something meaningful and relevant to say between each ball and each over. You are more relaxed commentating on cricket because of the slower pace: there aren't many ex-players doing radio commentary on football. One exception, back in the 1960s, was [BBC Radio commentator] Maurice Edelston, who had played for Fulham and Reading.*[22]

Nerves are not easily conquered, as Dellor attests: 'The first time I was on air, for Radio London, I was reading the results and got the intonation wrong. "Ilford NIL, BARKING nil", that sort of thing.' As with any desirable job, being in the right place at the right time has its advantages. It was through Edelston, indeed, that Peter Jones, Alan Green's predecessor as the voice of BBC Radio's football coverage, gained his big break. 'Edelston coached at Bradfield College, where Jones was a French teacher and sports master,' recalls Dellor.

*Edelston used to take him to matches with him and one day an opportunity arose for Jones to commentate for the BBC, purely because he was there. Frank Bough [*Grandstand *reporter and presenter] started out doing football commentaries for Forces radio in Germany,* *and got his chance when Gerald Sinstadt lost his voice. The big thing is getting those lucky breaks but the key is to recognise them. If you are no good, no matter how many chances you get you won't be able to take them.*[23]

DOCUMENTARIES

The exception to the broadcaster's time-starved lot is the documentary, fast becoming the most effective way to attempt to paint a rounder, fuller picture. In terms of research and output, a one-hour documentary is approximately the equivalent of a 100,000-word book. Yet even then, there is a vast amount of editing and squeezing. One BBC producer recently informed me that for every hour-long documentary he would expect to shoot 100 hours of material. Having spent an hour being interviewed for a BBC *Reputations* programme about Ian Botham and for an ESPN special on Sonny Liston, I can testify from humbling experience how miniscule a bite my allegedly sound contributions actually made (barely five seconds in the former case). 'Soundbite' may have come to be a term of derision, but it is the currency television has always dealt in. The 'sound' can be viewed in two ways, referring both to the act of producing something for aural consumption and to the appropriateness of the comment, i.e. the ability of the interviewee to encapsulate a sometimes complex matter both succinctly and in language that can readily be digested by a broad audience. In that interview for the Botham documentary, I was repeatedly asked to repeat snatches of my answer when the producer decided I'd found a line he liked, a form of off-the-cuff script editing that saves time while giving the viewer the impression that the interviewee is capable of getting to the point reasonably swiftly.

LIVE COMMENTARY

Lice commentary is arguably as valid a form of journalism as any, albeit the most instantaneous, least forgiving sort. Being licensed to pontificate on air can do wonders for the ego that print journalists can only envy. Instant responses, on the other hand, risk repeated derision, all the more so since the advent of the action replay in the 1960s. Small flaws can make you a national laughing-stock: a tendency to gabble or uncork awful puns; a misidentified goal scorer or misjudged assertion. Extemporising convincingly on air is all the trickier. Confronted by a high word-count, wary of the drawbacks of a dull game, a print journalist might compose half a dozen paragraphs of background before kick-off; notwithstanding John Motson's cannily inserted factoids and cringe-inducing coincidences, it is extremely difficult for a commentator to adequately script a foolproof response to a plot that, for all the endless duplication of certain scenes, even entire acts, never offers the luxury of infallible predictability. Caution, even more than with print journalists, is imperative. On the other hand, exhorted as they are by producers eager to wring drama from even the most tepid encounter, commentators are just as prone as newspaper reporters to over-dramatisation and injudicious sermonising. Hence the enormous admiration, even awe, inspired by the masters of this particular domain and the virtues they exude: the authoritative cucumber-coolness of Richie Benaud and Peter O'Sullevan, Martin Tyler and Barry Davies; the earthy wit and wisdom of Red Barber and Bill McLaren; the matiness of ESPN's Chris Berman and Sky's David Lloyd.

With his husky, deliberate, reassuring Hampshire burr, John Arlott was one of the foremost exploiters of the radio audience's blindness, not only putting the listener in the picture but colouring it in subtle shades, musings informed by the hinterland of a broad mind and working soul. That he also wrote about cricket and football was doubtless an asset, instilling the thoughtful deliberation that forestalled the rush to premature verdicts. When this converted policeman set quietly off on his illustrious broadcasting career shortly after the end of World War II he produced arts programmes for the BBC World Service; he would joke in later years that he was exceedingly fortunate that the audience was almost entirely of an overseas complexion, as his son Timothy put it, because they 'dare not complain for fear the service would be stopped'.[24] That Arlott Senior was a cut above first became widely apparent during the sun-drenched summer of 1947: while South Africa's spinner 'Tufty' Mann was causing Middlesex and England's George Mann no end of difficulties, he proclaimed it a case of 'Mann's inhumanity to Mann'. He was cherished, moreover, for his own humanity: when asked to complete a visa form upon entering South Africa two winters later, he identified himself as a 'human being'. Like Benaud, he empathised with the players, preferring to humanise than demonise or canonise.

According to Timothy Arlott, his father

> *always imagined he was not speaking to millions of listeners but to someone on their own sitting at home – perhaps his mother or someone who did not know about cricket, who needed to have it carefully and enthusiastically explained. That person would be as interested to know not just about the play but about what it was like to be watching the cricket at Hove that particular morning – 'The blue seaside sky, the white wedding-cake grandstand and the sea mist nine-tenths gone from the ground . . . '.*[25]

Because of its pastoral settings and regular lulls, cricket lends itself to this poetic approach – or did before Arlott's retirement in the early 1980s prompted a stronger emphasis on public schoolboy giggles and japes in the *Test Match Special* box. Perhaps Arlott Senior's most moving and memorable broadcast was one demanding little embellishment: the delivery from Eric Hollies that dismissed Don Bradman second ball at The Oval in 1948, in the final Test appearance by the man who would leave a legacy of statistical superiority unmatched in any other sporting sphere.

> *Hollies pitches the ball up slowly and . . . he's bowled . . . Bradman bowled Hollies nought . . . and what do you say under these circumstances? How . . . I wonder whether you see the ball very clearly in your last Test in England, on a ground where you've played some of the biggest cricket in your life and where the opposing side has just stood around you and given you three cheers, and the crowd has clapped you all the way to the wicket. I wonder if you see the ball at all.*[26]

In those few words, plucked from experience, knowledge, passion and the ether, Arlott contrived to impart the essential information while putting the scene firmly, and vividly, in context. And that, in short, is the art of radio commentary. The following tips, nonetheless, are eminently worthy of consideration and absorption. They were written by Paul Tinkle of Thunderbolt Broadcasting in Martin, Tennessee, and refer to his work covering school basketball games, but the principles are universal.

> *Don't call numbers. Call names and call them often. Give the score every time someone scores, and give the time often. Remember, the only things the listener really needs to know is: What's the score? Who's leading? How much time is left on the clock? What quarter is it?*
>
> *Describe the action. Describe how far out [a throw is made]. Don't yell, but sound interested and excited.*
>
> *Don't be critical of a call unless you're darn sure that the ref blew it – and then be kind. 'It looks like he missed that one but he's done a great job tonight, and it's difficult not to miss a couple.' Refs listen to the radio, and the last thing you want is a ref telling his or her buddies you've been hard on him or her.*
>
> *When interviewing the coach, keep your questions short: 'Coach, congratulations . . . ' Then hush up. They'll take it from there. I've broadcast a lot of games where the team played lousy but the coach thought they played great. The last thing the coach wants is my opinion on the front end. You want his or her opinion. Remember, you've been on the air for the last two hours giving your opinion. The interview with the coach is what you want, not more of your opinion.*
>
> *Finally, give the score again as you sign off. I've tuned in a hundred times to other broadcasters at the tail end of the interview and they failed to give the score again.*[27]

Just as Arlott was the radio commentator's radio commentator, so it is doubtful whether any television commentator of any ilk has won such pandemic praise as Benaud, who did his final stint in a British booth in 2005 having managed to pull off the possibly unique trick of enchanting viewers at opposite ends of the planet for four decades. He may be Australian, but the affection he stirred in 'the old dart' was no less pronounced, thanks in the main to his unerring impartiality. In a trade that promotes nationalism and regionalism, the use of 'we' and 'our', frowned upon on national newspapers, is a reflex action, bias the norm. Other assets included a resolute resistance to hyperbole, a refusal to utter the first thing that sprang to mind, expertise in the science of succinctness and mastery in the art of silence. So effortlessly – seemingly – did he adapt to his audiences' native tongue, marvels Dellor, he would fly back to England at the end of an Australian season and switch from saying 'sundries' to 'extras', and from revealing the total as 'four for 100' to '100 for four', without a hint of a blip.

Benaud expounded his philosophy thus:

> *Usually you are not required to give a running commentary, as is the case on radio, but to provide comments at what you hope is exactly the right time. I believe you should only talk when you can add to the picture on the screen and it is possibly for that reason I have the reputation of talking less than most others working on cricket telecasts. It is, I can assure you, very difficult to get the correct balance. You have, sitting out there, children, mothers and fathers, some of whom may not have seen a cricket telecast before or may be watching it in their first season – they want every bit of information you can give them. Then there is the*

> *person who might play club cricket, knows a lot about the game and requires a mid-way commentary – he wants some information but not merely as much as the novice. Finally, there is the one who considers he knows everything about the game and a lot more besides, and he wants to be told nothing . . . you have to try and strike a balance of conversation with the person to whom you're talking through the lens. That person needs to be a blend of everyone I have listed, requiring all the information available and, at the same time, needing none, so from that you may appreciate it is a difficult job.*[28]

That said, even giants are fallible. During one Test at Lord's between England and the West Indies a crowd disturbance broke out. The BBC crew was a camera short – this was long before two dozen were de rigeur. Benaud momentarily forgot this. He had one eye on the television monitor in front of him, enabling him to describe what the viewers could see; the other was on the unrest far to his right. Impelled by the news sense of a trained journalist, he elected to commentate on the latter. Unfortunately, he was ahead of the camera; worse, by the time it had swung towards the troublesome area, the kerfuffle had died down. In his left ear he heard the sarcastic tones of his producer: 'How *very* interesting, Richie – and how nice it would have been to show the millions sitting in front of their television sets the picture you were describing so beautifully.'[29]

That, though, was nothing compared with the faux pas perpetrated by Lamar Thomas, a TV pundit, during a college gridiron game in 2006 between local rivals Miami Hurricanes and Florida International University. Thomas, a former Miami student broadcasting for Comcast Sports SouthEast, a regional cable network available in 5.5 million American homes, let his colours show a little too readily during an onfield brawl: 'Now that's what I'm talking about. You come into our house, you should get your behind kicked. You don't come [here] playing that stuff . . . You'll get your butt beat. I was about to go down the elevator to get in that thing.'[30]

In theory, neutrality should be sought at all costs by every journalist, and, since they are journalists too, every broadcaster. Commercial reality dictates otherwise, as emphasised by Andy Colquhoun, who started out as a print journalist in Birmingham and now does radio commentaries on rugby union for SABC, South Africa's BBC: 'I've worked on commercial regional radio and it's actually compulsory – "our team on our station". And for the national broadcaster when commentating on national teams there is also a sense of "supporting" the team effort while being rigorously objective in relating the events.'[31] None of those alibis, however, could excuse Mr Thomas's pathetic schoolyard rhetoric. Not unexpectedly, Comcast handed him his cards and edited out his comments when the transmission was re-aired.[32]

The difference between Arlott and Benaud – and between Benaud and the rump of admired commentators – is that whereas the Englishman was a journalist and broadcaster with a possibly over-developed enthusiasm for sport in general and cricket in particular, the Australian was a world-class cricketer who served an apprenticeship in newspapers before becoming one of the most astute captains the game has seen. Even before he attained that exalted status – which, not unnaturally, boosted his prospects of employment as a pundit – he had the humility and foresight to take a three-week BBC television course at the end of the 1956 Ashes tour. The roots of his appeal to viewers lay less in that inimitable understatement than in the knowledge that, as the first man in Test history to aggregate 2,000 runs and 200 wickets, and as a leader of unquestioned sagacity and virtue, he knew what he was talking about. He could be trusted, to be accurate and perceptive but also to be fair. He may have been over-generous with compliments, and sparing with criticism, but his close-of-play summaries were a model of sincere, authoritative concision. Impersonators made merry hay with his inflections and minimalist sayings but when Richie took a stand, few argued.

Not that he lacked support. Apart from the producer, director and stage manager, there were statisticians, assistants and sound recordists, computer operators and video editors. Just as his chosen speciality was a team game, so is broadcasting.

Benaud alienated many by joining Kerry Packer's late-1970s breakaway as consultant and commentator, doing much to influence the direction of both the game and the way it was broadcast; as ever, his judgement was impeccable. The prescient David Hill was Benaud's innovative executive producer on Packer's Channel 9 network, advocating ever more camera angles, promoting the use of graphics and having an inestimable impact on the way Gary Franses would change the face of British cricket broadcasting with Sky Sports and Channel 4. At the outset of World Series Cricket, Hill produced the following list of ten points for his commentators which, warranted Benaud drily, 'could almost go under the heading of commandments'. He would not dream of picking up a microphone, he wrote, 'without bearing them in mind':

1. Keep one eye on the monitor, one eye on the field of play, and your third eye on your tongue and your fellow commentator.
2. Never talk over your fellow commentator – just as your fellow commentator shall never talk over you.
3. Remember, silence is the greatest weapon you have in your armoury.
4. Listen to your director with an ear as keen as a ferret's – just as your director will listen avidly to the commentary, thus ensuring your magic phrases are pertinent to the viewer's picture.
5. Think constantly of voice-over cassettes, animations, computers and anything which will help the viewer enjoy the telecast.
6. Make your commercial throws[33] as tight as the proverbial fish's ear, so no ball is missed.
7. Remember this is a game of many and varied hues. As a commentator you will keep foremost in your mind that cricket contains venom and courage, drama and humour, and you will not be backward in bringing out in your commentary those aspects of the noble and ancient pastime.
8. This marvellous game has many by-ways and secret things – and you as a commentator will remember that multitudes of viewers do not understand some aspects of the art, therefore you will endeavour always to add to the picture on the screen.
9. Remember at all times that, having practised this ancient art at the highest possible level, you may occasionally dwell on the sacred mysteries to the utter confusion of the uninformed. Therefore, you will keep it simple, never talking down to a viewer by using those bastard phrases: 'of course', 'as you can see' or 'as my fellow commentator said'.
10. Also remember your producer and director, aged and infirm as they may be, could ask you to do things which, at the time, you feel you do not completely understand. Although

> your producer and director may not be properly introduced into the subtle nuances of your ancient game of cricket, they have been introduced into the puerile art of communications, so . . . concentrate, and make it work![34]

These tablets of stone were plainly directed at ex-players in particular. That they can be applied, almost en masse, to other long-established sports, and to non-Australian booths, is indisputable.

All of which brings us to the difficulty in choosing the commentary booth as your ideal office. Why bother with a trained broadcaster when you can have a familiar name and face boasting a string of caps and winners' medals and/or an attractive line in laddish humour and rebelliousness? The presumption is that success in sport bequeaths an ability to assess the ebb and flow of a game, to anticipate and dissect tactics, to distinguish between technical efficiency and incompetence, thus compensating for any absence of the communication skills required of the unfamous. For all my earlier comments about players-turned-sportswriters, this is neither realistic nor fair. Would you expect Paul McCartney to be able to submit a credible review of a James Blunt single on air? Perhaps, but why? Articulating something you have long done by trained but often God-given instinct is no easy matter. Scores of accomplished sportsmen may have made a smooth transition to print, but broadcasting relies even more on celebrity, and hence comes unstuck more often (witness Olympic champion Sally Gunnell's short career at the microphone). Reacting instantaneously while on air, and offering a credible analysis, is vastly more demanding than taking time to contemplate before writing. It is not only thwarted broadcasters who contend that the trade-off is loaded too heavily in favour of dumbing-down.

Yet it would be insensitive, and probably rather ungrateful, to bemoan any of this too strongly. As mentioned earlier, sportspeople, who give us so much pleasure for our pounds, have difficulty adapting to life after the ball. In his study of cricket suicides, *By His Own Hand*, David Frith quotes the fictional character Sam Palmer, a Test veteran played by Jack Warner in the 1953 movie *The Final Test*, the words courtesy of that fine playwright Terence Rattigan: 'The trouble with making a game a profession is that you're at the top too young. The rest of the way's a gentle slide down. Not so gentle sometimes. It makes one feel so ruddy useless and old.'[35] Should we not be glad the slide is becoming gentler?

Besides, when two experienced, eloquent minds are in harness, broadcasting can enter a higher plane. Take the second day of the Adelaide Test in November 2006, when two former England captains, Mike Atherton and his successor Nasser Hussain, batted around the ethics of Shane Warne bowling negatively to silence the rampant Kevin Pietersen.[36] Back and forth they went: Hussain declaiming that a Test match was just that: a test of a man's ability to overcome obstacles; Atherton asking Hussain to justify his adoption of the same ploy to quieten the Indian maestro Sachin Tendulkar a few years earlier; Hussain pointing out somewhat gleefully that Tendulkar had blinked first, lost patience and got stumped, that end justified means; Atherton quoting the laws verbatim, stressing that the umpires were empowered to call a wide, that cricketers were primarily entertainers, and that bored viewers had been sending baffled emails to the studio; Hussain jabbing back, insisting that the mental battle between Warne and Pietersen was the very essence of sport. At one juncture, the camera picked the pair out: both men's eyes were twinkling, both caught up in the thrill of a good but even-tempered argument. It was broadcasting in its best suit and tie but with sleeves rolled up and muscles flexing. Broadcasting at its best.

For those who do scale the broadcasting ladder on the strength of their talent as opposed to their feats on the field, the glamour is often muted. The majority of radio commentators, for instance, are virtual one-man bands, working for hospitals or other small stations with meagre back-up and even fewer resources. Colquhoun is one such. Unlike Benaud, he does all his own research: since he is preparing for what is usually an 80–90 minute solo stint, this is no small mountain. Commentary is to newspaper reports what newspaper reports are to television reports. For a commentary he might spend three or four hours researching whereas for a newspaper he does it 'on the hoof, using yearbooks or delving into the web'.[37]

Colquhoun's most embarrassing experience occurred during a Currie Cup provincial match. 'I realised only after about 10 minutes that a replacement I'd been happily calling Francois Steyn was actually on the opposing team's bench: I should have been calling him Mark Harris. By the time the latter kicked the winning goal I'd got back on track but I felt crap about it.' At the other end of the spectrum was the 2003 World Cup final between England and Australia. 'Not because of my commentary but because of the magnitude of the occasion and the drama of the conclusion – and the fact that it was a marathon effort as, from the start of the second half to "off-air" after the presentations I spoke for 90 minutes on my own.'[38]

A good producer is worth his or her weight in gold, though Colquhoun is used to setting his sights low. 'In South Africa, if the [phone] line is up and works without dropping during a broadcast I'm happy. If they also chased team changes, found a comments man, provided the odd bottle of water, supplied a parking ticket so one doesn't have to run the gauntlet in downtown Jo'burg, and then actually listened to the broadcast to keep track of replacements and whether you're actually boring the listeners rigid, that would be very nice.'[39]

EXERCISE

Beg, borrow or buy a DVD of a pre-1980s FA Cup final, before the advent of regular live soccer broadcasts. Familiarise yourself, through research, with the teams' respective passages to the final, their form during the season and any relevant inside stories and contextual elements you would have expected to know at the time (to research the 1961 final, for instance, and not discover that Tottenham were chasing the first League-Cup double of the twentieth century, or that Alan Shepard had become the first American in space the previous day, would be remiss). Arm yourself for all eventualities (was any of the participants celebrating a birthday/anniversary? Did the referee have an interest in stamp-collecting?). Once primed, start the DVD, connect yourself to a working microphone and tape recorder – and don't forget to mute the volume on the television.

Chapter 12

The safety net

Editing and sub-editing

For aspiring sports journalists seeking employment at a newspaper or magazine, there are two profitable avenues to pursue. If you crave glamour and fame, the thrill of being there and rubbing shoulders with the movers and shakers, of seeing your name and observations in print, being out in the field is the better option. If your preference is for a less nomadic, more stable existence, perhaps even involving fairly regular contact with home, spouse and children, a desk job is for you. Having sampled each of these alternatives, I can only say that equipping yourself for both is highly recommended. Besides, finding full-time employment as a sub-editor can be a pragmatic way of advancing your writing aspirations while enhancing your sense of security. Once known and trusted by a sports desk for your diligence, knowledge and way with subordinate clauses, the transition to reporter is not illogical. As the likes of Matthew Engel, Simon Wilde (*Sunday Times* cricket correspondent) and Henry Winter (*Daily Telegraph* football correspondent) have shown, the road from down-table sub to marquee writer is not an untrodden one.

Having wittered on about the delights and perils of reporting, I therefore propose, in this chapter, to focus on the grossly underrated, wholly understated pleasures of being behind the scenes and comparatively anonymous.

THE EDITOR

It would not be too much of an exaggeration to state that, of all the uncontrollables a sports journalist has to contend with, the nature, attitudes and communication skills of his or her section editor are right up there with the weather. Find one who sees the world the way you do, cherishes what you do and how you do it (or no matter how you do it), and you can begin each day and each article with confidence unconfined. But no matter how experienced and justifiably self-assured you are, should that editor be replaced by someone who constantly questions your judgment, your phrasing, your jokes or your expenses claims, paranoia is guaranteed to creep in. Under those circumstances, even the hardiest hacks can be robbed of self-belief. In which case, given that this is a battle you are considerably unlikely to win, it is probably best to move on. Speaking as someone who has fallen foul of more than one editor, the best advice I can pass on is to urge you to recognise and accept that judging writing is subjective, a matter of taste. One man's notion of quality may be another's concept of garbage.

I asked two highly respected writer/editors to cite the qualities they most admired in a sports editor: the commonalities were not extensive. 'A cool head, a belief in quality, a passion for the subject, strong news sense, original ideas, and the ability to inspire others and nurture a range of voices,' listed Tim de Lisle, who won major industry awards for his creative work as editor of *Wisden Cricket Monthly*. To him, the contemporary who best fits this bill is Richard Williams. Once our sports editor at the *Independent on Sunday*, now chief sportswriter at the *Guardian*, he is the most versatile journalist it has ever been my privilege to work with. Nobody else's CV, certainly, spans the editorship of a pop weekly (*Melody Maker*) and a listings magazine (*Time Out*), fronting a TV rock music programme (*The Old Grey Whistle Test*) and being chief film reviewer (*Guardian*). Equally at home at a Grand Prix, a rugger international or a Test match, Williams remains one of the very few in this writer's experience who earn their corn as sportswriters but are equally good at orchestrating and overseeing the work of others.

Brian Oliver, a genial driving force on the *Daily Telegraph* sports desk when I worked for the paper in 1989 and for some years now an excellent *Observer* sports editor and African football specialist, plumped for the late, great Frank Nicklin. Having revolutionised newspaper presentation of sport at the *Sun*, it was Frank, a gruff character with a matey grin and a heart of homespun gold, who took on the somewhat less necessary task of supervising my initial steps at Hayters with endless patience, boundless enthusiasm and remarkably good humour. Oliver remembers him this way: 'Resourceful, inventive, innovative, hard-working, fearless, did a lot of work in the pub.' No less importantly, Frank was 'happy to have an argument with the editor/proprietor'.

The ideal sports editor, for me, is somebody with experience in the field. This permits empathy for, and understanding of, the reporter's often lonely lot as well as the vision to spot a fresh angle. At the same time, they must be able to stand back and see what so many of those consumed by the action in front of them cannot, namely the broader canvas. They have a boyishly undying affection for at least one sport and a firm understanding of why others command such devotion. They have few if any unshakeable prejudices and, of course, a sense of humour and proportion. They share their correspondents' enthusiasm while maintaining critical distance. They have a nose for news and want to be the first to publish it. They are perpetually on the phone to correspondents, keeping abreast of developments and gossip. They appreciate that they are in the infotainment business and put readers before the egos and sensitivities of staff, however marginally. They also appreciate the need to spare readers' eyesight by creative use of photographs and graphics. They have the capacity and, more important, the *desire* to acknowledge individuality. They follow their own muse but are also flexible, open to contradiction, persuasion or dissuasion. They also make reporters feel as much a part of the gang as those on the desk. They are also good managers, ensuring all criticism is constructive while protecting that team in the face of bullying from above and refusing to buy into the Wapping culture of rule by dread. In short, they make journalists, a notoriously grumpy breed, *want* to work for them. Not a job, then, for the meek or the wild. Curiously, the person in my experience who has come closest to this almost certainly unattainable ideal is Nick Pitt, briefly my *Sunday Times* sports editor at Wapping.

Perhaps the trickiest task facing a sports editor, any editor, is to decide which stories should be the most prominent. Indeed, the advent of separate sports sections has accentuated this: where once the biggest headache was how to lead the back page, now the front has to be considered. There is no longer any hiding place. The conventional meat and potatoes of the big match and its repercussions, once the no-brain option, now vies with tales of corruption, drug abuse and fiscal excess or chicanery, not to mention the slightest tiff between coach and player, chairman and manager or club and country. To help him prioritise, the sports news editor will compile a list of the day's major events, which reporters are covering them and what stories will have to be picked up from the wire services. Features and columns will be added to construct a running order whose main virtue must be flexibility.

Although one might imagine his department to be his personal fiefdom, free from interference, the truth is that the sports editor is subject to the same pressures and compromises as any other section leader. He will attend the paper's twice-daily conferences, where he will take directions from above: if the paper's editor quibbles with the running order, or suggests that another story or issue be covered, he will argue his corner in the knowledge that his superior is likely to have the final say. For all the inconvenience it may cause, it is always possible to revise that running order during the day and finalise it by late afternoon, enabling the production editor to design the pages, but this means being hostage to evening matches and breaking stories elsewhere, perhaps even a television programme. And the trouble with sport is that so much of it takes place in the evening: waiting for games to finish holds up the rest of the paper.

Television, in fact, is to be thanked for making desks more receptive and responsive to developments in the field. Where once a news or copy editor would spend the day scanning the wire services, wall-to-wall live transmissions of sporting events have brought sports desks closer to the action. If a surprise result is in the offing, a page may be torn up and redesigned during the course of a match, in which case the reporter who has been asked for 800 words and been writing accordingly, might receive a call halfway though the second half: 'Sorry old boy, but there's been a riot at Rochdale so I'm afraid we only want 200.' Early copy is always desired because, in theory, it makes life easier – and technological innovation, perversely, has brought deadlines forward, especially on a Friday – but again, flexibility, where possible, is more important.

There are risks, too, associated with headlines. Midweek football matches that kick off late or go into extra-time are the most regular thorns, forcing the sub-editor to write a non-committal headline that will hold until he can recast it for the next edition. Cricket also poses problems, the dangers of a pre-emptive strike even plainer: a first-edition headline on the Saturday of a Test match in England or the Caribbean (the latter because of the five-hour time difference), both of which would be written two-thirds of the way through the day's play, might read 'Flintoff's men home in on victory'; by the time stumps are drawn, however, the match might easily have been turned on its head, as happened that day in Trinidad in 1994, when England, chasing less than 200 at tea-time with a day to come, looked odds-on victors until Curtly Ambrose reduced them to 40 for eight en route to 46 all out. I was working at the *Independent* that night and I doubt passions were running any higher in the press box at Port of Spain.

I was also on duty, this time at the *Guardian,* that night in the late winter of 1999 when a magnificent innings by Brian Lara, possibly the best I have ever witnessed, led West Indies to an improbable one-wicket victory over the mighty Australians. Sky Sports covered the climax live; I don't think I have ever heard a group of Englishmen so roused by a contest between two overseas teams; the only people in the office not rooting for Lara were a couple of Australian subs. Much earlier that day, Mike Atherton had announced he was not going to be fit to participate in England's impending World Cup campaign: that was the designated back-page lead. I argued quite forcefully that the West Indies' feat was not only good news as opposed to bad, but worthier of prominence; support, fortunately, was near-unanimous. Was I proud to be working for a newspaper not only prepared to put joy before pain, but a foreign story ahead of what was, after all, merely a little local difficulty? Do Popes pray?

THE SUB-EDITOR

The relationship between reporters and subs is a peculiar, complex one: not quite Cain and Abel but not exactly made in heaven either. It is unquestionably one of mutual dependency, albeit frequently based on intense mutual distrust.

On the one hand, the reporter depends on the sub to make good his errors or oversights, resist the urge to introduce any mistakes of their own creation, edit his handiwork sensitively, and sell it. Selling an article means bedecking it with appropriate 'furniture', the collective trade name for the headline, subheading, pullout quotes and so forth (see Glossary). These disparate elements should feed off each other, not duplicate one another: a headline reading 'Cole brings goals to Newcastle' should not be followed by a longer subheading stating 'Cole grabs glory as Newcastle bid for Europe place' but rather 'Born-again striker puts spring in Geordies' step'. The most important item of furniture is the headline, which should make it abundantly plain that not reading on would be a crime against both self and humanity.

On the other hand, the sub depends on the reporter to file copy on time, know their onions, make as few errors as possible, write within three or four lines of the designated length, and not be too precious if an alteration or two is required, whether for clarity or fact. Although they are now easily contactable by mobile phone, which many regard as a curse, reporters should make what are termed 'check calls' to ascertain whether their copy has arrived safely and the sub-editor has any queries. The latter will check any unfamiliar spellings or confusing details, and perhaps point out something he has seen during the television transmission that the reporter has missed, or erroneously elected to gloss over. To ring up and hear the words 'no queries' shouted across the office can be more unnerving than reassuring: the suspicion that one's copy has been savaged is never far away. And while most reporters of my acquaintance imagine subs as envious monsters wilfully defacing their prose, just as many subs I know feel they could do the reporter's job a good deal better. That harmony is at all possible is something of a minor miracle, helped as the cause is, admittedly, by the fact that, with the exception of squabbles involving the more prominent and stubborn correspondents, the sub almost always has the final say.

Kim Fletcher, formerly editor of the *Independent on Sunday*, asserts that, whatever changes might emerge in the coming years, so long as there are newspapers skilful subs will be in demand:

What you tend not to hear from writing journalists is praise for colleagues who can synthesise copy, pictures and headlines to create compelling pages; direct a reader's eye with clever design; take information from diverse sources and turn it into a clear narrative. What you will never hear from journalists is that their copy is frequently ungrammatical, sometimes barely literate, usually over-written and typically misspelled. There are many writers who have won awards for the cleverness of their subs and few who have not been rescued from disaster by them.[1]

HEADLINES

If I had a penny for every time a sportsman or reader told me they thought reporters were responsible for concocting the oft-exaggerated and sometimes downright inflammatory headlines to which English newspapers are especially partial, I would be in a position to launch a takeover bid for Rupert Murdoch's NewsCorp and buy a controlling interest in the United States. Most memorable was a PBI (Press Box Incident) during the England–West Indies Lord's Test of 1988 involving the chairman of the home selectors, a former national captain by the name of Peter May. Everyone referred to May by his three initials, PBH. That morning, he stunned all and sundry by entering the press box. A normally reticent chap who had long acquired a deep mistrust of the Fourth Estate – dating back to the 1958–59 Ashes tour when his fiancée's presence attracted the interest of the popular papers – he had a few polite if well-chosen words with Paul Weaver, then cricket correspondent of the *Daily Mirror*: he'd been offended, not unsurprisingly, by that morning's back-page headline – 'Nuts to May'. Despite having spent most of his life being alternately hailed and criticised by the press, he was still convinced Weaver had been the perpetrator.

Even with the most unexciting material to play with, headlines can be tremendous fun to write. Their raison d'être, of course, is to act, not so much as the story's shop window as the over-eager sales assistant, grabbing you by the lapels and dragging you inside for a longer peek. It is that requisite sense of immediacy that lies behind the notesy style: no definite articles or personal pronouns here. They may span one column or the entire page: the wider the headline, the fewer the 'decks' or rows. The heavies tend to favour the wide and the wordy, the tabloids the big, the minimalist and the multi-layered. The one rule of thumb, if a headline runs for more than one deck, is that the top line should be longer than the rest: an F-shape rather than an L-shape.

Headlines should always contain at least one name. For a match report, whether or not the final score follows underneath, it should sum up the outcome while singling out at least one key player and, if appropriate, one of the teams. Let's say Manchester United, in poor form, sneak a win at Wigan thanks to a goal from Alan Smith. Depending on the space and hence words available to you, 'Smith strike boosts stuttering United' would do, or 'Stuttering United boosted by Smith strike'. Better, though, to stick wherever possible to active verbs. Again, for the same reasons such unwritten rules apply to the copy itself, exclamation marks, aka 'screamers', should be heard but not seen. Even the tabloids have been known to adhere to such restrictions.

The chief factors to consider are the length and depth of the headline and the size of type. If your match leads the page the production editor/page designer will apportion it the largest headline in terms of typesize, number of decks and probably width, too. The larger the type, the fewer the words available, the greater premium placed on your vocabulary and felicitous way with words. When I began subbing, I had to do a character-count: each letter counted as one, bar the skinny ones (i, j, l, r, t), which are worth half, and the fat ones (m and w), worth one-and-a-half. Because of the density of copy on newspaper pages, white space is much valued, so a three-quarter-full line is deemed preferable to a full one. Then, once I was satisfied, for the benefit of the printers, I would scribble the headline on the top of the sheet of copy, along with the column width, typesize and whether the copy should be bold, italicised or roman. My best and neatest scrawl would also be used to cross out and rewrite sentences and words, link up passages disrupted by biro, ensure that each page was properly numbered and finished with an 'm/f' (more follows) and, finally, that I had the last word – 'Ends'. Ah, such innocent, simple days.

Computer design programs have swept away nearly all those time-consuming obligations. All the requisite format details are stored, from column widths to fonts, though stylistic changes within copy mean you still need to be able to tell your Times New Romans from your Century Bolds. If your headline busts (breaks the confines of the layout) you will know straightaway. Similarly, the computer will inform you, in terms of the number of lines, how much longer or shorter the copy is in relation to the space allotted. Splitting a paragraph in two, or more, is one well-worn tactic when it comes to making up any shortfall, likewise the substitution of a longer word. Conversely, you can trim overmatter by deleting as little as a single word. Note the length of the last line in a paragraph: if it comprises a short word, through the wonders of technology, you may even be able to squeeze the paragraph, shrinking it in a way that is indiscernible to the naked eye. The same, no less helpfully, applies to headlines, via a process known as kerning.

All this automation has had a beneficial impact on the craft of sub-editing, freeing exponents to focus on the creative side. Though they, too, are subject to editing, by the editor and/or the revise sub, down-table subs are entertainers as well as correctors and adjusters. Many, indeed, are paid accordingly, especially on the red-tops. Filing a cracking match report, after all, is no more worthy of awe or respect than a ripping headline: both are created under pressure from the clock. Tabloid readers in particular are accustomed to having their news packaged with irreverent front-page rib-ticklers such as 'Freddie Starr Ate My Hamster' and 'Up Yours Delors': headlines sell more papers to newsagent browsers than reporters do. So why waste words – and why not have some fun? 'Wigan shoulder arms as Reds start firing' and 'Smith ends famine as Reds get hungry' both make the essential points while introducing metaphor and balance. Puns are permissible, even encouraged, albeit not if gratuitous. Feel free, too, to draw in outside references, as in 'Smith strikes as Reds finally emerge from under bed'. The odds are that regular readers of most newspapers in the western world will be familiar with the paranoia about 'Reds under the bed' during the anti-Communist witchhunt of the 1950s, though in ten years' time that may no longer be so.

Be wary, in other words, of asking too much of the reader. As with the reporter's use of non-sporting allusions, it is a case of assessing – never a precise science – the probability of a decent share of the audience being familiar with the reference. On one shift at the *Independent* I was rather chuffed when the revise sub, the sub who subs the subs, approved a headline containing no fewer than three nods to Pink Floyd. Well, the golfer's name was Ray Floyd:

how could a self-respecting rock-bore resist? Like Simon Barnes and his mention of Sam Goldwyn, I felt sure that a goodly proportion of the readership would 'get it': my insurance policy lay in the fact that the headline made sense regardless of whether or not *Dark Side of the Moon* meant anything to the reader.

CUTTING COPY

This, too, is now a far more precise art. Until computers began replacing copysetters in the late 1980s, it was a hit-or-miss affair: you would do a word-count and delete to fit, knowing that the compositors fiddling around with all that piping hot metal would be the ultimate arbiters: only they would know exactly how long the copy actually ran. While you would usually have an opportunity to make the requisite cuts on a page proof, it was far easier to cut from the bottom, hence the 'inverted pyramid' structure for news stories, allowing as it does for the least germane and/or necessary information to be comfortably sliced off. As mentioned earlier, times have changed. No longer do sports reporters structure their reports for ease of trimming.

So long as you have a decent vocabulary, reference material at your fingertips and the ability to capture the essence of a sentence in a more concise fashion, chipping out words and linking passages should never prove too arduous, though the original unedited copy must always be preserved for reference, primarily as evidence in case of a dispute between writer and sub, or between the paper and a party pressing a case for libel. Priority lies with the facts: preserve as many as possible.

For all that leaving a story untouched can give the impression that you are not bothering to read it properly, change for change's sake serves no purpose whatsoever. The desire to leave your imprint on somebody else's work should be staunchly resisted – unless, that is, you sincerely believe you can improve it, either through a more pertinent fact, a more succinct sentence or more appropriate word choices (it is not exactly unknown for reporters to get caught up in the heat of the moment and over-dramatise). Talk the reporter through any such alterations if you have time. The best normally find it.

HOUSE STYLE

When you arrive for your first day as a sub-editor on a newspaper or magazine, make sure you request a copy of the house style 'book' and keep it to hand at all times. A small pamphlet at most, it will outline how that particular publication treats copy. Do quotes take single speechmarks (*Observer*) or double (pretty much every other major newspaper in England)? Are numbers spelt out one to ten and numeralised thereafter (*The Times*, *Daily Mail*) or one to nine (pretty much every other national newspaper in England bar the *Observer*, which opts for eleven and so forth)? Is it judgement or judgment, instill or instil? Gypsy with an initial cap (capital letter) or gypsy without – or simply traveller? Kickoff or kick-off, fullback or full-back, all-rounder or allrounder? Consistency is all. Master these small but vital points and you will save the revise sub some time; fluff them consistently and future employment on that desk may prove elusive.

PROOFREADING

One time-honoured practice that does seem, regrettably, to be falling into disuse is that of proofing, or stone-subbing. On the sports desks I have worked most regularly, the *Sunday Times*, the *Guardian* and the *Independent*, I would proof pages before the first edition was put to bed – depending on the clock and the weight of reading – or at the very least well before the deadline for the second. In the summer, I would be asked to scan a blown-up photocopy of the cricket page, whose individual components would originally have been read and subbed by a number of different people: this overview facilitated detection of factual errors and inconsistencies. This was especially crucial during the latter stages of a Championship race, particularly pre-Internet: a reporter at one match might be following the others on Ceefax in the press box, but even if he was utterly convinced he was up-to-date in his calculations of the overall picture, to be human is to be imperfect.

The mounting pile of pages, however, compounded by a reluctance to raise the freelance subbing budget, has made this type of insurance policy less practicable. One example, however petty it might seem, highlights the not-so hidden costs of cost-saving. Writing in the *Sunday Telegraph*, Scyld Berry quoted Duncan Fletcher, the England coach, as saying the previous day that he would send 'at this stage five' reserve players to Perth during the impending Ashes tour. On the facing page, Steve James announced that the ECB 'have decided that six players' would do so.[2] Since it is not uncommon for English newspapers to have four reporters at a major event these days, bolstered by the ghostly pronouncements of a participant or ex-player, the potential for contradictory information has never been more obvious. Just as page-proofing is an invaluable aid in spotting duplications in headlines (another no-no), so it can throw up textual inconsistencies. Eliminating such sources of mistrust is crucial. Unfortunately, for all the time saved by new technology, writer-subs, the latest bright idea for improving efficiency (management-speak for reducing costs), suggests the editing burden, as Fletcher contends, will continue to mount.

EXERCISE

After completing a feature designated for a specific publication, imagine how it might look on the page and supply suitable 'furniture' – headline, standfirst and pullout quotes – according to the style indicated by close inspection of the publication concerned. Calculate, as precisely as possible, how many characters are required, and write accordingly.

Chapter 13

Views from the top

Let me introduce you, sheepishly, to Ahmer Khokhar, a foxy terrier who has overcome innumerable obstacles to find a kennel he can call home.

We met a decade ago in the Lord's press box. I had overheard a young Asian man sitting quietly at the back being harangued by an experienced journalist who had objected to his presence as a 'non-journalist'. The reporter in question, while a good friend, should, I felt, have known better than to trample on a young man's dream, and I duly apprised him of this. First, though, I went over to introduce myself and tell the young man not to take the blindest notice. Thanks in the main to a new-fangled piece of technology known as email, we struck up a mentor–pupil relationship; a recent university graduate, he pestered me incessantly: definitely a journalist in the making. He introduced me to his father, and kept me abreast of his myriad troubles: horrifying and alienating his parents both with his choice of would-be career and conversion to Christianity; fleeing England to escape an arranged marriage; striving to overcome a speech impediment. Early-morning phonecalls from various temporary homes in Australia were not infrequent. I have never met anyone more determined.

Come 2006, Ahmer was earning a decent living from Melbourne, reporting for a variety of national and regional titles in Britain, India and Australasia. A precarious, hand-to-mouth existence had blossomed into a regular supply of commissions. In pursuing his goal, he has observed the essential unwritten tenets of the freelance. I could fill another book on this subject alone, but, for now, here are the Alternative Ten Commandments:

1 Don't go for the obvious angle, or even the second most obvious – the newspaper's staff correspondents will probably have both covered.
2 Once you have had one article published in a particular newspaper or magazine, and established a working relationship, keep offering more ideas.
3 Do not, however, bombard desks with so many ideas that they invite suspicion as to depth of thought or, worse, you are labelled a pest (the tell-tale sign is silence: as somebody, probably Woody Allen, once observed of the movie industry, this is not so much a dog-eat-dog world as dog-doesn't-return-dog's calls).
4 Look for niches in which you can specialise, the more the merrier.

5. Recycle and re-angle stories for different markets, always ensuring every client receives something different.
6. Never kick up a fuss when your copy is rewritten – accept and move on.
7. Never, unless you have ethical objections, or the fee is too insignificant or offered by an unreliable source, decline a commission: the day does have 24 hours, after all, and there are 168 of those available each week.
8. Always chase payments (which can be notoriously and disgracefully slow), targeting the accounts department or even the managing editor if necessary, but not so forcefully that you anger and alienate – unless, that is, your bank manager absolutely insists.
9. If one door closes, have another up your sleeve that you can batter down.
10. Treat rough and smooth with equal mistrust.

'I started by interviewing Australian cricketers playing county and league cricket and selling the results to the corresponding regional newspapers in the UK,' relates Ahmer.

> *It was hard work but proved to be profitable as I was able to write follow-up articles and also season previews and reviews. I suddenly discovered a niche market for my work that nobody knew existed.*
>
> *Also, in Australia there are several high-profile former Gaelic footballers at Australian Rules football clubs. In general the Irish broadsheets had very few if any writers in Australia so I started to freelance for the Irish daily and Sunday papers, which helped to establish me as an Australian correspondent for both Irish and British regional papers.*
>
> *At this stage my focus was purely sport but a reduction in the numbers of Australians in county cricket and a lack of work from British nationals – some of whom still insist on receiving copy on spec [short for speculative, meaning uncommissioned and unpaid unless published] – resulted in my expanding into news, politics and business stories.*
>
> *I now have regular customers in the form of Irish, Scottish, Welsh and English papers who agree – as well they ought – to pay kill fees for unpublished work. Last year [2005] I was also published on a weekly basis in one of Australia's biggest Sunday papers, the* Sun Herald. *I discovered there was a huge demand for interviews with Australian cricketers, many of whom knew me from my days of interviewing them for British regional papers.*
>
> *It's been an amazing turnaround when I consider that less than five years ago I was living in Manchester as a frustrated medical sales representative. Despite the difficulties – no holidays for one thing – I have no regrets and I know that I am one of the lucky ones who is doing a job he loves and whose dreams have come true.*

By way of spreading the responsibility, and demonstrating that I am neither alone in my views and prejudices nor the only sports journalist whose experiences are worth passing on, I sent a questionnaire to the sports journalists I hold in the highest regard. They include editors, reporters, chief correspondents, foreign correspondents, feature writers, columnists and sub-editors with extensive records of distinguished service in the world of newspapers and agencies, magazines and websites, broadcasting and books, from Britain, Australia, India and South Africa. I will not embarrass them by revealing their ages, but suffice to say I have intentionally consulted a number who plied their trade in an age when a single telephone shared by a dozen reporters cooped up in a cramped wooden press box devoid of electricity or warmth was considered a luxury. Seldom have so many skills and virtues been represented by so few.

For ease of translation I have listed the questions and relevant comments followed by the initials of the respondent. First, though, the roll-call. The accompanying thumbnail CVs focus on the respondents' accomplishments specifically within sports journalism; many have dabbled in more serious waters, and worked in broadcasting, which lends their observations a suitably broad command of proportion and perspective.

I should also point out that one or two questions were more open to confusion than others, notably on the subject of editors: many thought I was specifically referring to editors of newspapers or magazines rather than sports editors specifically, which was my fault not theirs. The results, however, were so absorbing, and the comments so universal, so varied and so instructive, I have not sought to distinguish between the differing interpretations: after all, an editor is an editor, regardless of subject or section. On occasion, I have failed miserably to resist the urge to join in; I also apologise in advance for making any of my respondents' cheeks take on the pallour of a fresh raspberry (even if I have had to omit their myriad awards for reasons of space). Some of them, indeed, will make each other blush. I can assure you that, since none was apprised of the identities of their fellow correspondents, mutual back-scratching and ego-massaging were not on the menu. (Note: Year in brackets denotes contributor's work at time of writing.)

Scyld Berry (SB): Chief cricket correspondent, *Sunday Telegraph* (2006), *Observer*, *Sunday Correspondent*; contributing editor, *The Wisden Cricketer*.

Andy Colquhoun (AQ): Editor, *Rugby World South Africa*, *SA Rugby Annual* (2006); SABC radio commentator (2006); rugby union writer, *Sunday Telegraph* (2006); deputy sports editor, football correspondent, cricket writer, *Birmingham Post*.

Ted Corbett (TC): Chief cricket correspondent, *Daily Star*; sportswriter, the *Sun*, the *Daily Mirror*, the *Daily Telegraph*, *The People*, *The Scotsman*, *Scotland on Sunday*, *The Herald* and *Sunday Herald* in Glasgow, *The Hindu* and *Sportstar* in India (2006).

Peter Deeley (PD): Chief cricket correspondent, *Daily Telegraph*; reporter, *Guardian*, *Melbourne Age*.

Tim De Lisle (TdeL): Editor, *Wisden Cricketers' Almanack* and *Wisden Cricket Monthly*; chief cricket correspondent, *Independent on Sunday*; columnist, *The Times*, *Independent*, *The Wisden Cricketer* and *Cricinfo* (2006).

Stephen Fay (SF): Cricket reporter, *Independent on Sunday*, *The Wisden Cricketer*, *Wisden Cricketers' Almanack* (2006); editor, *Wisden Cricket Monthly*.

Gideon Haigh (GH): Cricket writer, *Guardian*, *Melbourne Age*, *Sydney Morning Herald*, *Observer Sports Monthly*, *Cricinfo*, *The Wisden Cricketer* (2006).

Murray Hedgcock (MH): London Bureau Chief, News Limited of Australia; reporter and sub-editor, *Geelong Advertiser*, *The News* (Adelaide); sports editor, *South London Advertiser*.

David Hopps (DH): Cricket, football and swimming reporter, feature writer and columnist, *Guardian* and *Observer* (2006); cricket correspondent, *Yorkshire Post*.

Rob Kitson (RK): Rugby union correspondent, *Guardian* (2006); sportswriter, Reuters, *Sunday Correspondent*, Hayters.

Kevin Mitchell (KM): Chief sports writer, *The Observer* (2006); investigative reporter, *Sunday Times*; sub-editor and boxing writer, *London Daily News*.

Paul Newman (PN): Deputy sports editor (2006), reporter and sub-editor, *Daily Mail*; reporter and cricket editor, *Sunday Telegraph*; reporter and sub-editor, *Daily Telegraph*.

Brian Oliver (BO): Sports editor, football writer, *The Observer* (2006); football writer; sub-editor, reporter, deputy sports editor, *Daily Telegraph*.

Steve Pinder (SP): Co-editor, *FullTime*; sports editor, *City Limits*; ice hockey and minority sports correspondent, *Independent*.

Nick Pitt (NP): Golf and tennis correspondent (2006), *Inside Track* reporter, boxing writer, sports editor, *Sunday Times*; chief sportswriter, *London Daily News*.

Mark Ray (MR): Cricket correspondent, *Melbourne Age* and *Sydney Morning Herald*; sub-editor, *Sydney Morning Herald* (2006).

Brian Scovell (BS): Staff football and cricket reporter, *Daily Mail*; football and cricket writer, *Sunday Telegraph*.

Sharda Ugra (SU): Deputy editor, *India Today* (2006); Sports reporter/sub-editor *Mid-Day*; Special Correspondent, *The Hindu*.

Richard Weekes (RW): Page designer, *Daily Mail* (2006); sports editor, *Sunday Times*; night sports editor and baseball writer, *Independent*; sub-editor, *Guardian*; Scottish sports editor, *Sunday Telegraph*; oversaw modernisation of longest established quality national newspaper in Kuwait.

HOW AND WHY DID YOU BECOME A SPORTS JOURNALIST?

'I simply drifted into the business – and not in the fashion we are told is typical in British experience: the drudgery of collecting local soccer results, or watching junior matches in appalling weather, keen to avoid upsetting local worthies. The first newspaper report of any sort I wrote (when a bank clerk) was on a badminton league final in country Victoria in 1948 or 1949, when the team in which I played beat the hot favourites. The motivation? To get publicity in the local bi-weekly for my teammates and friends (if I didn't write it, no-one else would do so).' *(MH)*

'Lying in hospital for much of two years I started listening to Raymond Glendenning and Howard Marshall on the ward's only radio and fell in love with football and cricket. Decided

I wanted to be a Fleet Street sportswriter. My hero was Tom Phillips of the *Herald* (I snaffled the one copy and read every word!). Back at home in the Isle of Wight, I started going to watch local matches and came home to write reports. My mother found one and took it to the editor of the IOW *Mercury* and said "My son is a better football writer than Fred whatever his name is!" I was 13 and was hired for 7/6d a game to write about the reserves. That year I contacted the *Daily Mail* and asked if I could come to Northcliffe House to see the paper being produced. I went on my own, something that would never happen now, and the conducted tour started at midnight. I left school at 15, worked as a road licence clerk at the County Council, while studying for four A GCEs and the two National Council of Journalist Awards, by post, and passed all of them. By 17 I was working full time at the IOW *Guardian* and for four years wrote most of it. Fantastic experience!' *(BS)*

'By accident, following my involuntary departure from the deputy editorship of the *Independent on Sunday* in 1992. I had been a generous colleague to the sports editor and, as a reward, he allowed me to do 350 words each Saturday in the summer – at 3.30 and close of play – on a county [cricket] game. I was constantly aware of how much I had to learn about a specialist subject, but I had a reporter's instinct, and I delighted in the work. My break came on the Saturday of the Oval Test against South Africa in 1994. Simon Kelner decided a sidebar might be necessary and my county game had finished early. Devon Malcolm obliged by taking nine for 57.

'I became editor of *Wisden Cricket Monthly* in 1999 because I had already edited a monthly magazine and I had become a committed cricket writer. The learning curve grew a bit steeper then, and has barely levelled off since. Recently Mike Atherton said I didn't know anything about cricket. (I replied that I must know something because I had learned a bit from him.) But the accusation did not upset me. I remain a reporter after all, and I know more about journalism than Mike does, though he is learning.' *(SF)*

'The Kemsley Group, which owned the *Evening Press* at York in those days [1951], sent a training officer called Alf Dow round every week and when he asked what ambition I had I told him I wanted to be a cricket correspondent. He told me, in blunt terms, that it was a step too far and that I should learn to be a proper journalist first.' *(TC)*

'At 53 I still needed a job of some sort having fallen out with [editor] Donald Trelford at the *Observer*, where I was home news editor. I freelanced for a bit for the *Daily Telegraph* then out of the blue their sports editor Ted Barratt offered me the job of cricket correspondent. They needed someone who knew cricket but had a strong news background. I had done sport as a youngster (football mostly in Birmingham) and during a freelancing period in Australia had done a lot of cricket for UK papers, including the Packer revolution. Now I still needed a job to keep body and soul together. I would have been tiddlywinks correspondent if he had asked.' (*PD*)

'*Maitland Mercury*, New South Wales, February 1970. Because I love to write.' *(KM)*

'I was 29 and joined the *Stratford Express* in East London. Happened to start on sports desk then did general subbing. Just wanted to get into journalism.' *(NP)*

'Because when I was 10 I thought that Don Warters, who covered Leeds United for the *Yorkshire Evening Post*, had the best job in the world. Then I came to my senses and decided that I wanted to cover cricket instead, because it is a sport that still allows an attempt at decent writing, and retains a degree of honesty. I wanted to write and I loved cricket. Seemed easier than working.' *(DH)*

'The journalism came before the sport. I went to university with vague ideas that I wanted to be a journalist, but only once I had worked on a newspaper as a proofreader during a sabbatical year in Mexico did this become an overriding goal. I threw myself into student journalism in my final two years at university, and here my longstanding interest in sport fed increasingly into the student journalism. My involvement in student politics led to a suggestion from a friend that the *Morning Star* might be looking for graduates. After I graduated I approached them with the suggestion that I would like to work for their sports department, and they accepted immediately.' *(RW)*

'Thought it would make a pleasant vacation job. And thus it has remained.' *(SB)*

'Because a vacancy came up on the weekly paper where I was working, and because I'd always wanted to be a sports journalist, ever since my days as a paperboy when I used to read the papers avidly.' *(BO)*

'My ambition was to not be one and continue being a news hack although I'd earlier worshipped Terry Brindle (*Yorkshire Post* cricket correspondent) and believed that he had the best job in the world.' *(AQ)*

'Sort of fell into it when the sports editor at the magazine I worked at left and, as a contributor to the section, I took over.' *(SP)*

'I had done a bit of writing for my student paper and got a summer job making Reg Hayter's coffee. It was supposed to be a six-week trial but I never returned for my second year at uni.' *(RK)*

'It was always what I wanted to do. I used to produce a little news sheet at junior school (writing out several copies by hand), started work experience with my local paper at 14 and joined them at 16. I was made sports editor when I was 18, basically because I didn't enjoy news and local crime stories.' *(PN)*

'I began as a newspaper photographer covering everything, including sport, mainly Australian football. This was in Launceston, Tasmania in 1983. I was in the middle of four seasons of Sheffield Shield cricket for that state so I had a strong background on the field.' *(MR)*

'Because the *Independent on Sunday* was launching [1990] and they couldn't persuade anyone better to be their cricket correspondent. The sports editor was Richard Williams, who I had worked with in arts and features at *The Times*. He knew I was mad about cricket and he was open-minded (or desperate) enough to give me a go.' *(TdeL)*

'It was exactly the same month as Sachin Tendulkar made his Test debut [November 1989]. It is the only thing we have in common. It sounds utterly fanciful, but I wanted to convey the experience of watching sport in a way that people would think that sportswriting can actually be an art. It was very much regarded as back of the paper, mundane stuff in India.' *(SU)*

WHAT HAVE BEEN THE MOST BENEFICIAL AND COUNTER-PRODUCTIVE ASPECTS OF TELEVISION IN TERMS OF SPORTS JOURNALISM?

'TV coverage means the reporter has valuable access to the camera-eye view and often to endless replays, slow-motion sequences, etc., which can clarify an incident or a phase of an event. At the same time this can become all-important (and you may get bogged down in detail), so that you risk focusing on highlights – or lowlights – without necessarily setting these into the broader context.' *(MH)*

'Counter-productive: 1) Newspaper deadlines had to be tailored to suit the needs of TV deadlines (after all TV was/is the sport paymaster). 2) The print media has been forced into an obsession with soccer by TV's omnipresence and wealth. Productive? I suppose the fact that in the press box with all the TV screens we now have the chance to replay close decisions and come up with the right answer rather than a guess.' *(PD)*

'Much wider access for the viewing public. Much wider access to the drivel that passes for commentary.' *(KM)*

'Benefits: the money made available to sport, which unquestionably has made it "box office" as far as newspapers are concerned. There wouldn't be as many of us working in sports journalism without it. And the pictures themselves help to explain what goes on in a game, and show up human error. Counter-productive: over-hyping tends to seep through to the higher echelons of newspapers, and senior editors/assistants/newsdesks often make unrealistic assumptions and demands based on what they see/hear on TV – i.e. they blow things out of proportion. Nothing is worse than a page preview of Middlesbrough v Charlton that's there just because the game's on the telly.' *(BO)*

'The slow-motion replay has been the greatest benefit. The correspondent doesn't have to watch every ball, as he had to before. The downside is that most cricket supporters have also seen the match, so accuracy is more essential than it was in the age of [Neville] Cardus, and more interpretation is required.' *(SB)*

'The growth of televised sport has in turn fed the growth of printed sports journalism, so there are many more opportunities for writers and sub-editors to work in sport. One negative effect is that print journalists tend to genuflect to TV over the stories they run. Just because Sky TV has run a report saying Manager X has been linked with Club Y is no reason to treat it any more seriously than if it had appeared in a red-top tabloid – but few seem willing to learn that lesson.' *(RW)*

'That we actually have a proper record of events but now rely on frequently anodyne quotes from the performer to interpret those events.' *(AQ)*

'The most beneficial is, of course, increasing the number of sports that can be covered – in theory. The counter-productive side has been the growth of pseudo-sports and the replacement of trained journalists by ex-players and "faces" who have the communicative skills of a log of wood.' *(SP)*

'The best thing is the information the cameras bring into play. The worst thing is that more fans feel they don't need to read about the game the next day.' *(TdeL)*

'If well-produced, television gives everyone, journalists included, a better idea of the sport they are covering and its inner workings. To use an example from cricket, you see the game differently through the Super Slo-Mo and learn more when Ian Chappell speaks about captaincy or tactics. When banalities, superficialities and clichés find their way into print, you know print journalists are not doing their jobs.' *(SU)*

'We're now the second or third draft of history, rather than the first. We have to be better, more imaginative, more illuminating. That's both beneficial *and* challenging.' *(GH)*

WHAT MAKES A GOOD INVESTIGATIVE REPORTER?

'Cheek and a thick skin. Lacking both, I never was one.' *(MH)*

'Patience, intuition, willingness to take risks, the ability to write a compelling narrative – and money.' *(SF)*

'A desire to write the story that the subject doesn't want.' *(BS)*

'Hunger for facts, a huge curiosity, a ratlike cunning.' *(PD)*

'Courage.' *(KM)*

'Inquisitiveness and doggedness.' *(NP)*

'The refusal to take no for an answer.' *(SB)*

'Mistrust, inquisitiveness and a sense of righteous indignation.' *(AQ)*

'Fearlessness, curiosity, doggedness, determination, resourcefulness, and the ability to sift the wheat from the chaff. And, naturally, a passion for sport.' *(BO)*

'The continued belief that it is important that people know about things.' *(DH)*

'A tape recorder that works.' *(RK)*

'Thick skin, being a good gossip, getting a buzz out of finding out something new or uncovering an injustice.' *(PN)*

'The willingness to ask not the one probing question but to ask many questions of as many people as it takes to find the answer.' *(SU)*

'The selfsame qualities you require to be a good reporter. All reporters, by definition, should investigate.' *(RS)*

'Investigative journalist is a tautology. If it's not investigative – that is, if it's not revealing something that the unpaid observer could not see themselves – then it's not journalism.' *(GH)*

DO NEWSPAPERS HAVE ANOTHER CENTURY IN THEM?

'I am increasingly doubtful. My own sons, for instance, never buy a paper. Sportswriters can only do their best to provide a more thoughtful, flavoured, even "literary" cover of their topic, which can offer a more permanent record and lasting appeal than is available on the transient web, where you can go back to the record, but are less likely to do so because of its "Now!" atmosphere and urgency.' *(MH)*

'Yes, though the form might be different. Newspapers may become more specialised and smaller, and their writers will be expected to write for the web and blog away as well.' *(SF)*

'They should survive forever. Reporters should go to the heart of it. Entertain. Pass on their love of their sports to the readers.' *(BS)*

'I doubt it. In a hundred years' time everybody will probably be walking around with tiny hand-held computers on which they can read/hear the news. All journalists, not just sportswriters, will have to adapt or die. As they always have had to do.' *(PD)*

'Definitely. They might not look like newspapers in a hundred years' time, but they will still be portable and easy to consume.' *(KM)*

'I doubt whether newspapers have 100 years left. But what will enable them to survive as long as possible is good writing. If newspapers contain reportage there is no incentive to buy them, the Internet will suffice. Good writing, which may invite a second reading, will make future readers buy papers.' *(SB)*

'Yes, but maybe the demand for quantity will transmute into a demand for quality. Writers have to carry on doing what they do best now – inform, entertain, irritate, speculate, etc.' *(BO)*

'I'm not sure. Anyone under about 25 has grown up reading from the screen of a mobile phone and maybe they will have no appetite for stories of more than 40 words featuring words of more than four characters. Sportswriting will be at the mercy of whatever kind of global society we become – in an "alliterate" future all forms of writing are in danger. But people will always watch sport and as long as some of them continue to enjoy intelligent interpretation there will be a place for the McIlvanneys and Barneses – it's just the rest of us that are under threat.' *(AQ)*

'Yes, and the sportswriters' task is the same as any print journalist – to offer a permanent, factual, entertaining record of an event, an individual, a news story.' *(PN)*

'No – or, if yes, in a much reduced form. Sportswriters have to stop conning their readers with cynical churning out of tired, witless quotes. Facts are readily obtainable, so the need is for entertainment and insight.' *(DH)*

'Doubtful. Sportswriters must do what they have so far failed to do, at least in Australia, and that is give readers what TV cannot. Here I still think we do newspaper match reports the same as they were done in the 1960s. We give a record of events with some cursory analysis and a few quotes alongside the more analytical columnist. I've always felt a match report should be more analytical, more theme-based – pick a key event/decision and go into it in depth – with the bare facts in the scoreboard and an accompanying fact box. The *Age* and *Sunday Age* have tried this but they have rarely designated someone in the office to do the facts in consultation with the writers at the match. It quickly became an added job for the reporters and became a burden. Only one sports editor has answered my question as to what is a good match report in the late-twentieth/early twenty-first century.' *(MR)*

'No. And Australian newspapers provide a good case for the medium's extinction.' *(GH)*

'I am an optimist who thinks people will always read the papers . . . and the sports pages in them. Sportswriters need to be able to convey detail and drama more than anything else; not indulgently but inclusively to draw the reader into the experience when they could not be there. We all see Michael Schumacher race and see him on TV, but if you are writing about him, the reader would want to know, what's he REALLY like? Tall, short? Grumpy? Aloof? Cheerful? Distant? Small details keep people hooked into stories. Also, sportswriters should refrain from trying to be the custodians of morality or some Utopian sporting ideal. A sense of perspective – it's only a game – from time to time is a useful thing and I don't think the reader of the future wants to be lectured to. The world is already full of boring old farts. I'm quoting my friend Rohit Brijnath here: "Strike buttons, entertain, move, educate, inform or make people laugh – as a writer, you must do one of them."' *(SU)*

WHAT WOULD YOU ADVISE A NEWCOMER TO THE PRESS BOX?

'Head down, eyes and ears open, make friends with your neighbours, check your laptop works – and learn fast where are the sources of information.' *(MH)*

'To concentrate just as hard on learning to write as on knowing the gossip.' *(SF)*

'Be patient. Ask questions. Don't keep tossing opinions in until asked. READ! I used to read six books a week in my formative years. That's how you learn to write.' *(BS)*

'Listen. Don't fall into the trap of becoming an instant, opinionated bore who is never wrong. There are far too many of them in there already. Try not to go with the herd. You'd be amazed how many times the herd is wrong.' *(KM)*

'Write conversational English.' *(NP)*

'Don't take the big shots too seriously. Try to find an ally of like mind and offer occasional favours, hopefully reciprocal.' *(RW)*

'It's tough out there. Keep trying.' *(BO)*

'That their real training has just begun and that they should keep their ears open and never carry an i-pod.' *(AQ)*

'The first, second and third qualification to be a journalist is the desire to be a journalist and the temperament to be excited by a story.' *(SB)*

'Be yourself. Develop a "voice". Don't slavishly follow the crowd. Don't be bullied by tabloid agendas. Never have a drink 'til you have finished working for the day – except in emergency. Recognise that expressing your views can be a lonely business – many people survive by adjusting their message depending on who they are talking to.' *(DH)*

'Do not assume the bloke in the next-door seat with egg-stains down his jumper hasn't got a clue.' *(RK)*

'Treat experienced journos with respect – until you're convinced they don't deserve it – and learn off everyone. Ask them questions. Listen to every word past players say about the game. They're not all right all the time but they know a lot about the game. Treat confidences with great respect. If you burn bridges you'll suffer in the long term. Watch practice sessions closely and great players up close. This will give you more of a feel for the game. And always remember there's a huge world outside the box and the world of sport.' *(MR)*

'Make your own mind up. And don't worry about the long-term residents – their bark is worse than their bite.' *(TdeL)*

'Always remember, this is the best job in the world.' *(SU)*

'What do they know of sport who only sport know?' *(GH)*

WHAT MAKES A GOOD EDITOR AND WHO, IN YOUR EXPERIENCE, BEST PERSONIFIES THIS?

'Graham Perkins – editor of the Melbourne *Age* who took an old dust-sheet and turned it into a modern questing vehicle – and Cliff Makins, sports editor of the *Observer* in its heydays of the 1960s–70s. He brought together a mixed bag of outstanding talent like MacIlviolence [Hugh McIlvanney], Peter Dobreiner (golf), Richard Baerlein (racing), Tony Pawson (cricket), Chris Brasher (athletics) and many others (e.g. photographers Eamonn McCabe, Chris Smith) – and by giving them their head but always exercising gentle control, produced the best sports pages of the Swinging Sixties.' *(PD)*

'Courage, again. It is the essential quality a journalist needs: the courage to be different, to ask hard questions, to have no friends in public life, to ignore celebrities, to walk away from a free lunch, to stay outside the comfort zone of metropolitan bullshit. An editor has a huge obligation to bring miscreants of all types to book. You can't do that if you're in the pocket of the famous. We are watchdogs. Also, a lot of editors succumb to "avalanche journalism", taking a lead from each other in the Groucho Club, rather than trusting their writers. They are, generally, sheep. If a celebrity is considered fair game by enough newspapers, a villain or figure of fun, a serially "bad" character, not many newspapers are brave enough to ignore him or her. So up he or she goes on the front page. Too much of modern journalism is about "fashion" in its widest sense. It's about what editors reckon the most number of people want. And that, almost without exception, is generated on TV, not for any idle reason called the "idiot box". They are like City dealers: it doesn't matter which way the market goes, as long as it's moving. A lot of editors are amoral, in that their values shift with fashion. They don't lead, they follow. For a much better and longer take on all of this, read Andrew Marr's wonderful book, *My Trade*.' *(KM)*

'A good editor is a sympathetic one who knows what it is like to be abroad for weeks or months on end, who offers ideas and constructive criticism, and who by his support gives confidence to the journalist without letting him become complacent.' *(SB)*

'The best editors are those who ask the right questions about any story. In other words, they direct the coverage of the story by a process of constant probing, often taking it where others have not thought to go. They also must show confidence in their team. Editors who shout at their staff and rule by fear – and there are more than a few of those – will never get the most from their fellow journalists. Journalists respond to an editor who is seen to roll his sleeves up and get stuck in himself, putting in extra hours alongside his staff on a big breaking news story. Strangely, I can't name a single editor who personified all these qualities. Andrew Neil at the *Sunday Times* was very good at directing an investigation, though something of a bully, while Roger Alton [*Observer* editor at time of writing] when deputy sports editor at the *Guardian* was a very good leader of a team.' *(RW)*

'A good editor is someone who dares to release the talent of the staff, and recognises that a newspaper should be a badge of honour for the reader, something that proclaims the reader's beliefs and philosophy. New Labour, in its blurring of traditional political thought, has confused newspaper identities – no more so than the *Guardian*'s. Newspapers should care far more about their core readers, and core philosophies, and make courageous and honest judgements, instead of chasing TV and tabloid agendas and trying to be all things to all people.' *(DH)*

'The ones who empathise with their writers as well as being layout wizards, smooth talkers or unabashed despots. There are fewer of them around these days but no-one has beaten Reg [Hayter] in my experience. If you're talking about a good sub-editor, I would nominate three (in no particular order): Ian Malin, Jeremy Alexander (both *Guardian*) and Ron Surplice (Hayters).' *(RK)*

'A good editor wants the best for his product and his people. My first editor, Malcolm Schmidtke, in the business section of *The Age*, remains the best I have worked for: completely dedicated, utterly selfless, devoted entirely to helping others do their best work.' *(GH)*

'Someone who encourages you to think differently, tells you the truth about your writing, drills in lessons about detail and is a non-cynic. I have had teachers and colleagues like this but few bosses of this kind.' *(SU)*

'The best sports editor I've dealt with was Geoff Slattery at the *Sunday Age* in Melbourne from 1989 to about 1991. A great lateral thinker, innovative and stimulating editor who had visual style and a great feel for the human drama of sport. He wanted to drag Australian sports journalism into the modern era, and although he left newspapers out of frustration after only about five years as a sports editor on two papers, he did influence a lot of younger writers. He had been a fine sportswriter before that. One example of his approach was when there was a controversy in the 1970s about excessive drinking at the MCG. In those days patrons were allowed to bring their own alcohol. Officials proposed a limit of 12 cans per person. So Slattery filled his esky with a dozen cans, sat in the sun and drank them then, the next day I think, wrote a feature about it. He could spice his pages with a sense of fun and creativity yet he also treated high-quality athletes with respect. Like the best editors, he thought outside the square, came at things from a slightly different perspective.' *(MR)*

'Writers can be fragile creatures and good editors talk to them wherever they are, to encourage them and to get a feeling for what is happening and for the most interesting next new thing. They all complain they don't have enough time but good ones make the time. They also say thank you. A herogram or a postcard ought to be rare but it is never forgotten. I've had only one for any length of time and the *Independent on Sunday* is fortunate that Neil Morton has remained uncommonly loyal to the paper, having turned down the sports editorship of a couple of the other Sunday "quality" papers.' *(SF)*

WHICH SPORTS JOURNALIST(S) DO YOU MOST RESPECT?

'Retired now, but the sports journalist I most respected was the one and only Rex Bellamy, tennis writer of *The Times*. When tennis introduced an award for the best writer on the game worldwide, Bellamy won year after year – to the point that the award was scrapped, as being pointless. Of today's writers – Ian Wooldridge, who has just passed on, was outstanding for his easy flow and feeling for many sports (despite an obsession with round-the-world yachting and the whole world of golf). John Woodcock, writing little these days, was the finest cricket writer of his time – precise, informative, offering judgments from sound reasoning and an awareness of the game's past, much of which he has seen. And Simon Barnes soars like an imaginative eagle into flights of fancy, mostly managing to stay within reach of Mother Earth as he relates a game to life, society and all that.' *(MH)*

'It is impossible to choose just one, though if I were forced to select one from my own generation, it would be Hugh McIlvanney. But I would also want to bow to the Sage of Longparish, John Woodcock, and Alan Ross, who covered five overseas tours for the *Observer* and never saw England lose. I don't believe Matthew Engel will ever run out of good jokes. Many chief sports writers – Richard Williams, Simon Barnes, Jim Lawton and Kevin Mitchell – are worthy of their grand role.' *(SF)*

'Hugh McIlvanney for obvious reasons. His gift has been to lift sportswriting out of the ordinary, to put events in a much wider context, and to do it with wit and perception.' *(KM)*

'The general sportswriter who has to swot up each sport every time he writes about it, provided he comes up with accurate insights, not uninformed opinions.' *(SB)*

'Christopher Clarey, *International Herald Tribune*. Well informed, thinks, writes very well.' *(NP)*

'Paul Hayward (*Daily Mail*). Whichever newspaper he hangs his hat on, he seems able to maintain his personal integrity free of that particular title's biases. His arguments are generally humane and reasoned, and his writing helps to reinforce my belief that sport can give us some of the most enjoyable moments of our lives.' *(RW)*

'Martin Samuel (*The Times*) – the only columnist I would ever buy a paper to read (apart from our own of course). And the late Frank Nicklin – a genius.' *(BO)*

'I am in awe of Hugh McIlvanney for often turning the prosaic into poetry, and Simon Barnes for his humanity and revealing the personal in the often impersonal.' *(AQ)*

'Nationally – David Lacey (still required reading) and Richard Williams. Internationally – George Plimpton, who invented participatory sports journalism and wrote of his exploits with jealousy-inducing flair.' *(SP)*

'The ones who make it look easy. Matthew Engel, Frank Keating, David Foot, Simon Barnes, Martin Johnson, Paul Hayward, Stephen Jones, Chris Hewett, John Woodcock, Raymond Robertson-Glasgow.' *(RK)*

'Red Smith was a great writer. Roger Angell, all those fine American sportswriters. I can recall a piece from *Sports Illustrated* in the mid-1980s about what happened to Muhammad Ali's entourage. Geoff Slattery gave it to his staff at the Melbourne *Herald*. It was brilliant. In cricket, R.C. Robertson-Glasgow and Australia's Ray Robinson. Contemporary: probably Matthew Engel more than anyone else. At his best, Peter Roebuck is creative and perceptive. Gideon Haigh is a good writer, though more an author than a daily journalist. David Hopps is a very good writer.' *(MR)*

'Different folks for different strokes. As a reader of cricket, Scyld Berry. As a painter of the big occasion, Gideon Haigh. As an ex-player columnist, Nasser Hussain. As a judge of people and situations, Christopher Martin-Jenkins. As a stylist, Matthew Engel. As an enthusiast, Frank Keating. As an all-round cricket writer, John Woodcock.' *(TdeL)*

'Stephen Fay. A great journalist, and a great bloke, still brimful of enthusiasm for his vocation.' *(GH)*

'More than one but will name just a couple: Rohit Brijnath for his use of language, large-hearted writing and sense of wonder even after nearly two decades in the business. Peter Roebuck for his ability to understand the mind of the athlete and convey it in the fewest words. Mike Marqusee, not technically a sports journalist, for his original mind.' *(SU)*

'A XV to beat *The Venusian Times*: Christopher Martin-Jenkins (fullback), Kevin Mitchell (left wing), Thomas Boswell (inside centre), Ray Robinson (outside centre), Simon Barnes (right wing); Red Smith (fly-half), Frank Keating (scrum-half); David Frith (tight-head prop), David Foot (hooker), David Lacey (loose-head prop), Brian Glanville (lock), Stephen Fay (capt; lock), Scyld Berry (blindside flanker), Matthew Engel (open-side flanker), Hugh McIlvanney (No. 8). Coaches: Mike Marqusee, Steve Pinder, Huw Richards and Sharda Ugra. Manager: Brian Oliver. Psychologist: Nick Pitt. Physio: Giles Smith. Motivational Speaker: Michael Henderson. All have/had the courage of their convictions, a winning way with words, a (mostly) unerring sense of fairness, an unshakeable grip on the wider context and the ability to treat sport as simultaneously vital and trivial. Equally estimable are the sub-editors who work in consort with reporters instead of at daggers drawn, enhancing their copy rather than seeking to impose their own judgements or letting resentment obscure objectivity. Springing most readily to mind are Ron Surplice, Paul Coupar at *The Wisden Cricketer* and that immaculate *Guardian* trio, Jeremy Alexander, Chris Cheers and Ian Malin.' *(RS)*

The preceding array of opinions, I trust, makes it quite clear that 1) technological advances have been an almost unalloyed benefit to sports journalists; 2) print journalists have about as much respect for their broadcasting brethren as a whale holds for plankton. The intention was to demonstrate that there are several ways to skin a cat. The fact is that the rules are unwritten, and changing continually. By the same token, though, certain verities persist – above all the need to inform, to entertain, to demand answers, to be constantly vigilant, to be a thorn in the side of unreasonable or poorly exercised authority and power, to support the downtrodden and, of course, to toil long and hard. Those truths will continue to be self-evident for as long as society sees a value in paying people to relay and explain how the world actually works, and to illustrate and propose what we can do to help effect meaningful change.

Admittedly, the landscape is changing. The colossal growth in websites, blogs and so-called 'citizen reporters' illustrates that, when it comes to their interests and passions, or simply seeing their name in print, people are quite happy to proffer their views for nothing – and editors are increasingly happy to regard the last in particular as cheap labour, as well as drawing on the first two for free copy. In a world where opinion is often respected more than fact, and the more wittily or trenchantly that opinion is expressed the better, there is a great temptation to maintain this cheapening of the profession. All that notwithstanding, a sports journalist, unlike John Lennon's outmoded working-class hero, remains something to be.

Further reading

In the main, the following list of the best 50 books I have read about the world of competitive artistry (or, in a few instances, *ought* to have read) comprises those celebrating, and offering priceless insights into, the art, craft, history and heart of sport and sports journalism. A few baseball-centric titles in particular – Jane Leavy's poignant biography of the elusive Sandy Koufax, David Halberstam's and Tom Adleman's meticulously researched recreations of the 1964 and 1966 seasons respectively, and Roger Kahn's *Boys of Summer,* which saw the author track down the heroes of his youth amid the rosy glow and dull thud of retirement – testify that journalism need not be of the daily or weekly variety to have value and impact. They also testify to my abiding regret that British publishers are so rarely willing to support such ventures. Along with the titles referenced elsewhere, all are highly commended to anyone wishing to pursue a career in this scruffy vineyard. Read and reap.

Adleman, T. (2006) *Black and Blue: The Golden Arm, the Robinson Boys and the 1966 World Series that Stunned America*, New York, Little Brown.

Angell, R. (1991) *Once More Around the Park: A Baseball Reader*, New York, Ballantine Books.

Barnes, S. (1989) *A Sportswriter's Year*, London, Heinemann.

Barnes, S. (2006) *The Meaning of Sport*, London, Short Books.

Boswell, T. (1985) *Why Time Begins on Opening Day*, New York, Penguin.

Boswell, T. (1994) *Cracking the Show*, New York, Doubleday.

Boyle, R. (2006) *Sports Journalism: Context and Issues*, London, Sage.

Bryant, H. (2005) *Juicing the Game: Drugs, Power, and the Fight for the Soul of Major League Baseball*, New York, Viking.

Chadwin, D. (1999) *Those Damn Yankees*, London, Verso.

Chapman, P. (1999) *The Goalkeeper's History of Britain*, London, Fourth Estate.

Davies, H. (1998 reprint) *The Glory Game*, Edinburgh, Mainstream.

Engel, M. (1985) *Ashes '85*, London, Pelham.

Engel, M. (Ed., 1987) *Guardian Book of Cricket*, London, Penguin.

Engel, M. (1989) *Sportswriter's Eye*, London, Macdonald Queen Anne Press.

Fleder, R. (Ed. 2004) *Sports Illustrated: Fifty Years of Great Writing 1954–2004*, New York, Sports Illustrated Books.

Foot, D. (1993) *Country Reporter*, London, Fontana.

Foot, D. (2001), *Fragments of Idolatry*, Bath, Fairfield Books.

Frith, D. (1987) *Pageant of Cricket*, London, Macmillan.

Glanville, B. (2005 reprint), *The Story of the World Cup*, London, Faber & Faber.

Haigh, G. (1993) *The Cricket War*, Melbourne, The Text Publishing Company.

Haigh, G. (1997) *The Summer Game*, Melbourne, The Text Publishing Company.

Haigh, G. (2005) *Ashes 2005*, London, Aurum.
Halberstam, D. (1994) *October 1964*, New York, Villard Books.
Hauser, T. (1991) *Muhammad Ali*, London, Robson Books.
Holt, R. (1989) *Sport and the British: A Modern History*, Oxford, Oxford University Press.
Holtzman, J. (1973) *No Cheering in the Press Box*, Toronto, Holt, Rinehart and Winston.
Hughes, S. (2005) *Morning Everyone – A Sportswriter's Life*, London, Orion.
James, C.L.R. (1999 reprint) *Beyond a Boundary*, London, Random House.
Jennings, A. (1996) *The New Lords of the Rings: Olympic Corruption & How to Buy Gold Medals*, London, PocketBooks.
Jennings, A. (2006) *Foul! The Secret World of FIFA: Bribes, Vote Rigging and Ticket Scandals*, New York, HarperSport.
Jones, S. (1993) *Endless Winter: Inside Story of the Rugby Revolution*, Edinburgh, Mainstream.
Kahn, R. (1998) *Memories of Summer: When Baseball was an Art, and Writing About It a Game*, New York, Hyperion Books.
Kahn, R. (1999) *A Flame of Pure Fire – Jack Dempsey and the Roaring 20s*, New York, Harcourt Brace.
Kahn, R. (2000 reprint) *Boys of Summer*, New York, McGraw-Hill College.
Keating, F. (1980) *Bowled Over – A Year of Sport with Frank Keating*, London, Andre Deutsch.
Keating, F. (1999) *The Great Number Tens*, London, Corgi.
Kuper, S. (2003 reprint) *Football Against The Enemy*, London, Orion.
Leavy, J. (2002) *Sandy Koufax: A Lefty's Legacy*, New York, Harper Collins.
Marqusee, M. (1996) *War Minus the Shooting*, London, William Heinemann.
Marqusee, M. (1999) *Redemption Song: Muhammad Ali and the Spirit of the Sixties*, London, Verso.
McIlvanney, H. (1994) *McIlvanney on Football*, Edinburgh, Mainstream.
McRae, D. (2002) *In Black and White: The Untold Story of Joe Louis and Jesse Owens*, London, Scribner.
Mott, S. (1996) *A Girl's Guide to Ball Games*, Edinburgh, Mainstream.
Moynihan, J. (1987 reprint) *The Soccer Syndrome*, London, Sportspages.
Newfield, J. (1995) *Only in America*, New York, Morrow.
Novick, J. (1996) *Winning their Spurs: Tottenham Hotspur Dream Team*, Edinburgh, Mainstream.
Povich, S. (2005) *All Those Mornings . . . At the Post*, New York, Public Affairs.
Richards, H. (2006) *A Game for Hooligans*, Edinburgh, Mainstream.
Robinson, R. (1975) *On Top Down Under*, Melbourne, Cassell Australia.
Smith, R. (2000) *Red Smith on Baseball*, New York, Ivan R. Dee.

The following dozen films, albeit shamelessly Hollywoodenised at times, all offer priceless insights into journalistic reality:

Ace In the Hole (1951, director Billy Wilder)
All The President's Men (1976, director Alan J Pakula)
Almost Famous (2000, director Cameron Crowe)
Between The Lines (1977, director Joan Micklin Silver)
Citizen Kane (1941, director Orson Welles)
Cobb (1994, director Ron Shelton)
Network (1976, director Sidney Lumet)
Shattered Glass (2003, director Billy Ray)
The Front Page (1974, director Billy Wilder)
The Insider (1999, director Michael Mann)
The Paper (1994, director Ron Howard)
The Sweet Small Of Success (1957, director Alexander MacKendrick)

Notes

1 THE HARDEST JOB EVER CRAVED

1 *The Meaning of Sport*, Short Books 2006.
2 *LA Times*, 29 September, 2006.
3 http://www.robertlipsyte.com/events.htm.
4 *The Word*, September 2006.
5 Interview with author, November 2006.
6 *Bowled Over! A Year of Sport with Frank Keating*, Andre Deutsch 1980.
7 *Yale Herald* 2000.
8 'The things they said', *Sportspages Almanac*, Sportspages 1990.
9 *Open Tennis: The First Twenty Years*, Bloomsbury 1988.
10 *McEnroe: A Rage For Perfection*, Sidgwick & Jackson 1982.
11 *Open Tennis: The First Twenty Years*, Bloomsbury 1988.
12 *Sports Journalism: Context and Issues*, Sage 2006.
13 *No Cheering in the Press Box* by Jerome Holtzman, Holt, Rinehart, Winston 1973.
14 Ibid.

2 BATTING AND BALLING

1 *Sport: A Prison of Measured Time*, Ink Links 1978.
2 *The Meaning of Sport*, Short Books 2006.
3 *Observer Sports Monthly*, 29 October, 2006.
4 *Far Foreign Land*, Naomi Roth Publishing 2006.
5 *The Victorians and Sport*, Hambledon & London 2004.
6 *Cricket's Burning Passion*, Scyld Berry and Rupert Peploe, Methuen 2006.
7 *Edinburgh Review*, January 1858, from *The Penguin Dictionary of Quotations*, edited by J.M. and M.J. Cohen, Penguin 1960.
8 http://www.litencyc.com/php/speople.php.
9 *The Victorians and Sport.*
10 Ibid.
11 *The Father of Modern Sport*, The Parrs Wood Press 2002.
12 *The Victorians and Sport.*
13 *Sport And The British – A Modern History*, Oxford University Press 1989.
14 Ibid.

15 The other major grammatical difference is that partial quotes are punctuated *outside* the speechmarks in Britain and *inside* them across the Atlantic – 'Jones said he was "sicker than a parrot".' as opposed to 'Jones said he was "sicker than a parrot."'.
16 *10 for 66 And All That,* The Sportsman's Book Club 1959.
17 *Tickle the Public: One Hundred Years of the Popular Press,* Gollancz 1996.
18 *Guardian,* 2 December, 2006.
19 *The Tumult And The Shouting,* Cassell 1956.
20 Ibid.
21 *Washington Post,* 6 September, 2006.
22 *Red Smith on Baseball,* Ivan R. Dee 2000.
23 *No Cheering in the Press Box,* Holt, Rinehart and Winston 1973.
24 Ibid.
25 *Red Smith on Baseball.*
26 Ibid.
27 Ibid.
28 *New York Herald Tribune,* 3 October, 1947, quoted in *Red Smith on Baseball.*
29 *Red Smith on Baseball.*
30 Interview with author, August 2006.
31 *Tickle the Public.*
32 Ibid.
33 Ibid.
34 *A Game for Hooligans,* Mainstream 2006.
35 Email to author, September 2006.
36 Email to author, September 2006.
37 *Argus Lite,* October 3, 2006.
38 Interview with author, September 2006.
39 *The Times,* 11 August, 2006.
40 *British Journalism Review,* Vol.17, Number 3, Sage 2006.
41 *Bloomberg News* article, reprinted in *The Arizona Republic,* 23 January, 1998.
42 *Sports Journalism: Context and Issues,* Sage 2006.

3 WHOSE AGENDA IS IT ANYWAY?

1 http://sportsillustrated.cnn.com/2006/writers/tom_verducci/09/19/a.rod/index.html.
2 *Guardian* 7 August, 2006.
3 Sports Journalists' Association Newsletter, August 2006.
4 Interview with author, September 2006.
5 *UK Press Gazette,* 2 November, 2006.
6 *The Economic History of Major League Baseball,* EH.Net Encyclopedia 27 August, 2003. http://eh.net/encyclopedia/article/haupert.mlb.
7 'The things they said', *Sportspages Almanac,* Sportspages 1990.
8 *Independent,* 13 November, 2006.
9 *MediaGuardian,* 20 November, 2006.
10 *How Soccer Explains the World: An Unlikely Theory of Globalisation,* HarperCollins 2004.
11 *Sports Journalism: Context and Issues,* Sage 2006.
12 'The rise and fall of Kirby Puckett', *Sports Illustrated,* 11 March, 2003.
13 Ibid.
14 Ibid.
15 Ibid.

16 *Baseball: A Literary Anthology*, edited by Nicholas Dawidoff, The Library of America 2002.
17 Ibid.
18 *Game Time: A Baseball Companion*, edited by Steve Kettmann, Harcourt 2003.
19 *Sunday Times*, 26 June, 2005.
20 Interview with author, November 2006.
21 Ibid.
22 *Sydney Morning Herald*, 15 November, 2006.
23 *Guardian*, 15 November, 2006.
24 *Washington Post*, 28 October, 1986.
25 *The Times*, 18 October, 2006.
26 Ibid.
27 Interview with author, September 2006.
28 *Sport and Society*, 2006.
29 'The importance of sports journalism in today's world', *The Sport Journal*, US Sports Academy 2003.
30 Ibid.
31 Interview with author, November 2006.
32 Interview with author, November 2006.

4 THE KNOWLEDGE

1 *Sun*, 15 November, 2006.
2 Interview with author, November 2006.
3 *Guardian*, 17 November, 2006.
4 *The Sunday Times Sports Book*, World's Work, 1979.

5 THEN, IN THE FINAL MINUTE ...

1 *Guardian*, 27 November, 2006.
2 *The Times*, 28 August, 2006.

6 BREAKING THE NEWS

1 Interview with author, November 2006.
2 Ibid.
3 Ibid.
4 *Daily Telegraph*, 23 October, 2006.
5 *Guardian Unlimited*, 22 August, 2006.
6 *Guardian*, 22 August, 2006.
7 *LA Times*, 22 August, 2006.
8 *The Times*, 4 November, 2006.
9 Cricinfo, 4 November, 2006.
10 *Sun*, 2 November, 2005.
11 *Guardian*, 2 November, 2005.
12 *Sun*, 2 November, 2005.
13 *Guardian*, 2 November, 2005.
14 *Guardian*, 11 February, 2002.

7 'HI,' SAID MUHAMMAD, AMIABLY

1 *Daily Telegraph*, 11 November, 2006.
2 *Sunday Telegraph*, 12 November, 2006.
3 *Sunday Times*, 28 May, 2006.
4 Interview with author, 20 October, 2006.

8 BENEATH THE MUD

1 *Observer*, 31 May, 1967.
2 *Sports Illustrated*, 22 April, 1974, reprinted in *Baseball: A Literary Anthology*, edited by Nicholas Dawidoff, The Library of America 2002.

9 ME, THE JURY

1 *The Times*, 22 August, 2006.
2 Interview with author, November 2006.
3 Email to author, September 2006.
4 *Hindustan Times*, 22 August, 2006.
5 *Daily Telegraph*, 24 November, 2006.
6 *The Times*, 29 August, 2006.
7 *Baseball: A Literary Anthology*.
8 *The Times*, 9 September, 2006.
9 Interview with author, November 2006.
10 Quoted in *The Times*, 18 November, 2006.
11 *The Times*, 24 October, 2006.
12 Quoted in *The Wisden Cricketer*, June 2006.
13 *Guardian Unlimited*, 25–28 September, 2006.

10 THE ADVANTAGE OF DISTANCE

1 *The Word*, October 2006.

11 LIVE AND EXCLUSIVE

1 Cricinfo.com.
2 *Cricket on the Air*, BBC Books 1985.
3 http://www.crystalpalacefoundation.org.uk.
4 *Guardian*, 1 December, 2006.
5 http://amch.questionmarket.com.
6 http://www.baseballlibrary.com.
7 www.boxingnews24.com.
8 www.crystalpalacefoundation.org.uk.
9 *Games and Sets – The Changing Face of Sport on Television*, BFI Publishing 1990.
10 http://www.psychology.iastate.edu/faculty/caa/abstracts/2000-2004/01BA.ap.pdf.
11 *Sport in Britain 1945–2000*, Blackwell 2000.
12 Ibid.
13 *Rothmans Football Yearbook 1975–76*, Queen Anne Press 1975.

14 *Games and Sets: The Changing Face of Sport on Television.*
15 Ibid.
16 Ibid.
17 *Manchester Evening News*, 26–29 July, 1956.
18 Oxford University Press, 1961–95.
19 *Sport and the British*, Oxford University Press 1989.
20 Interview with author, November 2006.
21 Ibid.
22 Ibid.
23 Ibid.
24 *John Arlott: A Memoir*, Timothy Arlott, Andre Deutsch 1994.
25 Ibid.
26 *Great Cricket Quotes*, David Hopps, Robson Books 2006.
27 http://www.americansportscastersonline.com/radiosportscastingtips.html.
28 *Benaud on Reflection*, Collins Willow 1984.
29 Ibid.
30 Associated Press, 16 October, 2006.
31 Interview with author, October 2006.
32 *Miami Herald*, 16 October, 2006.
33 The commentator 'throws' the viewer over to an advert of prescribed length, ideally by a recitation of the score the instant an over ends; the more he editorialises or witters, the more the viewers will miss of the next.
34 *Benaud on Reflection*, Collins Willow 1984.
35 Stanley Paul 1990.
36 Sky Sports 1–2 December, 2006.
37 Interview with author, October 2006.
38 Interview with author, November 2006.
39 Ibid.

12 THE SAFETY NET

1 *Guardian*, 13 November, 2006.
2 10 September, 2006.

Index